Acclaim for *The S*

"Fast-paced and witty. . . . Jaivin knows her stuff but wears her erudition lightly. Iconoclastic, informative, and more attentive to female figures than many comparable works.
Highly recommended."
—**Jeffrey Wasserstrom, author of *Vigil: Hong Kong on the Brink***

"Succinct, lucid, and with a keen eye for detail, this slim book is an indispensable primer on China."
—**Louisa Lim, author of *The People's Republic of Amnesia* and cohost of *The Little Red Podcast***

"Linda Jaivin's may be the shortest history of China; it's also one of the best. . . . Jaivin has the erudition of long study, and she combines it with a touch of the poetic and the playful in her absorbing, wonderful book."
—**Richard Bernstein, longtime journalist, China observer, and author of *China 1945***

"An electrifying and erudite ride through Chinese history. . . . An illuminating history book that is also a real page-turner."
—**Alice Pung, author of *Unpolished Gem* and *Her Father's Daughter***

"The book is a gem. . . . A virtual diorama of China's most significant events, personalities, and anecdotes, carefully curated by a seasoned China scholar and master storyteller."
—**Jaime FlorCruz, former CNN Beijing Bureau Chief**

# Also by Linda Jaivin

# THE SHORTEST HISTORY OF CHINA

## From the Ancient Dynasties to a Modern Superpower— A Retelling for Our Times

## LINDA JAIVIN

THE EXPERIMENT

NEW YORK

THE SHORTEST HISTORY OF CHINA: *From the Ancient Dynasties to a Modern Superpower—A Retelling for Our Times*
Copyright © 2021 by Linda Jaivin
Page 269 is a continuation of this copyright page.

Originally published in Australia by Black Inc., an imprint of Schwartz Books Pty Ltd. First published in North America in revised form by The Experiment, LLC.

The Experiment, LLC
220 East 23rd Street, Suite 600
New York, NY 10001-4658
theexperimentpublishing.com

The Experiment's books are available at special discounts when purchased in bulk for premiums and sales promotions as well as for fundraising or educational use. For details, contact us at info@theexperimentpublishing.com.

Library of Congress Cataloging-in-Publication Data

Names: Jaivin, Linda, author.
Title: The shortest history of China : from the ancient dynasties to a modern superpower-a retelling for our times / Linda Jaivin.
Description: New York : The Experiment, [2021] | Series: The shortest history series | Includes bibliographical references and index.
Identifiers: LCCN 2021025263 (print) | LCCN 2021025264 (ebook) | ISBN 9781615198207 (paperback) | ISBN 9781615198214 (ebook)
Subjects: LCSH: China--History.
Classification: LCC DS735 .J35 2021 (print) | LCC DS735 (ebook) | DDC 951--dc23
LC record available at https://lccn.loc.gov/2021025263
LC ebook record available at https://lccn.loc.gov/2021025264

ISBN 978-1-61519-820-7
Ebook ISBN 978-1-61519-821-4

Cover design by Jack Dunnington
Text design by Dennis Grauel
Maps and illustrations by Alan Laver

Manufactured in the United States of America

First printing September 2021
10 9 8 7 6 5 4 3

# Contents

*In memory of my parents, Lewis and Naomi Jaivin,*
*who encouraged me to study whatever interested me.*
*What interested me was China.*

| | | |
|---|---|---|
| **PALAEOLITHIC ERA** (2.5 million years ago) |  | |
| **NEOLITHIC ERA** (10,000–2070 BCE) |  | The Yellow and Fiery Emperors (c. 2852 to 2070 BCE) |
| **ANCIENT ERA** (2070–221 BCE) |  | Xia dynasty (2070–1600 BCE) |
| | | Shang dynasty (1600–1050 BCE) |
| | | Zhou dynasty, Western and Eastern, including the Warring States period (1050–221 BCE) |
| **IMPERIAL ERA** (221 BCE – 1911 CE) | | Qin dynasty (221–206 BCE) |
| | | Western Han (202 BCE– 8 CE), Eastern Han (25–220 CE) |
| | | Three Kingdoms and general disunity (c. 208–265) |
| | | Jin dynasty (266–420) Sixteen Kingdoms (304–439) |
| | | Northern and Southern dynasties (439–581) Sui dynasty (518–618) |
| | | Tang dynasty (618–907) |
| | | Five dynasties and Ten Kingdoms (907–979) Khitan Liao dynasty (907–1125) |
| | | Northern Song (960–1127), Jurchen Jin dynasty (1115–1234), Southern Song (1127–1279) |
| | | Mongol Yuan dynasty (1271–1368) |
| | | Ming dynasty (1368–1644) |
| | | Manchu Qing dynasty (1644–1911) |
| **MODERN ERA** (1912–today) |  | Republic of China (on the mainland, 1912–1949; Taiwan, 1949–) |
| | | People's Republic of China (1949–present) |

Gaps and overlaps in dates represent times of chaos, rebellion, and division. Pre-Han dates are approximations.

| | |
|---|---|
| Peking man | First Aboriginal Australians (50,000 years ago) |
| Yellow River civilization  | Stonehenge (c. 3000 BCE)<br>Great Pyramid of Giza (c. 2680 BCE) |
| Oracle bones | Mammoth extinction (c. 1650 BCE) |
| *I Ching*<br>*The Art of War*<br>Confucius, Mencius, Laozi, Hanfeizi  | Buddha, Plato, Aristotle, Socrates |
| Unification | |
| Invention of paper, the compass, and woodblock printing, Silk Roads, Wang Mang Rebellion (8–25 CE) | Rosetta Stone (196 BCE)<br>Roman Empire (27 BCE– 476 CE) |
| Battle of Red Cliffs (208) | |
| Gathering at the Orchid Pavilion (353) | Classic Mayan civilization |
| The Grand Canal | Middle Ages<br>Muhammad (571–632) |
| Spread of Buddhism<br>Golden Age of Poetry<br>An Lushan rebellion (755–763) | Viking civilization<br>Ghana Empire |
| Footbinding | Goryeo dynasty (Korea)<br>Battle of Hastings (1066) |
| Neo-Confucianism, urbanization | Islamic Golden Age, Crusades |
| Khublai Khan, Marco Polo | European Renaissance |
| The Forbidden City<br>Golden age of the novel<br>Zheng He's maritime exploration  | Inca Empire<br>Age of Exploration |
| Conquest of Xinjiang and Tibet, Opium wars | Enlightenment, Age of Imperialism and Colonialism |
| Hundred Days' Reform, Republican revolution | Industrial Revolution |
| Warlord Era, Japanese invasion and resistance, civil war | World War I, founding of the Soviet Union, World War II |
| Great Leap Forward, Cultural Revolution, death of Mao, Deng Xiaoping's Reform Era, Xi Jinping's "New Era" | Korean War, Cold War, dissolution of the Soviet Union, September 11, COVID-19 pandemic |

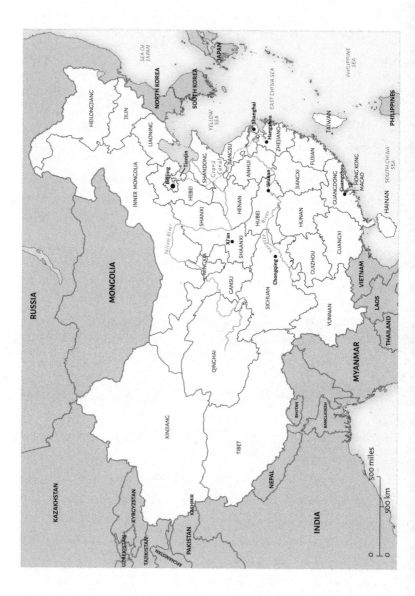

# Introduction

There is no Chinese curse that goes "may you live in interesting times." In any case, it would be redundant. Chinese history simmers with larger-than-life characters, philosophical arguments and political intrigues, military conflicts and social upheavals, artistic invention and technological innovation. It progresses in twists, turns, leaps, and returns. Chinese historical records are long and deep, stretching back at least 3,500 years. Their themes and lessons, as well as the memories of wounds and triumphs, pulsate under the surface of contemporary Chinese life, language, culture, and politics. The increasingly key role the People's Republic of China (PRC) plays in global affairs makes an awareness of this history essential, for it is the key to understanding China today.

Take, for example, the insistence of the Communist Party of China (CPC) that Hong Kong and Táiwān, along with Tibet, Xīnjiāng, and islands in the South China Sea, are part of China. The intensity with which the CPC pursues "reunification" has roots in the humiliation and semicolonization of China by imperialist powers in the nineteenth century and the civil war of the twentieth century. It also speaks to violent periods of division that occurred as long as two thousand years ago but have left their stamp on the national psyche. That the first great unification, in 221 BCE—which also involved the epic standardization of weights, measures, and the written language—came with a high dose of tyranny is also part of this history's complex legacy.

Nothing about China is small in scale. With some 1.4 billion people, the PRC boasts the world's largest population—nearly 1 in every 5 people on Earth (not counting another 45 million people worldwide who identify as Chinese). At 3.6 million square miles (9.3 million sq km), it occupies the third-largest landmass of any country after Russia and Canada and shares borders with fourteen nations. The PRC is the world's largest trading nation and second-largest economy, a manufacturing powerhouse, and an assertive military power, its army bigger than any other national armed force. It plays a steadily increasing role in global institutions and international affairs.

The PRC's trillion-dollar Belt and Road Initiative—with projects in countries as diverse as Afghanistan, Ecuador, Bahrain, Bulgaria, Ethiopia, and Vietnam—is the most ambitious global infrastructure-building project in history. Domestic schemes are often no less monumental, whether they involve constructing giant dams, establishing pervasive systems of surveillance, or creating the longest open-sea fixed link on the planet, the 34-mile-long (55 km) Hong Kong–Zhūhǎi–Macao Bridge. The PRC is also a leader in artificial intelligence, green technology, and communications network infrastructure, and aims to become a world leader in science and technology by 2050.

The rise of the People's Republic has inspired a range of reactions abroad, including concern about political influence operations and human rights violations. Běijīng's insistence that it defines human rights differently than the West does little to reassure its critics. Although the CPC claims to speak on behalf of all 1.4 billion Chinese nationals, history makes it clear that the people of this great land have always embraced a range of intellectual, philosophical, political, and cultural positions.

China is diverse in numerous ways. If more than 90 percent of the population claim Han ethnicity, the rest belong to fifty-five other ethnic groups, including Uyghurs, Mongolians, and Tibetans. Many speak distinct languages and retain their own religious and cultural practices, despite pressure to assimilate. The Han, too, may identify with different regional cultures and subcultures and speak discrete and even mutually unintelligible dialects, including Shanghainese and Cantonese— the latter claiming more native speakers (over sixty-two million) than Italian. The national language, Pǔtōnghuà, sometimes called Mandarin in English, is a constructed tongue. The PRC's own Ministry of Education admitted in 2013 that it was spoken with native fluency by less than 10 percent of the population and barely at all by 30 percent, though it aimed to change that.[1]

Northerners prefer wheat and southerners rice, but not always; some Chinese never touch chili, while others can't cook without it. Beijingers complain that Shanghainese are mercantile and petty; Shanghainese snipe back that Beijingers are bighearted but crude. All stereotypes fall apart in the face of Chinese diversity. The citizenry of the PRC includes subsistence farmers and jet-setting billionaires, Buddhist monks and nightclub owners, passionate feminists and steely patriarchs, avant-garde artists and aerospace engineers, yak herders and film animators, pro-democracy activists and loyal Communists. They may live in towering apartment blocks, courtyard houses built to a two-thousand-year-old design, European-style villas, longhouses, stilt houses, yurts, or even modified caves. They may be fans of Peking opera, Western opera, punk, throat-singing, Cantopop, chess, video games, Korean soap operas, calligraphy, photography, ballroom dancing, fan dancing, all or none of the above.

The heavily urbanized landscape of China's twenty-three provinces and five "autonomous regions" (Guǎngxī, Inner Mongolia, Tibet, Níngxià, and Xinjiang) is as varied as its people, ranging from frozen steppes to tropical islands, jungles, deserts, fertile farmland, tall mountains, and low floodplains. The PRC boasts several of the most populous cities on Earth. Its four provincial-level municipalities include Chóngqìng, home to more than thirty million, and Shànghǎi, with more than twenty-six million. Aside from the Yangtze—the third-longest river in the world—six of Asia's major rivers originate in Tibet: the Indus, Ganges, Brahmaputra, Irrawaddy, Salween, and Mekong. The construction of upstream dams, mines, and irrigation projects, and even the afforestation of the Tibetan Plateau, all have implications for the water security of almost half the world's population. President Xí Jìnpíng's pledge to the United Nations in September 2020 that China will reduce its net carbon emissions to zero by 2060, if followed through, could help address climate change and determine the future of the planet itself.

———

A disciple once asked Confucius (551–479 BCE) the first thing he'd do if he were in charge. Confucius replied, "Rectify the names." He explained: "If the names are not correct, if they do not match realities, language has no object. If language is without an object, action becomes impossible—and therefore, all human affairs disintegrate and their management becomes pointless and impossible."[2]

The first appearance of the name "China" in a European language is in a sixteenth-century Spanish text.[3] The word seemingly derives from references to the ancient Qín dynasty (221–206 BCE), via Sanskrit चीन (*cīna*) and Japanese 支那 (*shina*). In Chinese, the most common expression for China in the sense of a nation is *Zhōngguó* 中國 (中国 in simplified characters—more on those shortly). This expression dates back three thousand years to the ancient compilation of poetry, the *Book of Odes, Shījīng* 詩經. *Zhōng* 中 means middle, or center. The second character, *guó* 國, contains a mouth, *kǒu* 口, representing the people, and a dagger-axe, *gē* 戈, signifying defense, within an enclosure, *wéi* 囗. *Guo* originally referred to a fortified city, only later coming to mean a kingdom and finally a nation-state. Although *Zhongguo* is often translated as "Middle Kingdom," *zhong* originally referred to the center of the kingdom or city, rather than implying that the kingdom itself was at the center of the world.

Another popular way to refer to China is *Zhōnghuá* 中華. *Huá* 華 can signify splendor, radiance, or prosperity. It was the name of one of the two ancient tribes of settlers along the Yellow River from which Han Chinese claim descent. *Zhonghua* is less about a specific territory than a civilization, encompassing notions of myth, legend, history, and culture. It embraces the broader Chinese world, radiating out from the mainland, Taiwan, and Hong Kong to diasporic communities, from Canberra to California, Singapore to Senegal. Although there are other phrases that signify China, it's reasonable to say that the idea of China lies somewhere between *Zhongguo* and *Zhonghua*. The outline maps that appear in this book are not of the PRC but of territory that either is now or at one time has been part of something understood as *Zhongguo* or *Zhonghua*.

For most of history, people identified with their dynasty—as a man or woman of the Táng, for example, rather than as "Chinese." It was only after a republican revolution overthrew the last dynasty, the Qīng, in 1911, that the country incorporated "China" into its name. Both the Republic of China, founded in 1911, and the post-1949 People's Republic of China use *Zhonghua* rather than *Zhongguo* to stand for China.

Confucius also intended the principle known as the rectification of names to indicate who was privileged to speak. It was more than forty years ago that I began studying Chinese history and language, and I have lived and traveled extensively in the mainland, Taiwan, and Hong Kong. Although I am not Chinese, I take encouragement from the words of the historian Liú Xù (887–947), who drew this lesson about the writing of history from chess: "Those in the game see less clearly than those observing from outside."[4]

Controversy swirls around many Chinese historical events and actors. Confucius promoted moderation in all things and a strict social hierarchy. Did his ideas ensure the stability and continuity of Chinese civilization, or hold China back from progress? Chinese thinkers have hotly debated Confucius's ideas for thousands of years. I'll do my best to represent fairly, or at least note the existence of, diverse perspectives on this and other issues. Some readers might find this politically inconvenient or confronting. My loyalty is to historical truth as I best understand it.

For transcribing Chinese words and names in this book, I use Hànyǔ Pīnyīn, the official romanization system of the PRC, except where an older spelling will be more familiar to readers—Confucius rather than Kǒngzǐ, Sun Yat-sen instead of Sūn Zhōngshān, Chiang Kai-shek over Jiǎng Jièshí, the Yangtze and Yellow Rivers rather than Chángjiāng and Huánghé, and *I Ching* for the ancient book of divination *Yì Jīng*, for example. I do use *Dào Dé Jīng* instead of the perhaps more familiar *Tao Te Ching* for the Daoist ("Taoist") classic, as it is closer to the actual pronunciation; ditto Sūnzǐ rather than Sun Tsu for the author of *The Art of War*. The terms "chancellor" and "prime minister" both indicate the chief minister in an emperor's court.

Chinese is a tonal language—the contoured pitch at which words are spoken is integral to the meaning. When using Pinyin, I add diacritics to indicate the four tones of Putonghua in the first instance a word appears, as well as in the index, where you'll also find the Chinese characters for individuals' names.

Pinyin is a relatively straightforward guide to pronunciation for speakers of European languages, with a few quirks: *X* (as in Xi Jinping) is pronounced like the *sh* in "she"; *C* (as in Cáo Cāo) is pronounced like the *ts* in "its"; *Q* (as in the Qin dynasty) is pronounced like the *ch* in "cheese"; *Zh* (as in Zhōu Ēnlái) is pronounced like a *j*, but with the tongue curled almost to the roof of the mouth; and *Z* (as in Zūnyì) is like the *ds* in "adds."

When the CPC came to power in 1949, less than a quarter of the population could read or write. To promote literacy, they simplified many of the ten thousand most commonly used characters, including some of the two thousand to three thousand characters necessary for basic literacy. I use the traditional, complex forms until we reach 1949, and the simplified forms thereafter—except in reference to Taiwan and Hong Kong, where complex forms are still in use.

Chinese surnames come before given names—Aì is the surname of the artist Aì Wèiwèi and Sīmǎ the surname of the ancient historian Sīmǎ Qiān. Scholars, writers, and emperors

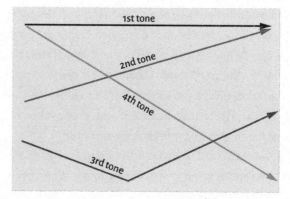

The shape of the diacritic roughly corresponds to the tone in Putonghua—
high and steady for the first tone, rising for the second, and so on.

typically went by several names or titles over a lifetime. To avoid
confusion, I choose the most common, identifying emperors
by their reign titles ("the Qiánlóng emperor"), using "Lady" for
imperial concubines (secondary wives) of different ranks, and
referring to authors by their pen names.

"China" and the adjective "Chinese" here mainly refer to
China in a historical or cultural sense: the China of the Tang
dynasty, or Chinese calligraphy, for example. I use the acro-
nym "PRC" when referring specifically to the People's Republic of China, and "the mainland" to indicate that part of the
Chinese world over which the CPC has exercised direct rule
since 1949. "Hong Kong" signifies the territory encompassing Hong Kong Island, Kowloon, and the New Territories,
formally known as the Hong Kong Special Administrative
Region of the People's Republic of China. "Taiwan" indicates
the geographical and political entity that officially calls itself

the Republic of China and that the CPC insists must be referred to as Taiwan, China.

Another thing: the *s* in "Great Walls" and "Silk Roads" is not a typo. The Great Walls are a series of discontinuous and sometimes parallel fortifications constructed over different historical periods. Similarly, there were several trading routes for silk and other goods in ancient times, including one also known as the Tea Road, originating in China's Southwest, where tea was first cultivated.

In writing a short history, a wise person might focus on a few key themes or personalities. I'm not so wise. Faced with deciding between key individuals, economic and social developments, military history, and aesthetic and intellectual currents, I choose ... everything. I highlight themes, events, and personalities that I think illuminate the essence of their time and the evolution of Chinese civilization and nationhood. I don't name-check all of China's many emperors, rebels, thinkers, artists, eccentrics, inventors, politicians, or poets. I do introduce you to some of the most influential and interesting ones and, to the extent possible in such a short volume, let them speak for themselves. You'll read quotations from the work of ancient historians, modern politicians, poets, and satirists. History is, of course, herstory as well—expect to meet a few more women on these pages than you may find in other general histories.

China contains a multitude. Its unruly complexity is part of its grandeur.

# ORIGINS

## An Egg Hatches and a Civilization Is Born

*Far, far back in time, a popular Chinese creation story tells us, primal chaos congealed into an egg, in which the complementary cosmic energies of Yīn 陰 and Yáng 陽 thickened around a hairy, horned giant called Pángǔ. Eighteen thousand years passed. Pangu hatched fully formed, holding an axe, with which he hacked apart the Yin and Yang. The Yin became the earth beneath his feet, and the Yang, the sky. As he grew taller, he pushed the two further and further apart. After Pangu died, his flesh turned to soil, his sweat to rain, and his breath to wind. His blood flowed as rivers and seas. His eyes became the sun and the moon. From his hair sprang plants and trees, and the fleas in his fur became animals and people.*

*Eons flew by. Warring deities laid waste to the heavens. Then Nǚwā, the daughter of the celestial Jade Emperor, repaired the sky with colored stones. Some say it was Nüwa who created humans, fashioning them from clay.*

AROUND 780,000 YEARS AGO, the Yellow River flowed much closer to the place we call Beijing than it does now, creating a fertile alluvial plain. Wild pigs, buffalo, sheep, and deer roamed the lush meadows that spread out from China's second-largest river, and birds nested in forests dense with nut and fruit trees. In caves in the surrounding mountains, Peking man (*Homo erectus pekinensis*) and other of humankind's Stone Age ancestors sheltered from saber-toothed cats, wolves, bears, panthers, and other predators, coming down to the flats to hunt and gather.

Two tribes, the Huá and Xià, from whom the ethnic majority Han Chinese claim descent, settled around the river's middle and lower reaches. At some point around thirteen thousand years ago, one of them carved a bird from singed bone, two centimeters in length and balanced on a pedestal—the most ancient animal sculpture ever found in East Asia. [1]

This carved bird, East Asia's most ancient animal sculpture, was found in a pile of dirt left behind by a construction crew digging a well in Língjǐng, Hénán province, in 2020.

Farming heralded the beginning of the Neolithic (New Stone) Age. In the relatively arid North, people cultivated millet, and in the fertile ground of the South, rice. Farmers raised pigs, sheep, and cattle and domesticated wild dogs. They built homes of mud brick, mud-plastered wood, and stone. In some places, their dwellings featured glossy, red pottery walls and roofs of fired mud and wood. The houses clustered in walled communities that would eventually dot the central plains. With more time for leisure, people crafted bowls, goblets, and musical instruments of fired clay, decorating them with abstract patterns and zoomorphic figures. They carved jade, turquoise, and bone into jewelry and objects for use in worship or burial rites.

A fragment of silk from the Yellow River Valley, the oldest in the world, shows that the Chinese practiced sericulture—the production of silk—as early as 3630 BCE. Sericulture seems to have been largely women's work from the start, from chopping mulberry leaves to feed the silkworms—the larvae of the *Bombyx mori* moth—to collecting the cocoons and boiling them to loosen their threads before spinning, dyeing, and weaving them into cloth.

Silk would eventually play an important part in China's diplomacy and trade, as well as in fashion, communications, and art (serving as paper and canvas). But how did anyone think of boiling moth cocoons in the first place?

One story goes that Madame Xīlíng, the principal wife of the semi-mythical Yellow Emperor, was sipping tea under a mulberry tree when a cocoon dropped into her cup and began to unspool. Gathering up the shimmering thread, she realized it was strong enough to weave.

The care and feeding of silkworms (which eat mulberry leaves) is the foundation of sericulture, which dates back to Neolithic times in China.

Other legends say it was Xiling's husband, the Yellow Emperor himself, who figured this out. Similar legends credit him with inventing many other things, from carts, boats, wooden houses, and the pottery wheel to the calendar, and even a bamboo pan flute tuned to the song of the mythical phoenix (a totem of the South, as the dragon is of the North). A mighty general, the Yellow Emperor fought fierce battles against his rivals—said to include horned demons and giants—to unify the tribes north of the Yellow River.

Accounts that also credit the Yellow Emperor with inventing writing underlie the popular claim that China has 5,000 years of recorded history. The earliest hard evidence of Chinese script, however, dates back 3,500 years, which makes it the third—or fourth—oldest system of writing in the world, after those of the Sumerians in Mesopotamia, the Egyptians, and possibly the Minoans (whose writing system developed around the same time as the Chinese).

It's unclear if the Yellow Emperor was an actual individual who, in the telling and retelling of his story, acquired godlike characteristics, or if he began as a god and was later given a human face. He has been a cult figure since the fifth century BCE. Han Chinese consider the Yellow Emperor and his successor, Yán Dì, the Fiery Emperor, their oldest ancestors.

Another semi-mythical dynasty, the Xia, began around 2100 BCE, after the reign of another three legendary emperors, Yáo, Shùn, and Yǔ. Historical records firm up around five or six hundred years later, when the Bronze Age began and, with it, the Shāng dynasty, which lasted more than six hundred years, beginning in the sixteenth century BCE.

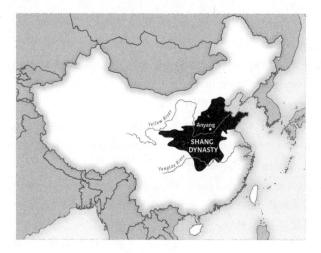

The Shang ruled over the fertile land on the lower reaches of the Yellow River from its capital of Ānyáng, in today's Henan province.

## RECORDS ON SHELL AND BONE

The rulers of the Shang dynasty were warlike and highly superstitious, worshipping a number of gods and conducting human sacrifices to them. They kept slaves, including musicians and dancers. Each king had a primary wife and many secondary ones, or concubines—for most of Chinese history, men with the means to provide for more than one wife were free to take concubines. (In the Chinese language, a man "takes," *qǔ* 娶, a wife, whereas a woman is "given," *jià* 嫁, in marriage.)

The Shang used a calendar based on both the cycles of the moon and the solar year, and invented a system of timekeeping that divided days into twelve two-hour blocks—a system that, with some revisions, remained in use for the next three and a half millennia.

We know all this because their shamans would anoint the shoulder blades of oxen and the plastrons (undershells) of tortoises with blood and heat them until they cracked. They interpreted the pattern of the cracks to answer such questions as "How will the harvests be this year?" "Should I go to war?" "Does my tooth hurt because I offended my ancestors?" The shamans inscribed the answers on the bones in the earliest recognized versions of Chinese characters, *jiǎgǔwén* 甲骨文—shell bone writing, also called oracle bone script.

Chinese characters may be concrete or pictorial: for example, *rì* 日 for sun and *yuè* 月 for moon. They may be conceptual: combining sun and moon makes *míng* 明, meaning "bright." Other characters are constructed from a "radical," or signific—typically a stylized form of a simple character indicating a class of meaning ("jade," "human," "fire," and so on)—and a phonetic, which suggests its pronunciation but gives no indication of tone (which, like pronunciation, can vary from place to place).

The character for horse, *mǎ* 馬, is highly pictorial: you can see the horse's galloping legs and flying mane. It can also be used as either a radical or a phonetic. It's a radical in the character *yù* 馭, which means "to drive a horse-drawn chariot," and a phonetic in the character *mā* 媽, meaning mother, where the radical is 女, woman.

**THE HISTORICAL DEVELOPMENT OF FOUR CHARACTERS**

| | 1. *xià* below, under, down | 2. *mǎ* horse | 3. *dé* to get, attain | 4. *qīng* mobility, court-official |
|---|---|---|---|---|
| Pre-historical marks | 丁 | | | |
| Oracle bone inscription | | | | |
| Great-seal | 丁 | | | |
| Small-seal | 下 | | | |
| Clerical | 下 | 馬 | 得 | 卿 |
| Grass | | | | |
| Regular | 下 | 馬 | 得 | 卿 |
| Running | 下 | 馬 | 得 | 卿 |

Oracle bone script is the earliest form of Chinese writing. Unlike alphabetic languages, which use letters to represent sounds, Chinese writing is logographic, using characters to represent words or ideas.

Oracle bones tell the story of a formidable woman, Fù Hǎo, who was the consort of the Shang king Wǔ Dīng (reign 1250–1192 BCE). A hunter and a warrior, she once led thirteen thousand men into battle against the king's enemies. (Some sources say her dowry included an army.) She also presided over divination and other ceremonies. When she died, she was buried with four battle-axes. Her military activities may or may not have been exceptional for the time, but her independent fortune and burial in her own tomb suggest that the Shang may have been a semi-matriarchal society.[2]

Fu Hao's enjoyment of hunting was typical of the Shang ruling class, who were often buried with their favorite hunting dogs. Sometimes they were buried with their servants as well, to ensure comfort in the afterlife. Fortunately for the servants, figurines eventually took the place of real people.

The common people had a lot to say about the behavior of the ruling classes. We know this thanks to one of the oldest collections of poetry in the world, the *Book of Odes*. Its verses and folk songs speak of love and courtship, sorrow and grief, housework, farming, the life of the soldier or soldier's wife— and exploitation:

> *You neither sow nor reap,*
> *So how do you fill so many bins with grain?*
> *You neither hunt nor trap,*
> *So from where come the quail hanging in your*
> *courtyard?*
> *The superior man*
> *Eats not the bread of idleness.*[3]

The invention of writing enabled rulers to govern a large kingdom, with couriers galloping from one part of the realm to the next, bearing transmissions brushed onto silk or strips of bamboo. Advanced communications, along with horse-drawn chariots and bronze-tipped spears and battle-axes, made the Shang a formidable military power. But, setting a pattern that would repeat itself many times throughout China's long history, its rulers grew corrupt, cruel, and negligent, and the people, suffering under misrule, rebelled. The Zhōu, originally a vassal state of the Shang, rose up and conquered the Shang around 1122 BCE.

The Zhou's first rulers reputedly governed so wisely that they presented future sovereigns and thinkers with a conundrum: how to recreate that perfect polity?

# THE ZHOU

## From Ideal Rule to Warring States

*After the death of the first king of the Zhou, King Wǔ, the throne passed to his young son, with his brother, the Duke of Zhou, as regent. The rule of the Duke of Zhou was reputedly a time of such peace and stability that for more than forty years not a single crime was committed. The hereditary, landowning nobility expressed their submission to the Zhou through an exchange of gifts and ritualistic ceremonies. It was China's first golden age, and it lasted until around 770 BCE, when nomadic tribes invaded from the northwest, forcing the Zhou rulers to flee eastward, following which the Zhou rapidly declined in strength and glory.*

THE FIRST, HALCYON ERA OF THE ZHOU became known as the Western Zhou. The second, the Eastern Zhou, which divides into the Spring and Autumn (771–476 BCE) and Warring States (475–221 BCE) periods, was a violent and volatile time. Once-loyal vassal states entered into increasingly violent conflict with both the rulers of the Zhou and one another. Large states swallowed smaller ones until only seven were left, these fighting ferociously among themselves for hegemony.

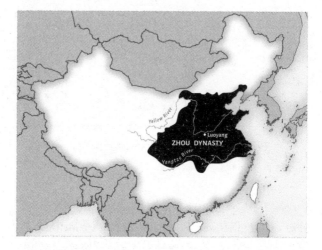

At its height, the Zhou's dominion stretched from south of the Yangtze River to the northern steppes.

The era, perhaps unsurprisingly, produced one of the world's most famous books of military strategy, *The Art of War* by Sunzi. Its thirty-six stratagems are primarily aimed at *avoiding* combat:

The highest realization of warfare is to attack the enemy's plans; next is to attack their alliances; next to attack their army; and the lowest is to attack their fortified cities. Thus one who excels at employing the military subjugates other people's armies without engaging in battle, captures other people's fortified cities without attacking them, and destroys other people's states without prolonged fighting.[1]

It was also an exceptionally fertile time for philosophy, and not just in China. In the lands to the west, the young Siddhārtha Gautama (circa 450 BCE) acquired the spiritual insights that would earn him the title of Buddha, or Enlightened One. In Asia Minor, a Grecian, Thales of Miletus (c. 624–548 BCE), explored ways of explaining the world that didn't rely on mythology, becoming the West's first philosopher, followed less than a century later by Socrates, then Plato and Aristotle. In China, a number of thinkers came along who would influence thought and politics there, and in other parts of Asia, to this day. Prime among them was Confucius.

## SAGE ADVICE

Confucius, or Kongzi ("Master Kong"), was born in 551 BCE in Qūfù, in today's Shāndōng province. Living in an age of extreme violence and disorder, he idealized the rule of the Duke of Zhou. He believed the duke's success was due to his attention to ritual and moral example. Confucius, who promoted education, believed that the *jūnzǐ* 君子, the educated or cultivated man, stood at the top of the social order and was duty-bound to use his knowledge to help guide his ruler. An intrepid traveler in dangerous times, Confucius wandered from place to place, trying to find a ruler to serve while expounding his ideas about society and governance in conversation with his talented disciples. He reportedly asked seventy-two different rulers if he could advise them. Briefly given a post as a minister in his home state of Lǔ, he so irritated the other men at court with his insistence on moral rectitude that they conspired to get rid of him.

Confucius considered loyalty a prime virtue. Loyalty involved speaking truth to power: "Can you spare those whom you love? Can loyalty refrain from admonishing?"[2] The ideal of the loyal yet critical "scholar-official" would endure, even if rulers didn't always welcome it in practice. If loyalty determined relations in the public sphere, filial piety—respect for and obedience to one's parents—was its analogue in the personal realm. The notion of "ancestor worship"—which in its most elemental form involved bowing before tablets inscribed with the names of male ancestors—preceded Confucius, though its rituals are strongly associated with his teachings.

He believed that if everyone in a society knows their place— if women respect and obey their husbands, sons their fathers, and men their prince—things are bound to go well for family, society, and state. It wasn't easy for those on top: "Women and underlings are especially difficult to handle: be friendly, and they become familiar; be distant, and they resent it."[3]

Another Confucian tenet was the "golden mean," *zhōngyōng* 中庸: moderation in all things. Told that a certain nobleman thought thrice before acting, he remarked that twice was enough. He frowned on vulgar displays of wealth as both distasteful and socially disruptive. He was also something of a realist: "I have never seen a man who loved virtue as much as sex."[4]

Confucius thought that rites reinforced moral teachings and embedded them in daily life. When his disciple Zǐgòng questioned if it was necessary to sacrifice a sheep on a particular occasion, Confucius replied: "You love the sheep—I love the ceremony."[5]

Nothing was too small or too insignificant for Confucius to comment on. He prescribed the correct length for men's nightgowns (to the knee), disapproved of conversation during meals and in bed, advised men that red and violet were not suitable colors to wear at home, and urged people to straighten their mats before sitting down. Music should not excite carnal or other desires but rather assist in the worship of gods or the praise of good rulers.

An apocryphal story has it that Confucius once became separated from his students in a strange city. They were searching for him when a local informed them that he'd seen a man who appeared "crestfallen, like a homeless wandering dog."[6] This clue led them to their master. When they told Confucius how the man had described him, he agreed it was fitting. This much-recited anecdote prompted the cultural critic turned democracy activist (and later Nobel Peace Prize laureate) Liú Xiǎobō (1955–2017) to remark cynically: "Had he found a ruler to take him in, the stray dog would have become a guard dog."[7]

Following Confucius's death in 479 BCE, two generations of disciples compiled his aphorisms into *The Analects*, considered one of the foundational texts of Chinese civilization. As the scholar-translator Pierre Ryckmans (pen name Simon Leys) has written, "No book in the entire history of the world has exerted, over a longer period of time, a greater influence on a larger number of people than this slim little volume."[8]

Mencius, or Mèngzǐ, (c. 372–289 BCE) was a prominent follower of Confucius. He identified four cardinal virtues, associating each with an emotional quality: benevolence with compassion, righteousness with scorn, propriety with respect, and wisdom with judgment. Everyone is born with these innate qualities, he believed, but needs to consciously cultivate them. He also stated that it is human nature to desire drink, food, and sex.[9]

Mencius's ideas would become the basis of the notion of the Mandate of Heaven, *tiānmìng* 天命, by which the emperor, or Son of Heaven, *tiānzǐ* 天子, enjoys a semidivine authority to rule. Mencius described politics as a cycle of "order and chaos." If an emperor forsook his mandate through immoral behavior or incompetence, rebellion and dynastic change was justified: "When the prince regards his ministers as his hands and feet, his ministers regard their prince as their belly and heart; when he regards them as his dogs and horses, they regard him as any other man; when he regards them as the ground or as grass, they regard him as a robber and an enemy."[10] Confucius said that for a *junzi* to serve a bad ruler was "shameful." Mencius went further—just as you'd execute a robber or a ruffian, you should kill an errant tyrant.[11]

## OTHER WAYS

Mòzǐ, another important philosopher, lived around the same time as Mencius. Mozi detested displays of wealth and elaborate rituals, advocating for an egalitarian, pacifist society animated by universal love. Few rulers ever embraced his ideas, though many people have speculated on how differently things might have turned out had they done so.

Lǎozǐ, "Old Master," believed that under perfect rule, people were unaware they even had a ruler: "When his tasks are accomplished and his work done, the people all remark, 'We have done it ourselves.'"[12] Laozi is attributed as the author of the aphoristic mystical text the *Dao De Jing*, the foundational text of the philosophy, and later religion, of Daoism. The word *dào* 道 signifies a path in both the literal and the metaphorical sense. It is often translated as "the Way." It can also mean "to speak." The first line in the *Dao De Jing* uses it in both senses: "The Way (*dao*) that can be expressed in words (*dao*) is not the eternal Way (*dao*)."[13] Daoism advocates flowing along the course that nature sets. The martial arts star Bruce Lee's famous invocation to "be water" pays homage to Laozi, who wrote:

> Water wends its way gently round every obstacle, avoids height, sinks to depths, bends with curves, fills and pours, fits into Square and Circle, into Small and Great, into springs and rivers, smooths the Surface of things, accepts all manner of filth, contains gold, extinguishes fire, brings Life to plants and trees, softens and moistens the soil, brings Benefit to the Myriad Things, never Contending, always lower, always beneath All-under-Heaven, Supremely Soft and Gentle.[14]

Perhaps the most famous line from the *Dao De Jing* is "A journey of a thousand miles begins with a single step."

We know very little about Laozi's life. We don't even know when he lived. The oldest known versions of the *Dao De Jing* date back to the eighth century BCE. Because the text was inscribed on strips of bamboo, no one can even say for sure in what order it is meant to be read. He's a mysterious figure in many ways, as suggested in this playful poem by the poet Bái Jūyì, who lived more than a thousand years afterward:

> *Those who speak*
> *Know nothing;*
> *Those who Know*
> *Are silent.*

*Those Words, I'm told,*
*Were uttered*
*By Lao-tzu.*
*If we're to believe*
*That he himself*
*Was someone who Knew,*
*Why did he end up*
*Writing a Book*
*Of Five Thousand Words?*[15]

Zhuāngzǐ, the best-known Daoist thinker after Laozi, lived around the fourth century BCE. He illustrated the abstruse ideas in the *Dao De Jing* with witty parables and arresting anecdotes. One of Zhuangzi's most famous stories involved a dream that he was a butterfly. Waking, he understood that he was a man who'd dreamt he was a butterfly. But then he wondered if perhaps he was a butterfly dreaming he was a man who'd dreamt he was a butterfly. How could one know?

The whimsical story of the butterfly dream is typical of Zhuangzi's use of parable to illuminate Daoist ideas of transformation, impermanence, perception, and reality.

Zhuangzi is the source of many apocryphal tales of encounters between Confucius and Laozi. In one, Confucius, wanting to put his ideas before the rulers of a kingdom, needed a contact to the court. He approached Laozi, who in this story was a retired palace librarian. As Confucius elaborated on his ideas, Laozi grew impatient.

"Give it to me in a nutshell," he said.

Confucius answered: "Goodness and duty."

Laozi replied that if goodness was innate to humanity, people only needed to reach inward and follow their nature: "The swan does not need a daily bath in order to remain white; the crow does not need a daily inking in order to remain black."[16]

Whereas Confucians were obsessed with the correct course of action in any situation, Daoists preached *wúwéi* 無為, "inaction"—flowing like water does in nature. Followers of Confucius yearned to serve a ruler; Daoists were famously uninterested in taking part in government. Their followers developed a diverse set of rituals and disciplines, ranging from meditation, alchemy, and energetic healing to the pursuit of immortality through sexual practices (such as non-ejaculation for men) and the consumption of potions. Daoists have irritated straight-laced Confucians for millennia.

The two streams of thought were united, however, in their reverence for the ancient and mysterious divination text the *I Ching*, or *Book of Changes*. The *I Ching* contains sixty-four hexagrams, representing all possible groupings of solid (*Yang*) and broken (*Yin*) lines in sets of six. Like the *Dao De Jing*, the *I Ching* first appeared as an unordered bundle of bamboo strips. No one knows who wrote it. Translator John Minford calls it "the strangest and most incomprehensible item in the [Chinese] canon ... a pillar of state ideology, and yet at the same time a subtle and powerful vehicle for a wide range of heterodox ideas." He credits its position as the ultimate "book of wisdom" in China to the fact that "the central *I Ching* concepts, Yin and Yang, the Tao, Good Faith, and Self-Cultivation, have preoccupied almost every Chinese thinker until the twentieth century."[17]

Yin and Yang, a cosmic duality of opposing but complementary and interdependent forces associated with ideas of feminine and masculine, dark and light, lie at the center of Chinese mystical thought.

Another prominent thinker of the Warring States period, Hánfēizǐ (280–233 BCE), wrote the first known commentary on the *Dao De Jing*. He also gives us the first mention of chopsticks, noting that a Shang king used an ivory pair. Hanfeizi was the founder of a school of thought known as Legalism. He argued that governing by moral example, as advocated by Confucius, was futile. Right and wrong were whatever the ruler wanted them to be. Confucius believed that laws only encouraged people to think of ways to get around them. Hanfeizi believed laws were the basis of efficient government. He proposed systems of mutual surveillance and a regime that rewarded desirable behavior and punished undesirable behavior according to standards set by the ruler: "The object of rewards is to encourage;

that of punishments, to prevent."[18] The contemporary writer Zhā Jiànyīng has written of the enduring importance of Hanfeizi's ideas: "In the art of Chinese-style imperial rule, if Confucianism is the outer shell, then Legalism is its inner core," she states. "To put it more bluntly, it is the abiding heart of darkness of the Chinese state."[19]

These three major streams of thought—Confucianism, Daoism, and Legalism—together with other different schools and variations, collectively known as the "One Hundred Schools of Thought," would compete, interact, and inspire society and governance in China for millennia.

## THE POET AND THE CONQUEROR

After one of the most aggressive states, the Qín, on the northwestern edge of Chinese civilization, conquered another called the Chǔ, in the central valley of the Yangtze River, the talented Chu poet Qū Yuán (343–278 BCE), in despair for his beloved homeland, committed suicide by throwing himself into a river. According to legend, local fishermen raced in their boats to save him; failing, they threw rice into the river so the fish wouldn't eat his body. To this day, on the fifth day of the fifth lunar month, people race "dragon boats" and eat glutinous rice steamed in bamboo leaves to commemorate Qu Yuan, whose name is synonymous with loyalty and patriotic sacrifice.

In 246 BCE, a thirteen-year-old boy called Yíng Zhèng became king of Qin, the powerful state that had conquered Chu. It took twenty-five years, but he vanquished the failing Eastern Zhou and all the other remaining states, bringing an end to this messy, if philosophically fertile, period of history.

# 3

## THE QIN

### Unification, Tyranny, and All Under Heaven

*In 221 BCE, Ying Zheng declared himself Qín Shǐhuáng, the First Emperor of Qin, appropriating a title previously reserved for mythical sovereigns and semi-deities such as the Yellow Emperor. Never before had so much territory—1.3 million square miles (3.4 million sq km)—been unified under one ruler. Although the Qin would barely outlast its founder's death, China scholar Geremie Barmé notes that its "imperial ambition and harsh rule has haunted Chinese politics ever since."[1]*

HAVING CONQUERED ALL UNDER HEAVEN, *tiānxià* 天下, by force, Qin Shihuang needed to secure it against hostile incursions. He ordered nearly a million soldiers and commoners—around one out of five of his subjects—to labor on a network of roads and tamped-earth border walls, signal towers, and watchtowers along the northern boundary of his empire. The Great Walls were primarily intended to keep out the loose confederation of warlike nomadic tribes the Chinese called the Xiōngnú 匈奴, sometimes referred to as the Hun in English.

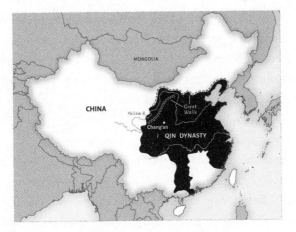

The Qin reinforced and linked existing border walls with new ones to create the first Great Walls, intended to secure its northern frontier.

## THE POWER OF ONE

Previously, as in the Zhou, it had been the custom for states to parcel the land into fiefdoms and award these to members of the royal family and their supporters. Qin Shihuang, wary of the subversive power of a strong landed gentry, instead carved his realm into thirty-six (later forty-eight) administrative regions. A joint civil and military bureaucracy were put in charge of these, reporting directly to him—the Qin was thus the first unified and centralized Chinese state. Its capital was at Cháng'ān (near present-day Xī'ān, in the Northeast). He introduced a single currency, round copper coins with a square hole in the middle—a template used until 1911. He also unified measurements for length and volume, and even standardized the width of cart axles—an inspired solution to the danger and inconvenience posed by unsurfaced roads furrowed by differently spaced wheel ruts.

One of his greatest legacies was the standardization of writing. Even the most common Chinese characters were written differently from place to place, having evolved independently. This hampered the Qin's ability to communicate its policies and laws. So Qin Shihuang ordered that characters be made uniform. Standardization of writing laid the foundations for both efficient government and a common literary culture.

Qin Shihuang had little time for the followers of Confucius, with their fixation on virtuous rule. He preferred the Legalist philosophy of strict laws and severe punishments—even if the Qin, during the wars of conquest, had imprisoned Hanfeizi himself. The Legalist philosopher died in custody in 233 BCE, forced to commit suicide, most likely by Qin Shihuang's chief adviser and, later, chancellor, Lǐ Sī (c. 280–208 BCE), who may have seen Hanfeizi as a rival. Li Si was wily and ruthless. When an educated man criticized one of the emperor's decisions in 213 BCE, Li Si advised his ruler to take drastic measures against dissent, which could take the form of unfavorable comparisons with the Western Zhou or other historical exemplars:

> I humbly propose that all historical records but those of Qin be burned. If anyone who is not a court scholar dares to keep the ancient songs, historical records or writings of the hundred schools, these should be confiscated and burned by the provincial governor and army commander. Those who in conversation dare to quote the old songs and records should be publicly executed; those who use old precedents to oppose the new order should have their families wiped out; and officers who know of such cases but fail to report them should be punished in the same way.

If thirty days after the issuing of this order the owners of these books have still not had them destroyed, they should have their face tattooed and be condemned to hard labour at the Great Wall.[2]

Works on medicine and agriculture and the *I Ching* were among those exempted from the conflagration. Luckily, some copies of the *Book of Odes*, *The Analects*, and other classics survived. According to the historian Sima Qian (c. 145–86 BCE), Qin Shihuang also had more than 460 scholars buried alive. This may not be entirely accurate: live burial wasn't one of the types of execution listed in the Qin legal code, and Sima Qian was writing more than one hundred years after the event. No one contests, however, that the Qin fiercely and widely persecuted scholars, especially Confucians.

The Qin would live on as a symbol of tyranny—the expression "burn the books and bury the scholars"[3] entered the language during the following dynasty, the Han, as a metaphor for the despotic repression of intellectual freedom. A famous essay by the reclusive poet Táo Yuānmíng, written five centuries later, describes a mythical place, Peach Blossom Spring, where the descendants of people who had *bì Qín* 避秦, "fled the Qin," could live in peace and isolation.

In 1958, Communist Party of China chairman Máo Zédōng embraced the notion that he could compare with Qin Shihuang in tyranny: "What's the big deal about Qin Shihuang? He buried only 460 Confucians alive; well, we've buried 46,000. . . . They attack us for being just another Qin Shihuang. Well, they're wrong. We're a hundred times greater than Qin Shihuang. They say we're dictatorial like Qin Shihuang. Certainly, we've never denied it."[4]

Zhāng Yìmóu's 2002 film *Hero* captures the ambivalence with which many still regard Qin Shihuang today. The eponymous hero sets out to assassinate Qin Shihuang. At the last moment, he considers the possibility that the unity of "all under heaven" is better than division and chaos, even if it means tyranny, and abandons his plan. Qin Shihuang has him executed anyway.

In 2019, the US-based physicist Yangyang Cheng asked, "How many libraries must be set on fire, how many ideas erased, so an empire can paint a mirage of national unity from the ashes, draw a border around different names and tongues, and call it 'all under heaven'?"[5] The phrase *bi Qin* continues to pop up in dissident writings in the twenty-first century.

Qin Shihuang, the first ruler to unify all the existing states and declare himself emperor, lives on as a symbol of both unity and tyranny.

Qin Shihuang made enemies of the feudal nobility when he took away their customary privileges. Mass conscriptions of labor and the high taxes needed to carry out his ambitious plans, from Great Walls to a lavish mausoleum, caused ordinary people to despise him. People still recite the legend of Mèng Jiāngnǔ, a young bride whose husband was abducted by soldiers and sent to labor on the Great Walls just days after their marriage. When winter fell, she packed his warm clothes and journeyed more than a thousand miles to find him. By the time she reached the place where he'd been working, he was dead. She cried so hard and long, it's said, her tears brought down the section of wall in which his bones were interred.

## A FISHY BUSINESS

Qin Shihuang died in 210 BCE while touring his empire. Some speculate he was murdered. There had certainly been assassination attempts. It's also possible he died of poisoning from drinking a Daoist immortality potion containing mercury. Li Si, who was traveling with him, shared the news of the emperor's death only with the emperor's second son, who was also in the imperial entourage, and several trusted eunuchs (castrated slaves). Li Si feared that if word of his father's death reached the boy's older brother, the crown prince, who detested Li Si, he might lead an army out to kill him.

Li Si trusted no one. To keep the death from the rest of the entourage, he is said to have ordered wagons loaded with fish to travel ahead and behind the emperor's carriage, to disguise the stink of his rotting body. He forged a secret decree in the emperor's name ordering the crown prince to commit suicide and contrived, upon their return to Chang'an, to have the younger one designated Second Emperor of the Qin. The new emperor, it turned out, wasn't a fan of Li Si either—launching a violent purge of the court, he had him executed, along with his entire family.

Qin Shihuang had ordered work to begin on his tomb when he became King of Qin at the age of thirteen. It took more than seven hundred thousand craftsmen and builders thirty-six years, working around the clock, to complete. The roof was studded with pearls that formed a map of the constellations, and decorating the floor was a topographical representation of the empire, complete with rivers of flowing mercury. But until 1974, when some peasants stumbled upon something unusual while digging a well, no one knew that guarding Qin Shihuang and his tomb in the afterlife was an underground army of almost eight thousand life-size terra-cotta warriors and five hundred terra-cotta horses.

Each terra-cotta warrior has unique features, which suggests that they were modeled after real people. Other pits house terra-cotta acrobats, fourteen-sided stone dice, and waterbirds cast in bronze.

Sima Qian observed that no matter how capable a dynasty's founder, once corruption set in, the dynasty was bound to fail. A new, vigorous house would conquer it and rule until its own vitality dissipated. By the time of Qin Shihuang's death, there was such widespread discontent with the Qin's overbearing punishments and oppressive taxes that, as an official of the dynasty that replaced the Qin put it, a rebel leader "had only to wave his arms for the whole empire to answer like an echo."[6] Looters broke into Qin Shihuang's tomb and stole or destroyed many of its fabled treasures, and the Qin's archives went up in flames. A eunuch murdered the Second Emperor. The Third— either a nephew, brother, uncle, or cousin of the Second, Sima Qian wasn't sure—sat on the throne for forty-odd days before surrendering to Liú Bāng, a former local law enforcer turned rebel leader. Despite the long shadow it would cast, the rule of the Qin lasted less than two decades.

Before the coup, the rebel leaders had agreed to divide the empire among themselves, but Liu Bang turned on his erstwhile allies. Within a year of the Qin's collapse, Liu Bang's sole remaining rival was a man known as Bà Wáng, or Hegemon-King. Liu Bang ruled the west, calling his domain the Han, after a river in current-day Sìchuān. Ba Wang ruled the poet Qu Yuan's homeland of Chu, in the east.

Liu Bang was a rough but jovial and charismatic peasant; Ba Wang was educated and aristocratic, arrogant and ill-tempered. As antagonists, they were well matched. One story goes that Ba Wang captured Liu Bang's father and threatened to boil him alive, to which Liu Bang replied, "Send me the soup."

At last, Liu Bang's army, swollen with defectors from Chu, had Ba Wang surrounded. In what would become one of the most famous (if quasi-fictional) episodes in Chinese history, Liu Bang ordered the men of Chu in his army to sing loudly the songs of their homeland. The phrase "Chu songs on all sides," meaning hopelessly besieged and isolated, entered the language.

With Ba Wang was his favorite horse and his beloved concubine, Lady Yú. Legend has it that when he set his horse free, it refused to run off, and Lady Yu killed herself with Ba Wang's sword rather than desert him—a story told, among other places, in the opera at the center of Chén Kǎigē's 1993 Palme d'Or–winning film, *Farewell My Concubine*.

Liu Bang, the rebel of humble origins, went on to found one of China's greatest dynasties, the Han. As the Gāozǔ emperor (r. 202–195 BCE), he preserved many of the Legalist institutions of the Qin, including the organization of society into units of mutual surveillance. At the same time, he lightened the burden of its onerous taxes, softened its harshest laws, and allowed banned books to circulate once more. The Han—which would rule over even more territory than the Qin, encompassing some of the Korean Peninsula as well as parts of what are now Myanmar and Vietnam, and which overlapped in time with the Roman Empire—would win renown for its intellectual accomplishments, advances in governance, and technological innovations. But first it had to survive one of the most dramatic and bloody succession crises in Chinese history.

# THE HAN

## Intrigue, Innovation, and a Brief Interregnum

*Gaozu's wife, Empress Lǚ, had married the emperor when he was still the commoner known as Liu Bang. They had a mild-mannered son, Yíng. Recovering from an arrow wound received while putting down a rebellion, Gaozu wanted to send Ying to the battlefield in his place. Empress Lü, protective of her son, went out to command the troops herself.*

*Trouble began after Gaozu became smitten with a young concubine, Lady Qī. Lady Qi pleaded tearfully with Gaozu to appoint their son, Rúyì, as his successor. But Empress Lü was not so easily defeated. After Gaozu died, she installed fifteen-year-old Ying on the throne with the reign title Huì, and herself as regent, imprisoning Lady Qi in the palace women's quarters. The young Hui emperor, suspicious of his mother's intentions, kept Ruyi close by his side. The one morning he rose early to go hunting, leaving his half-brother alone in their room, Empress Lü had the boy poisoned. She ordered her guards to chop off Lady Qi's hands and feet, gouge out her eyes, cut out her tongue, and throw her into a pit with pigs and human excrement.*

HUI WAS SO DISTRESSED by his mother's actions that he took to his bed, and the comforts of drink and concubines. He refused to rule, claiming that, as the son of a monster, he was unfit to govern—paradoxically leaving her to run the empire in his name.

The Hui emperor had several sons with his concubines. After he died of illness in 188 BCE, Empress Lü placed one of his sons on the throne and had all the concubines murdered to prevent them from making any play for power. Then, realizing that the new emperor knew she'd killed his mother, she had him dispatched as well, putting an infant half-brother on the throne in his stead.

After Empress Lü's death, the court replaced the infant with one of Gaozu's sons by yet another concubine and ordered Lü's entire clan exterminated. She has served as an exemplar ever since about the dangers of giving women too much political power—a situation said to be "as unnatural as a hen crowing at daybreak."[1] For all that, it's generally acknowledged that she oversaw a time of relative peace and rising prosperity.

In 141 BCE, the dynasty's fifth ruler, Wǔdì, the Martial Emperor, ascended the throne at the age of fifteen. Wudi was young, but he had big ideas and was determined to become the kind of exemplary ruler of which Confucius spoke. *The Analects* wasn't a coherent guide to policy, even when considered in tandem with texts Confucius venerated, such as the *Book of Odes*, *I Ching*, and *Book of Rites*. Wudi encouraged the ceremonial performance of rites to symbolize the ruler's adherence to Confucian values. If ordinary people placed offerings of rice and wine before tablets with their ancestors' names on them, the emperor did the same on a grander scale, to honor his dynasty's founder, with musicians and dancers contributing to the solemn pageantry. Other rites celebrated times of planting or harvest, or involved sacrifices to Heaven—the celestial order and the higher authority from which, he, the Son of Heaven, received his mandate to rule over All Under Heaven. The idea of Confucian statecraft, or "state Confucianism," would continue to evolve in the centuries to come.

In 129 BCE, Wudi ordered officials to carry out a rigorous census. This would form the basis for an efficient system of taxation, as well as conscription for corvée (labor) or military service. It revealed a population of some thirty-six million people, about 2 percent of whom lived in towns or cities. Among other policies designed to increase prosperity, Wudi loosened state control over iron production and the mining and trade of salt, allowing for private enterprise to thrive. He also expanded the money economy first introduced in the Zhou. A new landed gentry, with both agricultural and industrial interests, came into being. Economic stability allowed the state to maintain a military strong enough to deal with both internal rebellions and external threats.

The Xiongnu continued to menace the northern borders. Over four centuries, the Han would maintain and build some 6,000 miles (10,000 km) of Great Walls, extending them westward into what is today Gānsù province. To control such a large territory, its military developed a sophisticated system of signals, record-keeping, passport documentation, and policing, including monitoring the sandy northern deserts for horse or camel prints.

The Han also came up with the idea of "pacification marriages," héqīn 和親, which involved sending princess brides as peace offerings to nomadic chieftains, along with generous dowries of silks, alcohol, rice, and copper cash. This didn't always work out well, especially for the trafficked young women, but "princess diplomacy" would be practiced for many centuries to come.

Most princess brides faced a lonely existence, as one described in this poem:

> *In a place far, far away from my home,*
> *I was married to the King of Wusun.*
> *The sky is my house,*
> *Felt tent my bedroom.*
> *So much I miss my early years in Chang'an,*
> *I wish I could fly back like a swan.*[2]

The Wūsūn 烏孫 were a seminomadic, Indo-European people. Féng Liáo, the maidservant of another princess bride who was married to one of their leaders, went on to marry a Wusun general herself. Intelligent and capable, Feng Liao proved so adept at diplomacy that the Wusun called on her to mediate disputes among themselves. Impressed, the Xuān emperor (r. 74–49 BCE) appointed her an official envoy of the Han court, the first woman to hold such a position. It was thanks to Feng Liao that during a political crisis in 64 BCE, the Wusun allied themselves with the Han and not the Xiongnu.

The Han also initiated a practice of keeping foreign princes hostage in the court to prevent their tribes or states from attacking. The Han furnished the princes with a luxurious lifestyle and an education, sometimes even rewarding them with official positions. The assumption was that, on return to their homelands, they would become cultural ambassadors for the Han.

Trade and diplomacy grew in tandem. The Han rulers sent gifts—silk and other covetable goods, including lacquerware and jade—to neighboring states and tribes. In return, they received what they lacked, such as horses. The "tribute system," by which smaller states ritualistically acknowledged the dominance of the Han (and later dynasties), led to more informal trade along what would be called the Silk and Tea Roads. These routes of commerce linked Chang'an, where the Han, like the Qin, made their capital, to Central Asian kingdoms and Persia via the Taklimakan Desert in the region today known as Xinjiang.

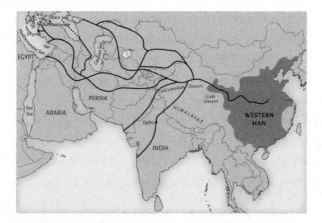

Shards of Han pottery found in Borneo and Korea testify to the extent of trade at this time, as does the arrival in China of jasmine, ivory, cucumber, and sesame from Persia and beyond.

## A CUT SLEEVE AND A CONFUCIAN REBEL

The burgeoning state required a competent civil service. Local officials put forward candidates, typically scions of the landed gentry, on the basis of their reputed virtue and incorruptibility, or because they had specific talents, such as military expertise, sought by the court. The appointees then took exams, the results guiding their placement in the bureaucracy. The system was plagued by nepotism and other forms of corruption. In 7 BCE, the twenty-year-old Āi emperor took the throne. Although intelligent, he was easily distracted, allowing the nepotism and corruption to flourish.

Ai's chief distraction was a minor official called Dǒng Xián, with whom he was enamored. In 2 BCE, he even made the twenty-five-year-old commander-in-chief of his armed forces. The story goes that one day, Ai and Dong were napping on the imperial bed when Ai was summoned to the court. Rather than disturb his beloved, whose head was resting on the long sleeve of his robe, Ai cut off the sleeve. The phrase "to cut the sleeve," *duànxiù* 斷袖, has entered the language as a metaphor for homosexuality. It is typically paired with "to share the peach," *fēntáo* 分桃, from an earlier tale related by Hanfeizi about a male lover of a prince who committed a great breach of protocol—for which he was not punished—by eating half a peach and giving the ruler the rest. "It is not women alone who can use their looks to attract the eyes of the ruler," Sima Qian observed. "Courtiers and eunuchs can play at that game as well. Many were the men of ancient times who gained favor this way."[3]

Castration was an ancient punishment in China. Castrates made useful servants, particularly for watching over wives and concubines, as there would be no doubts about the paternity of any children. Until the tenth century, a master could legally castrate his slaves for that purpose. (Although various emperors, including of the Han, moved to limit slavery, it was only legally abolished in 1910.[4]) Emperors also had eunuchs act as body-guards and maintain their palaces. Some impoverished families had their sons castrated in the hope that they could gain access to power and wealth. Different attitudes and rules governing eunuch-officials prevailed at different times. Most lived miserable lives performing menial tasks—what was described as "cleaning and sweeping," *qīngsǎo* 清掃—while a few enjoyed imperial favor and privilege.

Sima Qian had incurred Wudi's wrath by defending a general he believed the emperor had unjustly punished. He was given a choice: execution or castration. He had not yet finished writing his history, so he chose castration. As he explained to a friend in a letter: "A man has only one death. That death may be as weighty as Mount Tai, or it may be as light as a goose feather. It all depends upon the way he uses it. . . . The brave man does not always die for honor, while even the coward may fulfil his duty."[5] He researched his history, which he completed, through travel and interviews as well as the examination of documents; his *Records of the Grand Historian* remains one of the most ambitious, expansive, and influential books of the ancient world.

Before Ai died of illness in 1 BCE, he named Dong his successor. The court refused to honor this appointment. The official Wáng Mǎng led a rebellion, declaring himself emperor of the Xīn ("new") dynasty. An ardent Confucian who fancied that he embodied the spirit of the legendary Duke of Zhou, Wang Mang believed that "greed and vice" had weakened the Han social and political order: "The powerful counted their fields in thousands, while the weak had not even the space in which to insert the point of an awl."[6] He nationalized and redistributed farmland and outlawed slavery. He fined landowners who failed to cultivate their fields, urbanites who didn't plant trees, and citizens who refused to work.

After fourteen years in power, Wang Mang's regime grew corrupt. Nomadic tribes assailed the empire at its borders, internal rebellions erupted, and the Yellow River flooded—all taken as signs that he'd lost the Mandate of Heaven. In the year 23 CE, when pro-Han restoration forces broke into his palace, they found Wang Mang holed up with Daoist magicians, servants, and thirty-nine wives and concubines, his white hair dyed a defiant black. The Han soldiers killed him, dismembered his body, and cut out and ate his tongue.[7]

The restored Han relocated its capital from Chang'an to Luòyáng, in the east. The first half of the dynasty was retrospectively named the Western Han; the second, the Eastern Han. By the time order was restored, millions of people had died in the violence, floods, and famine—around half the population. The first emperor of the Eastern Han, Guāngwǔ, reinstated order, and the Han flourished once more.

### AN AGE OF INNOVATION

The Han (Western and Eastern) ushered in a remarkable number of scientific, technological, agricultural, and industrial innovations, including the production of steel. Han soldiers fought with iron weapons, and farmers used iron to devise waterwheels, ox-drawn plows, wheelbarrows, and winnowing machines. They practiced crop rotation, cultivating soybeans and vegetables alongside the barley, wheat, millet, and rice that had been staples since Neolithic times.

Cài Lún (48–121), a resourceful eunuch-official of the Eastern Han, invented the world's first paper by pressing flat felted sheets made of wet mulberry bark, rags, hemp, and other fibers. Paper is one of what are commonly referred to as the Four Great Inventions, along with the magnetic south-facing compass and woodblock printing—also Han innovations—and gunpowder, which came several centuries later. Cai Lun was later implicated in a plot to murder the consort-rival of an empress. Rather than endure the ignominy of imprisonment, he bathed, dressed in his best silk robes, wrote a poem, and committed suicide by poison.

Other inventions from this period include a seismograph and odometer carts, on which mechanical figures banged drums and gongs to mark the miles. A Han general used rice to create the world's first known topographic map, and Han astronomers compiled star charts. The doctor Huà Tuó, the putative author of the first major text on herbal medicine, performed surgery after putting his patients to sleep with an anesthetic drink, *máfèisàn* 麻沸散, concocted from wine and a kind of cannabis compound like hashish. According to the fourth-century *Chronicles of Huáyáng*, the people of the Han even worked out how to use bamboo tubes to extract and transport natural gas:

> There are fire wells, and they shine brightly at night. If people want to use their fire, they first bring some fire from home and drop it into the well. Thunderous noises follow, and flames come out, bright enough to be seen for ten miles. They store the fire in a bamboo tube and take it home, where it continues to burn for days.[8]

Han scholars, meanwhile, produced seminal works on music, pharmacology, acupuncture, astronomy, and mathematics, employing square and cube roots and introducing the concept of negative numbers.

With prosperity and social stability came an appetite among the elite for beautiful things. Artisans made great advances in lacquerware and jade carving, for which they began to use iron tools and a circular cutting drill, and potters employed glazes to portray scenes from both mythology and everyday life. Artists practiced portraiture and sculpture, including bronze casting. Burial customs, meanwhile, became increasingly elaborate. The extremely wealthy might be buried in suits made of thousands of rectangular pieces of jade held together with silver or gold wire. Even commoners were buried with objects they might need in the afterlife, including unglazed clay effigies of houses.

This Han funeral effigy is an early example of courtyard house architecture, which continued to evolve, with regional variations, into the twenty-first century.

Houses were built around central courtyards. The wealthier the family, the more connecting courtyards. The design could accommodate a large, multigenerational family. Women who didn't need to work were expected to stay home: one phrase meaning "wife," *nèirén* 內人, literally "inside person," was already in use by this time.

Bān Zhāo (c. 45–117), who helped her brother, a court official, work on a history of the Western Han, was commissioned by the emperor to finish it after her brother died in 92. As China's first female historian, her contribution—including an account of the first emperor's matriarchal line—was widely praised. But she was no proto-feminist: her influential text *Lessons for Women* admonished women to guard their chastity, not to "weary others with much conversation," and to devote themselves to sewing, cooking, and other such "womanly work." *Lessons for Women* helped transform abstract ideas about women's place in *The Analects* into an increasingly strict code of behavior.[9]

## COURTING TROUBLE

Toward the end of the Han dynasty, conflict between the scholars and the eunuchs in the court sharpened. Even if scholars sometimes forged opportunistic alliances with eunuchs, most found castrates abhorrent, a double affront to the Confucian virtue of filial piety: the bodies given them by their parents had been mutilated, and they could not carry on the family line.

The eunuchs enriched themselves by selling official posts. This undermined the system that allowed scholars the possibility of advancement on merit. Sometimes, eunuchs even stripped scholars of their positions to sell them on to others. The Han military leadership resented the eunuchs, too, for they did the same with military office. The scholars and soldiers failed to unite in common cause. The political order decayed beyond repair, and with it, social order.

By the late Han, wealthy landowners were exploiting peasants' labor with impunity. Floods and famines increased general misery, and mass rebellions, including one led by Daoist faith healers—the Yellow Turban Rebellion (184–185)—broke out across the realm. The eunuchs assassinated the commander of the army, displaying his head at the gate of the walled capital, and the army responded by massacring the eunuchs. Anarchy ensued and independent kingdoms arose; the Han lost control over much of its empire, including most of the land south of the Yangtze. The military man, politician, and poet Cao Cao (155–220), the adopted grandson of a eunuch, describes the toll on the people in "Graveyard Song":

> Ten thousand families were all wiped out.
> Their white bones lay and bleached in the wilderness.
> For a thousand leagues not a cock was heard to crow.
> Of the people, barely one in a hundred survived.
> Remembering this is enough to break your heart.[10]

There's a saying that's the equivalent of "speak of the devil": it's "speak of Cao Cao and Cao Cao appears." The thirteenth Han emperor, Xiàn, was eight years old when he was enthroned in 189. He became a pawn in the scramble for power, abducted by one general after the other. In the year 192, he had just managed to escape an exceptionally cruel captor, who was in hot pursuit. He was about to send an appeal for help to Cao Cao; the messenger had barely saddled up when Cao Cao's troops arrived to save the day.

With the emperor now his grateful puppet, Cao Cao set out to reunite the fractured Han empire. By 220, having conquered the last of the Han's northern rivals, he led a huge army south, and into the most legendary battle in Chinese history—Red Cliff.

# THE GREAT DISUNITY

## Three Kingdoms, Two Women Warriors, Seven Sages, and a Five-Mineral Powder

*Luó Guànzhōng's* Romance of the Three Kingdoms *is a fourteenth-century novel based on the history of the tumultuous period that began with the troubles of the late Han. The novel's opening sentence is among the most famous in Chinese literature: "In the way of All Things Under Heaven, that which has long been divided must come together, and that which has come together must fall apart." The cycle of order and chaos noted by Mencius is a common theme of Chinese history. The chaotic era that began with Cao Cao's march south has served ever since as a cautionary tale of the dangers of disunity.*

BY THE TIME THE HAN ARMY led by Cao Cao arrived at the Yangtze, his troops were exhausted, weakened by disease and low in morale and supplies. The marshy wetlands of the South bogged down the cavalry, recruited from assimilated Xiongnu and other northern tribesmen. Cao Cao's greatest military asset was an armada of warships his troops had captured from a rebel state they'd conquered along the river. His goal was to subjugate the Han's last two big rival states, which together commanded the land south of the Yangtze. To the east lay the kingdom of Wú, led by the young military leader Sūn Quán; to the west (incorporating current-day Sichuan) was Shǔ, led by a distant relative of the imperial Liú clan of the Han and pretender (claimant) to the throne, Liú Bèi (161–223). Wu and Shu formed a tense alliance to meet the common threat.

## BATTLE OF RED CLIFF

After an initial skirmish with the combined forces of Wu and Shu, Cao Cao made a tactical retreat to give his men a rest. They chained the warships together against the banks of the Yangtze at a place the histories name as Red Cliff. Having calculated the direction and strength of the winds, Zhōu Yú, a divisional commander acting for Wu and Shu, sailed toward Cao Cao's fleet with a squadron of boats, claiming that he and his men wanted to defect. As they came close, the men set fire to their own boats, which they had filled with kindling and combustible oil, escaping onto smaller craft. The wind slammed the flaming vessels into Cao Cao's chained-up fleet. Many of Cao Cao's men and horses died in the inferno or drowned trying to escape. The fire spread to their encampment on land, by now under attack from the combined southern armies as well. Cao Cao and his army fled, his enemies in pursuit.

The Battle of Red Cliff has achieved such legendary status that it's hard to verify every detail. What is undeniable is that the battle heralded the final fall of the Han.

Not long afterward, Sun Quan attempted to cement the alliance between Wu and Shu by arranging a marriage between his younger sister and the widowed Liu Bei. Known to posterity as either Sūn Rén or Sūn Shàngxiāng, his sister was reputedly a fierce warrior, the military equal of any man, and has enjoyed a long afterlife as a pop-culture hero. Historians record that her cohort of sword-wielding handmaidens made her much-older husband so nervous that whenever Liu Bei entered her bedroom, "he felt a chill in his heart."[1] Three years later, when Liu Bei was away on a military campaign, Sun Ren returned to her brother's side.

Director John Woo reimagined the Battle of Red Cliff for his two-part 2008–2009 film. The exact location of the battle remains a mystery—even if various river towns have claimed the label to capitalize on tourism.

Among those wary of Sun Ren from the start was Liu Bei's chancellor, Zhūgě Liàng, the most celebrated strategist in Chinese history after Sunzi. He was also the inventor of the "wooden ox," a wheelbarrow for transporting supplies onto the battlefield and stretchering out the wounded, and had improved on another of the era's inventions, the repeating crossbow. He once modestly summed up his achievements by saying, "I did whatever it took to save my skin in a turbulent world."[2] He's also remembered for gladly marrying a woman who was described to him by her father as no beauty but his equal in talent. (History, sadly, did not record her name.)

Liu Bei's reliance on Zhuge Liang displeased another legendary military man close to him, Guān Yǔ (160–221). Guan Yu might have found comfort in the fact that some four centuries after his death, he would attain immortality as Guān Gōng, the God of War. If Confucius has come to symbolize "literary" or "civil" China, *wén* 文, Guan Yu stands for the military tradition, *wǔ* 武.

As Guan Gong, Guan Yu is typically depicted as a huge, muscular man with red skin—evidence of his Yang masculinity.

Guan Yu died in battle against Cao Cao's forces in 219. One year later, Cao Cao died of illness. Suffering from agonizing headaches, he had summoned the physician Hua Tuo. There are several versions of the story. One goes that Hua Tuo proposed to split Cao Cao's skull with an axe to extract the infection. All versions see Hua Tuo executed and Cao Cao dying several days later. Cao Cao would be remembered as much for his poetry and outsized personality as his political and military adventurism.

Cao Cao left instructions that after his death, his concubines and dancing girls were to be confined to the Brazen (or Copper) Bird Tower overlooking his grave. They were to behave as though he were still alive, bringing meals to his curtained bed and performing for guests on the fifteenth of every month. One of his most famous poems, "The Empty City," implores:

> Come drink with me and sing,
> For life's a fleeting thing.
> Full many a day has fled
> Like the morning dew . . .[3]

After Cao Cao's death, Cáo Pī, one of his twenty-six sons, forced the hapless Xian emperor, who'd been hanging on to power all this time, to abdicate, marking the formal end of the Han dynasty. Cao Pi pronounced himself emperor of the state of Wèi, which remained in enmity with Wu and Shu—the "three kingdoms" for which the era is named. One of the main achievements of the Wei, in accord with Cao Pi's Legalist bent, was to create China's first comprehensive legal code. Another was to refine the Han system of official appointments by ranking candidates according to objective criteria—though powerful clans still managed to manipulate the system to advance their own interests.

During the reign of the child ruler Zhèngshǐ (r. 240–249), the Wei court hosted a coterie of eccentric but brilliant scholars whose circle included Zhengshi's co-regent Cáo Shuǎng. Infusing Daoist and other mystical ideas into Confucianism, they both captivated and scandalized the court with their libertine ways, cheeky badinage, and indulgence in "the ecstatic drug" Five Minerals Powder, a hallucinogen and alleged aphrodisiac.[4] Zhengshi's other regent, unamused, massacred them all in 249.

These eccentrics were contemporaries of another lively group of independent thinkers known as the Seven Sages of the Bamboo Grove, who wanted nothing to do with any court. Legend has it that they gathered in a bamboo grove to take intoxicants, banter, and compose poetry and satire. They detested conformity, Confucian ritual, displays of propriety and modesty, and the notion that men of learning had a duty to enter public service. They were natural Daoists.

They were also committed drinkers, none so much as Liú Líng (225–280), revered by inebriates ever after as the Wine Immortal, *jiǔxiān* 酒仙. Once, some acquaintances called on Liu Ling at home and found him drinking naked. When they expressed their shock, he retorted: "I take heaven and earth for my pillars and roof, and my house with its rooms as my pants and jacket. What are you gentlemen doing in my pants?"[5]

Jī Kāng (223–262) was another colorful member of the group and author of an epic and witty repudiation of the Confucian ideal of service:

There are seven things about serving the court that I could never tolerate, and two things I do that would not be permitted . . .

The seven things are: I like to stay in bed late and ignore calls to rise. I enjoy playing the lute and singing, fishing, and wandering in the countryside. How could I feel at ease with government attendants always at hand? I would have to sit still respectfully for long periods although I am by nature restless, and I like scratching when bitten by lice. But how would this be possible when wrapped in official robes and paying my respects to my superiors? I hate writing letters and ignore my correspondence. Fifth, I detest attending funerals, although they are treated with the utmost seriousness by the worldly. I could not help offending people and they might want revenge. I could make a show of weeping but would be unconvincing and be disparaged for it. Then, too, I despise common men and could not tolerate working with them or socializing with them at banquets, having to listen to their prattle and observe their carryings-on. And finally, I have no patience for official tasks and could not tolerate the cares and worries that go with office. . . .

The two things that would never be permitted are: I criticize Confucius and the sage kings he praises. I would be found severely wanting by "proper" society for this. I am also given to saying whatever I think. This, too, is forbidden.[6]

The Three Kingdoms period lasted a mere seventy years or so. Yet its personalities, battles, and politics live on in the national imagination. *Romance of the Three Kingdoms*, more than the third-century history *Records of the Three Kingdoms* on which it is based, has inspired popular culture for centuries, from classical operas to contemporary film, television, and storytelling in China and beyond. English-language online gamers in the twenty-first century can even play *Total War: Three Kingdoms* (tagline: "Unite China under your rule and forge the next great dynasty").

In 280, a new dynasty, the Jìn, conquered all three kingdoms and unified the country once more. In the early years of the Jin, one of the Seven Sages, Shān Tāo, accepted a position in the court. He offered Ji Kang a post as his assistant. The passage quoted above was Ji Kang's riposte. It so angered the Jin emperor that he ordered Ji Kang executed for "disturbing the times and confusing correct doctrine"—a crime not dissimilar

Ji Kang was one of the Seven Sages of the Bamboo Grove. Most of the Sages were friends, though not all were acquainted. There may not even have been a particular bamboo grove.

to the charge of "disturbing social order" used against dissidents and free thinkers in the PRC today. Three thousand scholars wrote in Ji Kang's defense, begging for clemency, to no avail.

Within decades of the establishment of the Jin, droughts, locusts, and famine ravaged a population already devasted by more than a century of ceaseless warfare. A number of the non-Han nomadic tribes that had formed settled communities within its borders—including proto-Tibetan, Turkic, and Mongolian peoples—took advantage of the anarchy, carving up the edge of the empire from the Yellow Sea in the east to Sichuan in the southwest, and establishing separate states on the Chinese model.

With so much warfare, the armies were in constant need of soldiers. Forced conscription was common, and as times grew desperate, not even old men or boys were exempt. A girl called Huā Mùlán disguised herself as a boy to take the place of her elderly father in one of these armies. After serving with distinction for twelve years, she was offered an official post, which she turned down. When some of her fellow soldiers later ran into her dressed in women's clothes, they were astonished, never having guessed her gender. Or so goes the "Ballad of Mulan," written hundreds of years later, in the sixth century.

Certain retellings of her story stress her womanly virtues, along with her bravery and filial piety, with an arranged marriage following her homecoming. In one seventeenth-century version, however, she bonds with a fellow woman warrior and, upon returning home, commits suicide rather than submit to an arranged marriage. The Disney versions of Mulan are historically and culturally fanciful. For one thing, she fought on behalf of the Northern Wei dynasty, whose ruling clan were

Mulan is probably a composite of several women warriors of that era.

the Xiānbēi, a proto-Mongol tribe, which, as one commentator noted, makes her "more Hun than Han."[7]

During the wars of the first part of the fourth century, about a million refugees fled south, shifting the heart of Han civilization to the fertile lands below the Yangtze for the first time.[8] Among the refugees were scholar-officials who had followed the Jin court to Nánjīng, nearly 200 miles (300 km) from present-day Shanghai, where the dynasty reestablished itself as the Eastern Jin.

The third day of the third lunar month was the Spring Purification Festival and the official birthday of the Yellow Emperor. It was customary to picnic by rivers or streams to symbolically wash away illness and misfortune. One such party in 353 would make an indelible contribution to Chinese literature and calligraphy. A group of forty-two scholars, including Daoists and freethinkers, gathered at the Orchid Pavilion on a mountain in today's eastern Zhèjiāng province. They played a drinking game, floating cups of wine in a winding stream—when a cup bumped against a bank, the nearest person had to either drink from it or compose a poem. One member of the party, Wáng Xīzhī, commemorated the gathering in an essay, "Preface to the Orchid Pavilion Poems," a work as renowned for its calligraphy as its expression and sentiment:

> Young and old congregated, and there was a throng of men of distinction . . . what with drinking and the composing of verses, we conversed in whole-hearted freedom, entering fully into one another's feelings. The day was fine, the air clear, and a gentle breeze regaled us, so that on looking up we responded to the vastness of the universe, and on bending down were struck by the manifold riches of the earth . . . men of a later age will look upon our time as we look upon earlier ages—a chastening reflection. . . .[9]

Centuries later, the Táng Tàizōng emperor (*tàizōng* means "great ancestor") would so treasure Wang Xizhi's essay that he reportedly had the original buried with him—fortunately ensuring that careful copies were made first.

In 1965, the Communist scholar and archaeologist Guō Mòruò (1892–1978), then head of the Chinese Academy of Science, threw the Chinese academic world into turmoil when he suggested that the text and the calligraphy of the "Preface" postdated Wang Xizhi. That argument was still being waged in the Chinese press decades later. Discussing this controversy in his lecture "The Chinese Attitude Towards the Past," which also addressed the relative lack of preserved ruins in China (compared to European piles like the Colosseum, for example), the China scholar Pierre Ryckmans reflected:

> The vital strength, the creativity, the seemingly unlimited capacity for metamorphosis and adaptation which the Chinese tradition displayed for 3,500 years may well derive from the fact that this tradition never let itself be trapped into set forms, static objects and things, where it would have run the risk of paralysis and death.[10]

Poetry and Daoism consoled the elite, and Buddhism solaced many more, through difficult times. Buddhism had first arrived in China during the Han via the Silk Roads. By the sixth century, it had found converts across the land, with more than ten thousand monks and nuns resident in Chang'an alone. Eunuchs proved enthusiastic converts, comforted by the promise of reincarnation; they carried their severed parts, their "precious," *bǎobèi* 寶貝, in a special container so that they could be reunited with them in the next life. Women, for whom Confucianism offered limited consolations, also readily adopted Buddhist beliefs. Chinese society was developing a syncretic, pragmatic approach to philosophy and faith. A strict Confucian might have disliked Buddhism no less than Daoism; yet his wife might well have prayed to Buddha for sons while taking a Daoist fertility potion.

Neither poetry nor prayers could save the Jin, which collapsed in 420. Historians have given the even more chaotic and violent period that ensued different names, including the Sixteen Kingdoms of the Five Barbarians, the Northern and Southern Dynasties, and the Six Dynasties. It was during these uneasy and dangerous times that Tao Yuanming conjured up the ideal of Peach Blossom Spring, the utopia to which one could "flee the Qin."

In 589, a new dynasty, the Suí, reunited North and South. Its legacy included the Grand Canal, which, together with its parallel post road, would eventually link Beijing with Hángzhōu. Five million men, women, and children labored to build the 131-foot-wide (40 m) canal; only three million survived.

The north-south Grand Canal, the world's oldest and longest artificial river, transported goods and people until the middle of the nineteenth century.

The Sui put all land under dynastic control and distributed it to the people on the basis of their ability to cultivate it. Because the land reverted to the ruling house for reassignment after its cultivator's death, this prevented the emergence of powerful landowning families that could challenge the central authority. Agricultural production revived, and the economy grew. But the Sui, after that promising start, began its decline under its second emperor, who was fatally fond of both luxury and ill-considered military campaigns.

Along the densely populated reaches of the Yellow River, land reclamation and deforestation caused by farming led to worsening floods. A catastrophic flood in the late Sui, earning the Yellow River the moniker "China's sorrow," appeared to augur the dynasty's loss of the Mandate of Heaven.

Rebellions broke out across the land. One of these was led by Lǐ Yuān, the general charged with defending the Sui's northern border. Li Yuan, of mixed Han and nomadic heritage, conquered the Sui in 617 and founded the Tang, ushering in what would become one of the most celebrated and open-minded eras in Chinese history.

# THE TANG

## From Golden Age to Everlasting Sorrow

*In the period leading up to the Tang dynasty, women tended to veil their faces in public. Not long after the new dynasty's founding, they began experimenting with headdresses and hairstyles that showed off their features. Hair ornaments grew increasingly intricate. Makeup, too, became more elaborate and even outlandish in the privileged circles of the court, from which women of means took their cues. For a time, women were even covering their faces with decorative stickers crafted from gold foil, mica, colored paper, or textiles. They used so much makeup, the poet Wáng Jiàn wrote, that when they washed it off at night, "the water in the golden basin was turned into red mud."[1] There's something to be said for an era in which male poets can complain about the mess made by women in golden basins.*

BY 660, THE TANG HAD PACIFIED its northern frontier and secured access to the Silk Roads, over which it extended its influence throughout Central Asia. To the east, it controlled most of the Korean Peninsula and stationed a governor-general

Fashionable women in the Tang dressed their hair elaborately, shaped their eyebrows into styles with names like "mandarin ducks," "five mountains," and "horizontal smoke," and painted floral and other designs onto their lips.

in the city today known as Hanoi. To the west, Tibet, which had controlled large parts of the Southwest in the Sixteen Kingdoms period, remained a potent military threat. Employing "princess diplomacy," the Tang sent Princess Wénchéng as a bride to the Tibetan warrior king, Songtsen Gampo. Wencheng and another of the king's wives, the Nepalese Bhrikuti Devi, introduced Buddhism to Tibet, which merged with aspects of Tibet's native animistic Bon religion to become Tibetan Buddhism. Later claims that Wencheng also brought Chinese civilization (in the form of paper, among other things) to Tibet are central to official assertions that Tibet has "always" been part of China.

In addition to settling its borders, the Tang court, based in the historic capital of Chang'an, needed to address the challenges to its central authority posed by local power holders.

Unlike the hereditary aristocracy of Europe, China's landed gentry owed their influence to a fluid mix of lineage, wealth (including land ownership), education, and official position. It was a stable identity insofar as inherited wealth made it easier to get an education, making it easier to secure an official position, making it easier to accumulate wealth. The civil service had fallen into disarray in the chaotic years preceding the Tang. The Tang curtailed the power of local gentry by dividing the country into ten (later fifteen) provinces, to which it dispatched administrators, including magistrates, selected from an empire-wide pool of educated men. These administrators ideally had no personal ties to the place they were sent, enabling them to resist pressure from powerful local clans. Some provinces retain their Tang-era names—Héběi, a toponym meaning "north of the (Yellow) River," is one example.

The Tang also instituted a new penal code, laying out crimes and punishments in great detail. The latter ranged from the corporeal (such as beatings with a cane) to banishment to the harsh northern frontiers or pestilential South to execution. Torture was a legal means of extracting confession. The foundation for all dynastic codes to follow, the Tang code also sanctioned collective punishment—the execution of a rebel's entire family, for instance—for crimes such as sedition. But no judge could hand down a death penalty without first reviewing the case on three separate days while abstaining from meat and music, in order to emphasize the seriousness of the ruling.

Social standing, determined by the Confucian moral schema that privileged scholar-officials above others, influenced the application of the law. This is illustrated in a famous episode from a later (Ming dynasty) novel, *Outlaws of the Marsh*. The lowly born Wǔî Dàláng, a peddler, is murdered by his adulterous wife,

Pān Jīnlián, and her lover and accomplice, Xīmén Qìng. Wu Dalang's brother, Wǔ Sōng, avenges his death, killing them both. The law can forgive Wu Song the murder of his sister-in-law. But because Ximen Qing is an official, Wu Song must be punished.

To ensure both social stability and tax revenue—which was paid in the form of grain, cloth, or corvée for public works such as canals and granaries—the Tang guaranteed farming families approximately 16.5 acres of land each, offering special incentives to cultivate virgin land. Merchants and artisans paid other taxes, such as transportation tolls. The system hinged on conducting an accurate census. Demographers today believe that Tang censuses underreported migrant populations and members of non-Han ethnicities, as well as monks, entertainers, laborers, and eunuchs. Although the census of 754 counted about fifty-three million people, the actual figure was likely to have been closer to sixty-five or seventy million.[2]

Within the capital was a walled Imperial City, some 1.7 square miles (4.5 sq km) in size, encompassing the palace, government ministries, and the only court allowed to impose the death penalty, along with the chancellery, which checked and transmitted imperial decrees, and the censorate, which accepted petitions from the general public and monitored corruption and abuses of power by officials. Later dynasties would adopt an architecturally and administratively similar model.

The first emperor of the Tang was succeeded by his son Lǐ Shìmín—who ensured his own ascension by murdering his two brothers. Despite the bloody origins of his reign, as the Taizong emperor (r. 626–649), he proved a dynamic and intelligent ruler who fostered social stability and general prosperity, in part by further refining the workings of the civil service.

Taizong gathered about himself a coterie of devoted and talented ministers. His chief minister was Wèi Zhēng. This staunch Confucian, who offered criticism as well as advice, has gone down in history as China's most famous zhěngyǒu 諍友, a loyal friend who is capable of speaking hard truths, a "friend with arguments." When Wei Zheng died, Taizong wrote: "One looks at a reflection in a mirror to see if one's dress is in order. One studies history to understand the changing fortunes of time. And one seeks wise counsel to avoid mistakes. Wei Zheng has died, and I have lost my mirror. To have a zhengyou is to be fortunate indeed."[3]

## A SHINING LIGHT: EMPRESS WU

In 637, when he was thirty-nine, Taizong took a twelve-year-old girl, Lady Wŭ, as a concubine. He died twelve years later and was, it's believed, buried with Wang Xizhi's original "Preface," among other treasures. As was now the custom after an emperor's death, his palace women, including the intelligent, well-educated, and pretty Lady Wu, now twenty-four, entered a Buddhist convent, presumably for life. The new emperor, Gāozōng, Taizong's son, a few years older than Lady Wu, fetched her back to the palace and made her empress. Lacking both her aptitude and interest in politics, Gaozong gradually turned the tasks of government over to her. She ruled well, in the tradition of her husband's father and grandfather. After Gaozong died, in 684, their twenty-eight-year-old son ascended the throne as Emperor Zhōngzōng.

Less than two months later, the empress had her minions physically drag Zhongzong off the throne, accusing him of wanting to turn the empire over to his father-in-law. She replaced him with his younger brother, Ruìzōng, with herself as regent. In 690, she dispensed with the Tang altogether, declaring herself Empress Wǔ Zétiān (r. 690–705), founder of her own dynasty, the Zhōu, and becoming the only woman in China ever to rule in her own name. She reformed the civil service to entrench the principle of meritocracy. Mandating that civil service examinations be held on a regular schedule and made accessible to candidates of humble background, she insisted on blind marking to eliminate favoritism. The exams, which previously tested knowledge of the ancient classics, were altered to focus on subjects she deemed more useful for governance, such as history and rhetoric. Wu Zetian also invested in public works and commissioned scholars to write biographies of exemplary women.

Among her more unusual accomplishments was the invention of nineteen Chinese characters, including *zhào* 曌, which places *míng* 明, meaning brightness, over *kōng* 空, space. It signifies brightness that shines through space, or universal enlightenment. She intended *zhao* to describe her effect on the world. The Buddhists, who enjoyed her patronage, proclaimed her the reincarnation of the bodhisattva Maitreya, who hears all the suffering of the world and offers solace.

Writing about Wu Zetian in the mid-twentieth century, the popular author Lín Yǔtáng stated that she "shattered more precedents, created more innovations and caused more upsets than any male schemer in history."[4] Her personal life—she had several lovers—scandalized the court. And by the end of her reign, corruption had reared its familiar head. She had promoted two of her lovers, who were brothers, to high positions. They abused their power, even murdering their critics among

The features of Empress Wu Zetian, a great patron of Buddhism, became the basis for representations of the female bodhisattva.

the royal family. A coup, in which the brothers were assassinated, forced her to give the throne back to Zhongzong in 705, restoring the Tang dynasty.

Five years later, Zhongzong's empress reportedly poisoned him to death. Perhaps inspired by Wu Zetian, it's said she wanted to place their daughter on the throne. Following more palace intrigue, Ruizong returned to power. Eager to restore stability, he posthumously honored those persecuted during both Wu Zetian's and Zhongzong's reigns and then, after just two years, stepped down in favor of his son, the Xuánzōng emperor, in 712. Xuanzong's forty-year reign over what was then the world's most populous state is remembered as one of Chinese history's golden or prosperous ages, *shèngshì* 盛世.

## THE GOLDEN AGE OF THE TANG

At its height, the Tang capital of Chang'an was one of the wealthiest and most intellectually, artistically, and socially vibrant, cosmopolitan places in the world. Persians, Japanese, Indians, Central Asian Sogdians, and other visitors thronged its bustling streets, lined with wineshops, teahouses, and markets. The Tang elite played Persian polo, cooked with Indian spices, danced to Central Asian music, and dressed up in Turkish costume. Tang women's fashion, in turn, inspired the Japanese kimono and Korean *hanbok*, and the city of Kyoto modeled itself on Chang'an. The Japanese, like the Koreans and Vietnamese, adopted written Chinese for the composition of official documents and some forms of literature.

The Tang were eclectic in matters of belief. Its ruling clan, who claimed Laozi for an ancestor, insisted that candidates for the civil service be tested on the *Dao De Jing* as well as Confucian texts.

Buddhism had by now woven its way into the fabric of Chinese civilization. Frustrated by possible translation errors of Buddhist holy writ, the scholar-monk Xuánzàng traveled to India via the Silk Roads to collect more authentic texts in the original Sanskrit. He returned to Chang'an in 645 with 520 boxes of sutras. Teams of translators set to work, translating one quarter of them within eighteen years. It would take six hundred years to finish the rest.

Scripture didn't matter so much to practitioners of *chán*, a melding of Daoist and Buddhist traditions that dated back to the fifth century. *Chan* rejected the study of texts in favor of meditation aimed at enlightenment, *wù* 悟, a sudden apprehension of truth. The Japanese proved keen adopters, pronouncing it "zen." (Both "chan" and "zen" derive from the Sanskrit *dhyāna*, meditation.)

When the Confucian official Hán Yù (768–824) learned that the court planned to welcome a relic, a bone of Buddha, into the imperial palace, his blood boiled. He wrote what was called a memorial to the throne—so-called because one never presumed to tell an emperor anything, only to "remind" them. In the memorial, he attacked the "barbarian cult" of Buddhism, arguing that Buddha "understood neither the duties that bind sovereign and subject, nor the affections of father and son."[5] Quoting Confucius's injunction to "respect ghosts and spirits but keep them at a distance,"[6] he despaired that the emperor was introducing this "loathsome thing" into the palace without taking even the most basic precautions, such as the employment of exorcists. Han Yu so detested Buddhism and Daoism that in another memorial he called for the closing of their monasteries, the burning of their sacred books, and the conversion of their temples into dwellings.

The battle wouldn't be won in the short term. Confucianism, on the wane since the end of the Han, declined further in influence in the freewheeling Tang. Han Yu's memorial infuriated the emperor, who banished him to the South. Han Yu would have the last laugh: his anti-foreign, prescriptive style of Confucianism would become the guiding philosophy of the Sòng, the dynasty that followed the Tang.

### THE AGE OF POETRY

The ability to write poetry, including at short notice or for a special occasion, was considered an essential attribute of the educated man—along with fine calligraphy, which was regarded as the highest art. During the Tang, poetic genius flourished as never before. Poets were the celebrities of their day, their work popularized by singers in teahouses and wineshops; some fans got tattoos of their favorite lines. The authoritative *Complete Poems of the Tang*, compiled in the eighteenth century, contains some fifty thousand poems by about two thousand poets.

Tang poetry frequently drew on the pictorial nature of Chinese characters as well as rhyme, meter, and imagery. The following line from a poem by the Tang poet Liú Chángqīng is about approaching the home of a hermit on a mountain and finding that wild plants have grown over his door:

芳 草 閉 閑 門

*fāng cǎo bì xián mén*

The characters signify, in order: fragrant, plants, cover, idle, door. In *Chinese Poetic Writing*, François Cheng comments that the line's last three characters suggest

> the increasingly coherent, the increasingly clear, vision of the poet as he approaches the dwelling of the recluse. The line culminates in the final image, a bare door as if at last stripped of all that is superfluous. This idea of successive stages of "stripping away" is reinforced on a deeper level by the meanings implied in the third and fourth characters in the line: 閉 contains the element 才 "talent," "merit," and 閑 contains the element 木 "plant," "ornament"; they seem to signify that to arrive at true spirituality one must first free oneself from all worldly care for exterior merit and ornament.[7]

This example just hints at the richness of the Chinese poetic tradition, which, like the interrelated arts of calligraphy, painting, and music, reflects on and encompasses *qì* 氣 (sometimes spelled *ch'i* in older texts)—a notion combining life force, energy, rhythm, and breath. Tang poetry is incredibly varied in subject and mood—it can be playful, meditative, sardonic, melancholic, worshipful, or irreverent. Poems celebrate spring in the mountains, the songs of fishermen, the fluttering of garments in a pine forest breeze. The burdens borne by the common people, including military conscription, are another common theme. More Tang poems extol male friendship than romantic love—unsurprising in a time of arranged marriages. There are many that express the sorrow of parting when a friend is called to take up a distant official post, for example.

Lǐ Bái (701–762) was among the most popular of Tang poets. A powerfully built man of Turkic and Han heritage with piercing eyes, Li Bai wrote poems that were sung by entertainers in wineshops across the empire. Everywhere he went, fans treated him to meals and plied him with wine just to hear him recite. Yet he yearned for an official position as a policy adviser to Xuanzong. He traipsed about the empire, hoping to find an official who would recommend him to the court. His much-loved poem "Bring on the Wine," one of many he wrote about drinking, homesickness, and the company of friends, features the plaintive line "Heaven gave me this talent, it must surely find a use."[8]

Another celebrated poet of the era was Xuē Tāo (768–831), the educated daughter of an official, who became a courtesan to support her family after her father's death. Her "Ten Poems of Separation" are masterpieces of simplicity, wit, and metaphor:

> *Yes, she's a good dog,*
> *Lived four or five years*

*Within his crimson gates,*
*Fur sweet-smelling,*
*Feet quite clean,*
*Master affectionate.*
*Then by chance she took a nip*
*And bit a well-loved guest.*
*Now she no longer sleeps*
*Upon his red silk rugs.*[9]

The arts thrived under Xuanzong's patronage. He even established the first imperial school for (mainly female) actors, singers, and musicians, in the part of his palace known as the Pear Garden, *líyuán* 梨園. To this day, the world of Chinese opera—which in later, more conservative times became a male preserve—is called the Pear Garden; stage actors traditionally burn incense to Xuanzong before a performance. Xuanzong himself wrote poetry and music—including a battle song that was performed to the accompaniment of 120 armored dancers wielding spears.

## A FATEFUL LOVE AFFAIR

When Xuanzong was sixty, he fell in love with his son's wife, Yáng Gùifēi. Her voluptuous beauty was legendary: in the words of the poet Li Bai, she "stops others from pining for goddesses."[10] The besotted emperor loved to watch her bathe in the hot spring pools of Huáqīng, some 25 miles (40 km) east of Chang'an, where, legend has it, their affair began.

A canny political operator, Yang Guifei soon became her former father-in-law's favorite concubine. She persuaded Xuanzong to appoint a number of her relatives to official positions,

Ceramic sculptures in tricolor—amber, green, and creamy off-white—are among the Tang's most iconic artifacts.

including her first cousin, who became prime minister. Dù Fǔ, considered the greatest of Tang poets along with Li Bai, wrote a thinly disguised reproach to the nepotism and venality of the Yang clan, "Song of the Beautiful Ladies," which describes a group of women bedecked in gold and pearl ornaments.

It was around this time, 742, that Li Bai made it into the court, albeit as a writer of poems commemorating official occasions, a position far below that of political adviser. He enjoyed the favor of the court for three years, alternately amusing and scandalizing the people of Chang'an with his drunken antics. Although he praised Lady Yang in his poetry, they shared a mutual antipathy. The emperor admired his talent, but Li Bai's enemies in the court and his own impulsive behavior stymied his chances for advancement. In the end, he tendered his resignation to a relieved Xuanzong.

A different kind of talent arrived in the court a year after Li Bai. Ān Lùshān (703–757) was a polyglot with a heritage that possibly included Sogdian and Turkic ancestry. Having entered the military as an officer's slave, he rose to become a general. Hugely fat, he played the uncouth barbarian to an amused if condescending court, endearing himself to Xuanzong and Yang Guifei. He submitted cheerfully to mockery, including allowing Yang Guifei to dress him up like a baby, all the while cultivating his power and influence. Around 750, Yang Guifei's first cousin, the prime minister, accused An Lushan of plotting a rebellion. An Lushan's tearful protestations convinced the emperor of his loyalty.

The prime minister had been right. In December 755, commanding an army of two hundred thousand men and thirty thousand horses, An Lushan captured the Tang's secondary capital of Luoyang and, on Lunar New Year's Day of 756, declared himself emperor of the new dynasty of Yàn. He then marched on Chang'an, capturing the capital. The emperor and his court fled.

At a place called Mǎwéi, the troops guarding the imperial refugees mutinied. They blamed Yang Guifei's indulgence of An Lushan for the debacle. After executing the prime minister, a eunuch strangled her with a silk scarf, devastating the seventy-two-year-old emperor. A later Tang poet, Bai Juyi—author of the humorous riposte to Laozi's *Dao De Jing*—wrote an epic ballad describing this episode, "The Song of Everlasting Sorrow":

> *On the ground lie gold ornaments*
> *with no one to pick them up,*
> *Kingfisher wings, golden birds*
> *and hairpins of costly jade.*
> *The monarch covers his face,*
> *powerless to save;*
> *And as he turns to look back,*
> *tears and blood flow mingled together.*[11]

An Lushan's revolt ended 132 years of peace. Du Fu's family was among the many forced to flee from the rebels' destructive path. His poem "Road to Péngyá" describes sleeping under trees, his infant daughter biting him in her hunger, and the confused bravery of his little son as for "Ten days, half in rain and thunder, through mud and slime we pulled each other on."[12]

The disconsolate Xuanzong abdicated in favor of his son, who, as Emperor Suzong, raised an army of Chinese, Central Asians, Turks, and Arabs to crush the rebels.

In the end, it was one of An Lushan's own sons who took him down. An Lushan was going blind. Ill-tempered, he often beat his eunuchs, including one called Lǐ Zhū'ér ("Piggy Li"). After the second son was named An's successor, his firstborn feared his father might kill him to foil any potential challenge. Under his orders, Piggy Li attacked and killed An Lushan at night, when he couldn't see well enough to find his sword.

Two years later, one of An Lushan's old friends murdered the patricidal son and proclaimed himself the new emperor.

The Tang dynasty never fully recovered. In 763, not long after the Tang had retaken Chang'an, a Tibetan army captured and ransacked the city. The Tibetans and the Tibeto-Burman Tangut people also occupied large parts of Sichuan and Gansu, establishing the Western Xià kingdom and severing the Tang's access to the Silk Roads. The Xia crippled the Tang's cavalry by driving the horses off the state-run stud farms. Historian Jacques Gernet, who has written eloquently of the role of horses in the Tang, cites the court's inability to source good horses from then on as decisive in its decline—and a fatal weakness of the following dynasty, the Song, as well.[13]

The empire began to fray. The Korean kingdom of Silla declared its independence. Indigenous tribespeople founded the kingdom of Dali (937–1253), which commanded a great swath of the Southwest.

Few emperors of this post-rebellion period managed to reign longer than a decade. Yet throughout all these northern-centered upheavals, the South grew populous and prosperous, producing silk, tea, and salt and coming up with new methods for rice cultivation that gave greater yields and meant more secure incomes for farmers. The pride in the flourishing civilization of the South during this period is reflected in the Cantonese language: unlike northerners, Cantonese today tend to call themselves not Han but Tang people. (Chinatowns in the West, first settled by Cantonese immigrants, are still called "Tang people streets," *tángrén jiē* 唐人街, in Chinese.)

In 881, another rebel army sacked Chang'an, forcing the emperor to flee. The Tang official Wéi Zhuāng witnessed the terror, describing it in a poem titled "The Lament of the Lady of Qin": "Every home now runs with bubbling fountains of blood / Every place rings with a victim's shrieks—shrieks that cause the very earth to quake."[14]

Chang'an would never serve as a dynastic capital again. The Tang struggled on for another chaotic twenty-seven years, until 907, when it collapsed, and the Five Dynasties period—which actually involved eleven rival states—began.

In 960, a group of soldiers belonging to one of those states was traveling toward their capital, on a mission to protect their infant ruler. Night fell, so they set up camp. In the middle of the night, their general, Zhào Kuāngyìn, awoke with a start to the sight of his men crowding into his tent with swords drawn.

They demanded that he usurp the throne of the infant they'd been sent to guard and held out a yellow robe—a color exclusive to emperors. The general was furious, but under duress, he donned the robe. The Song dynasty was born.

# THE SONG

## Proto-Socialists, Neo-Confucians, and Urban Living

*Zhao Kuangyin learned a hard lesson about the power of the military that night. Although he gave in to his men's demands, he demanded their absolute obedience in return. He ordered them not to harm the infant ruler, the royal family, or anyone else in the capital. As the Song Tàizǔ emperor (r. 960–976), he limited the power of the military and strengthened that of the civil service. In his quest to unite the realm, Taizu preferred to negotiate with the rival states or, where that failed, intimidate them, avoiding direct conflict wherever possible. These less-violent tactics served the Song well—at first.*

BY THE TIME THE LAST OF THE RIVAL states joined the Song in 979, the throne had passed to Taizu's younger brother, the Song Tàizōng emperor (r. 976–997), who may or may not have murdered his brother to get the throne, which should otherwise have passed to Taizu's sons.[1] Stories circulated about ax blows in the night.

Taizong tried to regain some of the old borderlands of the Tang but met fierce resistance from the Tibetans, as well as the indigenous tribes of the Southwest and the Khitans, a nomadic, proto-Mongolian people from the lands northeast of the Great Walls. The Khitans had founded the Liáo dynasty in 916, incorporating a good portion of today's Hebei province, and making what is now Beijing their capital. Although the Song's territory was smaller than the Tang's—approximately the size of the Qin's, in fact—its population would grow to a hundred million, exceeding that of the Tang by at least thirty million.[2]

Taizong's son and successor, the Zhēnzōng emperor (r. 997–1022), made peace with the Khitans in 1004. The settlement involved paying the Liao dynasty a substantial yearly goodwill fee. It bought the Song more than a hundred years of relative peace—relative because the Tibetans never stopped their harassment. Also, although the Dali kingdom, in what is now Yunnan province, maintained cordial relations with the Song, the seminomadic Jurchen warriors of the Northeast were on the rise. Overall, though, the Song's pacifism and generosity to those who surrendered to it served it well.

## TAKING THE BAIT

In the time of the fourth Song emperor, a new appointee to the imperial board of finance, Wáng Ānshí (1021–1086), appeared on the scene. The twentieth-century essayist Lin Yutang wrote that Wang

was a curious man, extraordinary in mind and character. He was an industrious student, a good scholar except in his abominable philology and certainly a major poet.

Unfortunately, he combined a Messianic sense of mission with a deplorable lack of tact and inability to get along with anyone but himself . . . The story is told that he never changed his gown. One day some of his friends went with him to a bathhouse at a temple. The friends stealthily left a clean robe while he was in the bath and wanted to test whether he would find out his dress had been changed. [Wang Anshi] came out of his bath and put on the new robe, totally unaware of what his friends had done.[3]

Another story has it that the emperor invited his ministers to dine by a pond, setting out fish bait so that each could catch the fish that would be cooked for their dinner. Wang Anshi, who couldn't be bothered fishing, ate the bait.

Having served as a local official for several decades, Wang Anshi had observed how the accumulation of vast estates by powerful families allowed them to exploit those who tilled the land. He didn't see why the rich deserved to own so much more than anyone else. Besides, the wealthy, he observed, were adept at tax avoidance, allowing the burden of taxation to fall on those least able to support it. Confucian moral example and rites weren't going to solve these problems. Only Legalist methods would bring about social justice and equality.

Tax loopholes for the rich should be closed, he argued in a lengthy memorial to the throne. This would provide the empire's administration with the funds to pay commoners for work such as building or repairing the Great Walls. Lavish weddings and funerals, justified by the wealthy on the grounds of Confucian propriety, should be banned—they shamed poorly paid low-level officials unable to meet such extravagant standards, leaving them vulnerable to the temptations of bribery and graft. Low-level officials needed to be better paid in general. The state should lend money to the farmers, and on better terms than offered by the usurious rich. It also ought to establish public granaries and other institutions promoting the public good. Wang Anshi proposed the *bǎojiǎ* 保甲 system, by which ten households were bound into one unit, a *jiǎ* 甲, and ten *jiǎ* into a *bǎo* 保, for mutual defense, tax collection, and law enforcement. This concept of mutual defense, surveillance, and collective responsibility continues to inform ideas about policing and social organization to this day, as exemplified by the PRC's ubiquitous urban Neighborhood Committees.

The neo-Confucians, as the intellectual heirs of the sclerotic Confucian Han Yu became known, found Wang's ideas as outrageous as his demeanor slovenly and eating habits repulsive. His repudiation of the ideal of the scholar-official as a man steeped in learning and morality but without specialized skills offended them. But he had the ear of the sixth emperor of the Song, twenty-year-old Shénzōng (r. 1068–1085), as he had had that of the fourth, and with the emperor's enthusiastic backing, he drafted laws incorporating these ideas.

One year after Shenzong's death in 1085, Wang Anshi's enemies in the court convinced the regent governing on behalf of Shenzong's young son and successor, Zhézōng (r. 1085–1100), to force Wang Anshi into retirement, bringing the two-decades-long experiment to an end. Bureaucratic foot-dragging had already undermined much of his program. Wang died soon after retiring.

When Zhezong began to rule in his own right, however, he ordered Wang's disciples to carry on with the reforms.

His successor, Huīzōng (r. 1100–1126), continued to back the reforms until the vexed conservatives of the court wrested back control of the system once more.

Historians still debate the character and ideas of Wang Anshi. Was he ahead of his time—a proto-socialist, as Mao would claim? An impractical dreamer? A snake-oil salesman? An original political thinker, his lasting legacy includes the maintenance of publicly funded institutions such as orphanages, hospitals, schools, cemeteries, and granaries.

## CLASSIC MOVES

The stricter Confucians would have the last laugh. The Neo-Confucians completed the transformation, begun in the Han, of Confucian philosophy into state ideology. Idolizing the mythical kings Yao and Shun, as well as the Duke of Zhou, they stressed the importance of ritual for everyone from the emperor down. Rites propagated Confucian norms and reinforced social hierarchies. Not even a village archery competition was to take place without a proper ceremony.

The most influential neo-Confucian thinker was Zhū Xī (1130–1200). Widely read in Daoism and Buddhism, he drew on these spiritual traditions as well. In his view, the cosmic force or "energy matter" of *qi*, which encompassed the five dynamic elements of metal, wood, water, fire, and earth, existed alongside *lǐ* 理, reason, a concept incorporating Confucian concerns such as propriety and righteousness. Like Mencius, Zhu Xi believed that people were basically good; through proper behavior and moral cultivation, anyone could develop a noble spirit. Also like Mencius, Zhu Xi believed that a *junzi*, gentleman, was duty bound to rebel or speak out against a ruler's corrupt or ignoble behavior.

In 1195, a powerful minister labeled Zhu Xi's teachings a "school of lies" and banned all who subscribed to it from public office. Zhu Xi died not long after. Several decades later, he was posthumously back in favor, his ideas official doctrine. The canonical list of the Four Books and the Five Classics he helped to compile, which included *The Analects* and the writings of Mencius, as well as the *Book of Odes*, *I Ching*, and *Book of Rites*, became the basis of civil service examinations.

Rancorous court politics kept the Song rulers so preoccupied that they failed to notice the storm clouds gathering to the north, where the Jīn (Gold) kingdom of the Jurchens was gathering strength. In 1122, the Song allied itself with the Jin against the Liao dynasty, on which they staged a joint attack. The Song and Jin agreed to divide the territory of the Liao between them.

In 1125, the Jin, having conquered the Liao with minimal help from the Song, demanded a considerable sum of silver and silk from the Song in return for a portion of the Liao's territory. Two years later, the Jin advanced on the Song capital of Kaifeng. The Song military used gunpowder, which had been invented in the Tang, in weapons including "thunderclap bombs" (firecrackers), to no avail. The Jurchens kidnapped the emperor, his father, and some three thousand members of his court and carted them off to the north. Jurchen men raped and enslaved the women of the Song court while presenting the Song princes with captive Khitan women—revenge on the Khitans for their rape of Jurchen women.

The Song heir apparent had himself enthroned as Gaozong in the southern city now known as Hangzhou. The previous period became known as the Northern Song. The new Southern Song was much diminished, having lost all its territory north of the Huái River.

Among the dynasty's most loyal warriors was Yuè Fēi, who had first marched north against the Liao in 1122 as a nineteen-

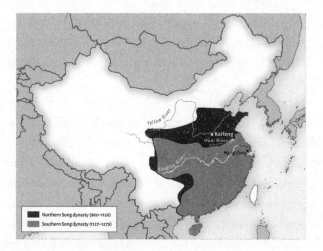

Under the Southern Song, the land south of the Yangtze River became a political as well as cultural center for the first time in China's history.

year-old. He was renowned both for his military prowess and his mastery of Sunzi's *The Art of War*. He is also credited as the inventor of Eagle Claw kung-fu—the style practiced by Jackie Chan's antagonists in the 1978 film *Snake in the Eagle's Shadow*.

In 1130, a faith healer led a peasant uprising, burning down markets and temples and murdering scholars, monks, and wealthy landowners. He was murdered, in turn, by a bandit who went on his own rampage. In 1135, using a combination of military strategy, offers of amnesty, bribes, and ambushes, Yue Fei restored order. The court rewarded him with a noble title. Yue Fei didn't want honors—he wanted to march north to retake the Song's former territory from the Jin. The emperor, who was trying to negotiate a new treaty with the Jin, refused.

By 1138, talks between the Song and the Jin had collapsed. Yue Fei was preparing to march north at last when jealous rivals at court accused him of plotting a rebellion. During his interrogation, he whipped off his upper garments to show them the most famous tattoo in Chinese history: the phrase, inked on his back, "Serve the country with undying loyalty," *jīngzhōng bàoguó* 精忠報國.

It is impossible to verify this story; the first written source on Yue Fei is a biography by his grandson. Its significance lies in its iconic expression of patriotism. When the Chinese Jews of Kaifeng wanted to convey their loyalty to the state some three centuries later, they carved those same words onto the stone tablets that recorded their community's history. Among the many representations of the scene in popular culture is the opera *Mother Yue Tattoos Her Son*, which adds a note of filial piety to the story. When Mao saw that opera for the first time in 1960, he jumped to his feet to applaud.[4]

Yue Fei's enemies, unmoved, garroted him in his cell in 1141. The Jin rejoiced at the news. Not long after, they forced the Song court to sign a humiliating treaty that gave the Jin ruler a higher status than their own emperor.

## THE FLOURISHING SOUTH

Despite all the conflict, the Southern Song enjoyed remarkable prosperity. By 1123, an unprecedented 15 percent of its ninety million people lived in large urban centers that were among the world's most populous. Hangzhou, with its beautiful West Lake, served as a magnificent and well-managed capital. Although its wooden buildings were susceptible to fire, there was a sophisticated system in place for preventing and detecting fires, involving signal flags, protective clothing, and the construction of stone towers for households to store their most precious possessions. The state was the city's main landlord, and in both times of celebration and times of need, when harvests were bad or disasters struck, it reduced or forgave rents.[5]

The loss of the North meant the Silk Roads were now entirely inaccessible. The Song turned to the sea. They were aided in this pursuit by the Han invention of the south-facing compass and the Tang innovation of dividing a boat's cabin into separate, waterproof compartments, or bulkheads, so that if one part of the hull was breached, the vessel could still stay afloat—a revolutionary development in maritime safety.

Over time, the Song became a great maritime power. The coastal entrepôt of Guangzhou (later called Canton in English) welcomed Malay, Persian, Indian, Arab, Vietnamese, Khmer, and Sumatran merchants to its bustling streets.[6]

The Song was also an age of great technological achievement. The production of high-grade iron led to innovative uses of hydropower for spinning wheels, clepsydra (water clocks), irrigation, and milling. Agriculture thrived with the introduction of early-ripening varietals of rice and the cultivation of a greater range of vegetables and fruits—thirty-two species of lychees alone.

The upper classes, more urbanized and sedentary than those of the Tang, valued the arts. Literati were avid collectors of jade, coins, paintings, and large decorative stones from Lake Taihu in the Yangtze Delta, which they installed in their gardens and courtyards. Their garden retreats in the canal city of Suzhou, not far from Hangzhou, are considered the apex of Chinese garden design and are today listed as UNESCO World

Heritage sites. The lyrical poetry of the time is considered the apogee of the Chinese poetic tradition alongside that of the Tang. Publicly funded and privately endowed colleges and libraries, from village schools to imperial academies, fostered an unprecedented boom in literacy, further aided by the invention of cheap woodblock printing.

Treatises appeared on everything from the raising of silkworms to the farming of fish, the growing of chrysanthemums, the nature of crustaceans, and the cultivation and fermentation of tea. There were manuals of architecture and astronomy, as well as works on geography and the customs of foreign lands. Cartographers created maps of unprecedented accuracy.

The Song also made great advances in mathematics, medicine, and pharmacology. Imperial patronage promoted research into dentistry, pharyngology, and obstetrics, as well as acupuncture and herbal remedies. It even produced the world's first monograph on forensic medicine, detailing methods for conducting autopsies and exhuming corpses, recognizing different kinds of knife wounds, identifying time of death, and distinguishing between suicide and murder. Song physicians understood both the principle of infection and the notion of psychosomatic illness.

Antiquarianism, called "the study of metals and stone," *jīnshíxué* 金石學, grew popular. Discoveries of bronzes from the Shang era excited historians and collectors and inspired artists and counterfeiters alike.[7] Historians aspired to compose sweeping works of literary grandeur, with Sīmǎ Guāng's *Comprehensive Mirror for Aid in Government*, which covered the years 403 BCE to 959 CE, becoming a model for generations of historians to come.

Vernacular literature flourished. Storytellers entertained audiences from the streets to the court with chivalric, supernatural, and romantic tales, true crime, and stories drawn from mythology and history—the Battle of Red Cliff was a favorite. Disapproving neo-Confucians promoted a classical literary style based on ancient literature, with the availability of inexpensive copies of the classics a boon for their cause.

A twelfth-century scroll, 17 feet (5.25 m) long and 10 inches (25.5 cm) wide, painted in monochrome ink on silk, offers a unique insight into urban life in the Southern Song. Attributed to the painter Zhāng Zéduān, it's called *Qīngmíng shànghé tú* 清明上河圖, which might mean "life on the river during the Qīngmíng festival," or simply "peaceful life on the river."

In one section, a crowd on a bridge eat snacks from food stalls while gawking at an argument between a man on horseback and one in a sedan chair about who has the right of way. Others help boatmen tether a vessel with a snapped towline. Multistory restaurants line the boulevards alongside stores selling furniture, toys, and funerary offerings. Wheelwrights, barbers, and pharmacists ply their trades.

Beyond the crumbling city wall, a caravan of camels plods along. Further out, we see irrigated fields and farmhouses. Everything is rendered in fine detail.

The few women who appear are glimpsed in sedan chairs or on boats, though at least one is washing laundry in the river. Neo-Confucian mores had pushed women indoors. Foot-binding—the increasingly prevalent practice of deforming a young girl's feet into a hooflike shape through the use of ever tighter bandages that eventually broke the bones of the foot—further restricted their movements.

The *Qingming shanghe tu* depicts a lively parade of fortune-tellers, guards, Buddhist monks, Daoist priests, gowned scholars, laborers, servants, children, and others on the streets of the unnamed city.

The origins of foot-binding are obscure. The attractiveness of small feet is a feature of a story by the famed Tang writer of supernatural fiction Duàn Chéngshì. Considered one of the earliest "Cinderella" legends that appeared around the world, it tells of a young, beautiful, and talented girl, Yè Xiàn, who is tormented by her mean and ugly stepmother and stepsister. A magical fish befriends her, but they kill it. As a spirit, the fish still manages to provide her with beautiful clothes and tiny golden slippers for her to wear to a gathering hosted by a king. After her stepmother and stepsister see her there, she flees, losing one slipper. The slipper eventually leads the king to Ye Xian, and he makes her his wife.

The practice of foot-binding may have begun after a late Tang emperor fell in love with a dancer who performed for him atop a six-foot platform in the shape of a golden lotus. Some say she had naturally small feet, others that she bound them in white silk to resemble crescent moons. The aesthetic rippled outward from the court and became ever more cruelly restrictive. Bound feet became the object of sexual fetishism: ancient erotic fiction describes men licking bound feet and drinking wine from miniature cups placed inside elfin shoes.

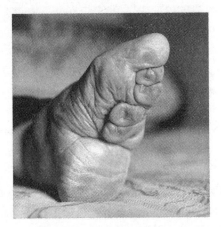

By the end of the eleventh century, foot-binding was de rigueur for women of the ethnic Han majority. The ideal "three-inch golden lotus" required binding the feet of very young girls. It was crippling and painful.

Only the poorest women, who labored in the fields, could afford the shame of not conforming to the practice, by then seen as a sign of womanly virtue, especially among the Han.

Neo-Confucians such as Zhu Xi approved of foot-binding as a means of constraining the mobility of women, whom they considered dangerously lascivious by nature. If the Tang had been a time of relative liberation for women, who could take lovers or remarry without incurring social disapprobation, and whose learning and talents were celebrated, the Song shut that party down.

Yet the Song didn't want for talented women. Lǐ Qīng-zhào (1084–1155), who made a name for herself as a poet at seventeen, is one of China's most respected writers. She and her husband built up a legendary library, where they amused themselves by playing literary-themed drinking games. The Jin invasion of 1125 forced the pair to flee, hurriedly packing their precious books onto carts. Only two volumes survived, which Li Qingzhao wrote she treasured like "life itself."

Of similar mind to Yue Fei, Li Qingzhao demanded that the Song fight back against the Jin, writing powerfully on the theme of heroism. After her husband died, Li Qingzhao defied social mores and remarried. She divorced her second husband just months later, the whole scandalous episode glossed over by historians reluctant to sully her lofty image. (Others smeared her for it.) Though only a small portion of her writing survived, schoolchildren still study it and pop songs quote it. During the COVID-19 pandemic, a line from one of her poems, "In life be a hero, in death a courageous ghost," was turned into a social media meme in praise of frontline health workers.[8]

The detailed realism that characterizes the *Qingming shanghe tu* and many other paintings of the time reflected the spirit of reason that so obsessed the neo-Confucians. Yet other artists of the Song would take painting to new heights of intuitive expression, creating a fresh pictorial language in the process. Paradoxically, this also owed something to neo-Confucianism, which considered displays of technical virtuosity unworthy of the Confucian gentleman.

This ideal achieved its highest expression in Song landscape, or "mountain and water" paintings, *shānshuǐ huà* 山水畫. Combining the arts of painting, poetry, and calligraphy—often literally, with poems calligraphed onto the paintings themselves—such paintings aimed to capture the poetic essence of a scene, exploring the tension between abstraction or emptiness, *xū* 虛 (the void),

In Chinese "mountain and water" paintings, such as this one by Xià Guī (1180–1230), there may be multiple points of perspective. Human figures are typically dwarfed by the landscape.

and representation, *shí* 實 (what is real or solid). A poet of the Song dynasty, Sū Dōngpō (1037–1101), wrote of the Tang poet-painter Wáng Wéi (699–759), whose work is considered a forerunner: "Savor his poetry, and there is a painting in each poem; look carefully at his paintings, and each one contains a poem."[9]

Su Dongpo's real name was Sū Shì. As a neo-Confucian official who had opposed Wang Anshi's reforms at the time when they had had the emperor's blessing, Su had lost his post and retired to a farm called Dongpo ("eastern slope"). While visiting a presumed site of the Battle of Red Cliff, the fact that not a trace of the epic battle remained in the landscape struck him as a metaphor for life's ephemerality. In retrospect, the poem seems also to foreshadow the end of the once-great Song dynasty itself:

> *East flows the mighty river,*
> *Sweeping away the heroes of time past;*

*This ancient rampart on its western shore*
*Is Zhou Yu's Red Cliff of Three Kingdoms' fame;*
*Here jagged boulders pound the clouds,*
*Huge waves tear banks apart,*
*And foam piles up a thousand drifts of snow;*
*A scene fair as a painting,*
*Countless the brave men here in time gone by!*
*I dream of Marshal Zhou Yu in his day*
*With his new bride, the Lord Qiao's*
*younger daughter,*
*Dashing and debonair,*
*Silk-capped, with feather fan,*
*He laughed and jested*
*While the dread enemy fleet was burned to ashes!*
*In fancy through those scenes of old I range,*
*My heart overflowing, surely a figure of fun,*
*A man grey before his time.*
*Ah, this life is a dream,*
*Let me drink to the moon on the river![10]*

The Jin, having confined the Song to the South, controlled the coal and iron ore deposits in the North and learned advanced ironmongery from the Song. Imprudently, they sold iron to the nomads of the northern grasslands, including the Mongols, who were talented equestrians and fierce warriors. The Mongols replaced their horn and bone arrowheads with iron and forged swords and armor.[11]

A century and a half later, under the leadership of Genghis Khan, the iron-clad cavalry of the Mongols thundered south to conquer both the Jin and the Song.

## THE MONGOL YUAN

### From "Glorious Slaughter" to the Splendid City

*Genghis Khan (1162–1227) once stated that the greatest pleasures in life were vanquishing one's enemies, seizing their horses and possessions, and ravishing their weeping women. In 1215, he led his troops in a bout of "glorious slaughter" that razed the Jin capital to rubble, leaving its streets littered with corpses and awash in blood. Census records show a drop in the number of Jin households between 1207 and 1236 from 8.41 million to 1.1 million, suggesting the Mongols may have killed seven out of eight people in their path of conquest.*

*Yelü Chucai, a Khitan adviser to Genghis Khan, argued that, as enjoyable as pillage and slaughter was, the Great Khan would profit more from his subjects if he let them live and taxed them. Or, as the polymath Buddhist monk and geomancy expert Liú Bǐngzhōng would tell Genghis's grandson, Khublai Khan (1215–1294), "You can conquer 'all under heaven' on horseback, but you can't govern it from there."*

KHUBLAI KHAN, WHO ADMINISTERED the Chinese portion of the Mongol empire, was fortunate to have good advisers and smart enough to listen to them. One of his advisers was his mother, Sorghaghtani Beki (c. 1190–1252), of whom a Syriac scholar remarked that should he encounter just one other woman like her, he'd happily pronounce women superior to men. From 1232, she had been in charge of governing parts of northern China, gleaning valuable insights on how to rule a non-nomadic, agricultural people, which she shared with her son.

In 1271, Khublai Khan formally established the Yuán dynasty, using a character (元) that indicated "ultimate origin" in the I Ching. It was the first major dynasty not to be called after its founder's birthplace.[1] No other non-Han dynasty, including the Jin, had ever ruled over so much territory. The Yuan built its white-walled capital, Khanbalik, near the ruins of the Jin (and former Liao) capital. Apart from a few brief interludes, the site—that of present-day Beijing—would serve as China's capital ever after.

When Samuel Taylor Coleridge wrote "In Xanadu did Kubla Khan / A stately pleasure-dome decree," he was referring to Khublai Khan's "upper capital" Shàngdū, in today's Inner Mongolia. Liu Bingzhong, who had designed Shangdu, was entrusted with the plan for Khanbalik. The palace complex, dubbed the Forbidden City, was situated on the city's central north-south axis so that the emperor on his throne could be the pole star to his court and domain. The throne itself sat within three concentric sets of walls—those of the Forbidden City, the Imperial City (encompassing parklands, workshops supplying the palace with its material needs, and noble residences), and the city itself—symbolic of Heaven, Earth, and Humankind. The streets of Khanbalik, from grand avenues wide enough for nine chariots to run side by side down to the narrow *hutong* (a Mongolian word apparently signifying a lane with a drinking well), ran parallel and perpendicular to the central axis in a gridded design intended to guarantee peace, stability, and prosperity. The Han capital of Luoyang and the Tang capital of Chang'an had been laid out according to similar principles, but Khanbalik saw their finest expression.

Like the Tang, the Yuan was a time of bustling international commerce and exchange. Around 1274 or 1275, the young Venetian Marco Polo, barely out of his teens, arrived in Khanbalik with his merchant father. At the time, Europeans knew China as "Cathay," from the word "Khitan." The Venetian marveled at the city and the Khan's palace, which he described as "the greatest palace that ever was," with its marble stairways, gold- and silver-covered walls, and a hall for feasting that could accommodate six thousand guests. He thought it "altogether so vast, so rich, and so beautiful, that no man on earth could design anything superior to it."[2] He admired Khublai Khan so much that he learned Mongolian and stayed on to serve in the court.

## THE HEAVENLY CITADEL

Khublai's mother was a Nestorian Christian. His wife, Chabi, another astute political adviser (and a fashionista whose hat and robe designs would influence Mongolian costume for centuries), was a devout Buddhist of the Tibetan school. She prompted him to restore some of the area's ancient Buddhist temples and dagobas (dome-shaped shrines). Under the guidance of his mother and wife, Khublai welcomed to his realm

Khublai Khan, Genghis's grandson, was literate in and respectful of Chinese tradition and culture—but he didn't trust the Han Chinese themselves.

people of all religions and races. His grandson and successor, Temür Khan, would even host a papal envoy, the Franciscan friar John of Montecorvino, who built two churches in the Yuan capital and claimed to have baptized more than ten thousand Mongols during his time in China.

Khublai founded the Confucian Temple and the Imperial College, which still stand today, adding a state library to the complex in 1313. He diligently performed Confucianist state rituals at altars to the Sun, Moon, Heaven, and Earth, and planted sesame, beans, melon, and rice in symbolic offering to the God of Land and Grain at the altar just west of his palace.

He was also well aware that his grandfather's conquest of China had been brutal, and that the Han had long considered Mongolian and other nomads to be crude barbarians. With a few exceptions, such as Yelü Chucai, he didn't feel able to count on the loyalty of scholar-officials who'd served the Song or the

Jin, including Sinicized Khitans, Jurchens, and Koreans. He froze them out of the highest ranks of the civil service, including financial administration and tax collection. Top appointments were made hereditary and went to Mongols. Other prestigious and powerful positions went to Sogdians, Persians, Arabs, and Europeans like Marco Polo. Northern Chinese were favored over Southerners. These policies effectively demolished the exam-based civil service system established in the Han and refined over centuries to select officials for posts across the empire and promote them to the court according to merit. It rankled many educated Han Chinese to see the Yuan court dominated by barely literate Mongolians.

The Arabs, Persians, Central Asians, and Tibetan monks employed by the Yuan as tax collectors developed a reputation for corruption, rapaciousness, and brigandry—one Tibetan monk even looted the tombs of the Southern Song emperors. After a Chinese resident of Khanbalik used a bronze hammer to smash in the skull of the widely detested finance minister Ahmad Fanakati, the city exploded with jubilation. Although the assassin was executed, Khublai, on learning the facts, posthumously cleared his name.

Adding injury to insult, the Yuan legal system mandated more severe punishments for Han Chinese than for Mongols: execution for a Chinese who murdered a Mongol, fines for a Mongol who murdered a Chinese. Educated, underemployed Chinese channeled their discontent into the writing of plays and operas, some of which, like the tragedy *The Injustice Done to Dou E That Moved Heaven and Earth* by Guān Hànqīng, were barely disguised political allegories. The Yuan became known as a golden age of theater, which evolved from an elite to a popular entertainment. Satirical songs and literature mocking the Mongols and their foreign retainers circulated widely.

Despite the declining fortunes of the scholar-officials, the South thrived. Hangzhou was now home to five hundred thousand people—one million counting the surrounding areas. Located at the terminus of the Grand Canal, and close to the East China Sea, it had grown to become a center for both domestic and international commerce. Its merchants traded Chinese textiles, porcelain, tea, and precious metals for perfumes, incense, spices, ivory, and crystals from places as far-flung as India and Africa.[3] There were streets devoted to gilding, tailoring, and candle-making, as well as shops offering every sort of product or produce.

In the Tang, the wealthy deposited their cash and silver with agents, who issued promissory notes that could be used to purchase goods, with sellers collecting the cash from the agent. The Yuan introduced *chāo* 鈔, paper currency. This was several hundred years before Europe's first paper currency. (The contemporary unit of currency, the *yuan*, was originally written with a different character, 圓, meaning round, referring to the traditional coin shape. It has nothing to do with the Yuan or its currency.)

As the Yuan relied on the wealthy South for almost half of its tax revenue, Khublai Khan dispatched Marco Polo to Hangzhou (which, due to a linguistic misunderstanding, he referred to as "Quinsai") to audit the city's finances. The Venetian found its beauty and wealth breathtaking: he was struck by its elegant canals and bridges, beautiful lake, and the cleanliness, fine silk robes, civility, and hospitality of its people. He observed that the city's streets were paved with stone or brick, making them

passable even in wet weather, and admired the painted pleasure boats on the lake.

Medieval European towns could not compare to Hangzhou
for sophistication or material splendor. According to the great
cataloger of Hangzhou life at the time, Wú Zìmù, shops sold
"early rice, late rice, new-milled rice, winter-husked rice, first
quality white rice, medium quality white rice, lotus-pink rice,
yellow-eared rice, rice on the stalk, ordinary rice, glutinous rice,
ordinary yellow rice, short-stalked rice, pink rice, yellow rice,
and aged rice." Fishmongers offered a great variety of fresh,
salted, and frozen fish, as well as shellfish and eels. Life revolved
around the city's wineshops, restaurants, and noodle houses,
which collectively served some six hundred distinct dishes.
These included stewed pork belly with aromatics, milk-steamed
lamb, mock (vegetarian) duck, and honey-roasted quail.[4]

Beggars and peddlers, scam artists, pickpockets, acrobats,
jugglers, courtesans, and prostitutes jostled for the crumbs of
prosperity. Many establishments employed women to provide
conversation and formal entertainment. Men sought excite-
ment and romance outside their arranged marriages among
women who, as the saying goes, "sold their smiles."

One plucky Southern woman, Huáng Dàopó (c. 1245–1330),
fleeing an unhappy marriage and cruel in-laws, boarded a boat to
Hǎinán Island. There she learned from the indigenous Lí people
how to gin, fluff, spin, weave, and dye cotton. When she returned
to her hometown in Jiāngsū decades later, she taught local women
these skills, while inventing a better cotton gin, a three-treadle
loom, and other machines for textile production. Thanks to Huang
Daopo, the region is a center for the textile industry to the
present day. A temple in Shanghai honors her memory.

Responding to the needs of and opportunities offered by the greater Mongol empire, more Chinese than ever before traveled abroad, either privately or on official missions. By the fourteenth century, Han Chinese had established communities in such diverse places as Moscow, Japan, Vietnam, and the island that would become Singapore.[5] Chinese hydraulic engineers worked on the irrigation of the Tigris and Euphrates basins. Persian miniatures, ceramics, and architecture from this time reveal Chinese influences, while methods of Chinese woodblock printing spread to parts of Europe. Firearms, which the Chinese used against the Mongols in the final battles of the Song, transformed warfare forever after the Mongols introduced them to Europe at the Battle of Mohi in Hungary in 1241.[6]

Marco Polo called Hangzhou, home of the beautiful West Lake, "the most splendid heavenly city in the world."

"My descendants will go clothed in gold-embroidered stuffs; they will feed on the choicest meats, they will bestride superb steeds and press in their arms the most beautiful of young women. And they will have forgotten to whom they owe all that."⁷ Such were supposed to have been Genghis Khan's last words. Legend holds that when the construction of Khanbalik began, the turning of the first sod revealed a nest of redheaded worms. This unnerved the monk-planner Liu Bingzhong, who saw it as a bad omen for the future of the dynasty.

Not long after Khublai's death in 1294, the old pattern of corruption, infighting, and rebellion took hold. In 1368, the Yuan was on its eighth khan in just over seven decades. The people had been pushed to the limit by the tax collectors. Inflation had rendered the currency worthless. The Yellow River broke its dikes once more. The bubonic plague, believed to have originated somewhere in present-day Kyrgyzstan, swept the land in 1331, compounding the suffering wrought by floods, locusts, and famine. It's recorded that disasters led to the death of nine out of ten people in parts of central China, though that way of expressing mortality in Chinese can also simply be a formulation meaning a great number. By way of comparison, the bubonic plague probably killed something like half the people of Europe, where it was known as the Black Death.

Countless rebellions broke out, some led by salt smugglers and pirates, others by leaders claiming to be reincarnations of Buddha. A peasant monk from the South called Zhū Yuánzhāng (1328–1398) led a rebel force called the Red Turbans. In 1368, they overran Khanbalik like redheaded worms. The last Yuan emperor fled.

Zhu Yuanzhang razed the magnificent palace that had so impressed Marco Polo and announced the founding of a new dynasty—the Míng, meaning "bright."

# THE MING

## Splendor and Decay

*The Hóngwǔ emperor (r. 1368–1399), as Zhu Yuanzhang titled himself, distrusted scholar-officials no less than Khublai Khan, but in his case it was because they were more educated than him, typically from a higher social class and opinionated. He did not welcome zhengyou, "friends with arguments," in his court. He would observe Confucian rituals while barring the publication of inconvenient Confucian texts, such as those of Mencius that sanctioned killing tyrants. Paranoid about challenges to his authority and sensitive to insult, he had tens of thousands of scholar-officials and generals, including former allies, executed on charges ranging from corruption to treason.*

*Hongwu's antagonism toward scholar-officials prompted him, some twelve years into his reign, to abolish the position of prime minister, concentrating both civil and military power in his own hands. Although the Ming would last almost three hundred years, Hongwu's decision to place the emperor at the center of decision-making ultimately condemned the dynasty to incompetent government and endemic corruption.*

AFTER HE DROVE THE MONGOLS all the way to Siberia, Hongwu's realm was as large as continental Europe. He established the capital in southern Nanjing. Inspired by the Tang's division of the land into administrative units, Hongwu redivided the country into fifteen provinces. The boundaries of most provinces today date back to the Ming.

Hongwu raised armies of corvée laborers to restore roads, canals, and dikes, and repair or build nearly forty-one thousand reservoirs. His mother had died of starvation; preventing famine was a guiding concern for him as emperor. He rewarded those who moved to depopulated areas with arable land, ordering them to plant fruit trees, including mulberry (to feed silkworms). A billion trees were planted in his reign, fifty million of them near Nanjing. Some were earmarked for shipbuilding, for the Ming had grand maritime ambitions. The dynasty, which in 1393 ruled over a population of just over seventy million, began to enjoy peace and prosperity.

Hongwu's legal code mandated harsh punishments for corrupt officials. High-level offenders were to be flayed after execution, their skins put on public display. Mindful of the crisis prompted by the nepotism of the Tang consort Yang Guifei, Hongwu barred all relatives of empresses and consorts from official positions. He also sought to constrain extravagance among palace functionaries, limiting official banquets to four dishes and one soup (a formula that modern leaders, including Dèng Xiǎopíng and Xi Jinping, would invoke in their own campaigns against official profligacy).

Hongwu was wary of eunuchs, mindful that there was little reward for their grievous personal sacrifice apart from self-enrichment. To lessen their chances of meddling in state affairs, he banned them from receiving an education and ordered any who interfered in politics be put to death. They were to guard the harem and to "clean and sweep."² Yet because they also staffed the imperial bodyguard and the secret police, eunuchs enjoyed personal access to the emperor, giving them ample opportunities for blackmail and influence-peddling. For all Hongwu's efforts to control them, eunuchs would play a large role in the eventual downfall of his dynasty.

Hongwu's dozens of wives and concubines gave birth to twenty-six sons (twenty-four survived infancy) and sixteen daughters. He sent his sons to govern different parts of the empire, discarding the system of independent administrators established in the Tang. In 1370, he dispatched his fourth son, ten-year-old Zhū Dì, to the ruins of Khanbalik, in the charge of a trusted general whose mission was to rebuild the old Yuan capital into a garrison city for defense against Mongol incursions. Zhu Di was intelligent and ambitious, resembling his father in vigor and temperament. After his eldest brother died, he expected to be named his father's successor. When Hongwu died in 1398, Zhu Di was thirty-eight and ready to rule.

Zhu Di was infuriated to learn that Hongwu bequeathed the throne instead to his eldest brother's bookish twenty-one-year-old son. As the Jiànwén emperor (r. 1398–1402), the young ruler was determined to restore regional governance to the realm of civil service. He demanded that his uncles relinquish power, imprisoning those who refused. He hadn't been on the throne a full year when Zhu Di galloped south at the head of an army fifty thousand strong. Three years later, in 1402, Zhu Di burnt his nephew's palace to the ground. Jianwen's body was never found; some believe he escaped and secretly lived the rest of his life as a Buddhist monk. Tens of thousands perished in the coup, including Jianwen's chief adviser, whom Zhu Di had sliced in half after he refused to endorse him as the new emperor. Zhu Di then executed every member of the advisor's family to ten degrees of kinship, along with 870 of his associates.[3]

Zhu Di took the reign title of Yŏnglè (eternal joy) and moved the Ming capital to his base in old Khanbalik, renaming it Beijing (Northern Capital). He disarmed his surviving brothers, mollifying them with generous pensions.

It was one thing to make Beijing the new capital. It was another to force a reluctant court, content with the ease, warmth, and sophistication of the South, to shift to the cold and dusty North. Yongle dispatched troops to work alongside convicts and peasants to cultivate the barren wilderness around the new capital, planting millet, wheat, barley, and sorghum plus hardy vegetables such as turnips, carrots, and cabbage, and commissioned painters and poets to extol the beauty of the North to their fellow literati.

Teams of hundreds of laborers hauled barges up the newly repaired Grand Canal from Hangzhou laden with everything needed to build and supply the new capital. This included hardwoods for the construction of the Forbidden City, which twenty-four emperors of two dynasties—the Ming and its successor, the Qing—would call home. He ordered the repair and construction of the Great Walls (left to decay in the Yuan dynasty) to block incursions by Mongol and other tribes, replacing the Han-era tamped-earth-and-stone bulwarks with sturdier ones of stone and brick. Yongle inaugurated his capital in 1421 with grand ceremony.

The Yongle emperor had an instinct for spectacle: his entourage included thousands of musicians who literally sang his praises.

Yongle commissioned more than two thousand scholars in Nanjing to produce a compendium of all knowledge. When completed, the Yongle Encyclopedia, *Yongle Dadian* 永樂大典, consisted of 22,937 chapters in 11,095 string-bound volumes. For Yongle, who, like his father, had a tense relationship with scholar-officials, this was both an act of self-legitimization and a means of exerting control (busywork for busybodies). It was "not intended to generate, preserve, or disseminate knowledge, but rather to fix and consolidate existing knowledge and to make it more readily available" for purposes of governance.[4]

The northern tribes continued to harass the capital. Yongle personally led five military campaigns to secure the borders, pushing the troublesome Jurchens north of the Amur River. His troops also occupied part of Vietnam until the Vietnamese drove the Ming out again in 1427. To placate the Tibetans, he adopted Tibetan Buddhist practices and commissioned the building of Tibetan Buddhist temples, including along the border with Tibet, a gesture aimed at both conciliation and territorial marking.[5]

## EUNUCH HEROES AND VILLAINS

Yongle commissioned the first expeditions of the intrepid eunuch admiral Zhèng Hé (1371–1433). A Muslim from southwestern Yunnan, Zheng He led seven epic voyages, each involving dozens of seafaring junks (ships with battened sails) and tens of thousands of sailors. The armada suppressed pirate activity in the East China Sea, carried out diplomacy on behalf of the court as far the Persian Gulf, the east coast of Africa, and the south coast of Arabia, and projected an image of Ming confidence and power. He also solicited tribute and acquired exotic luxuries for the court, such as Japanese swords, Sri Lankan and Indian gems, and African gold.[6]

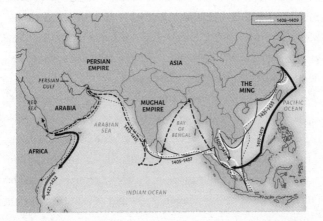

The savvy diplomat and intrepid explorer Zheng He carried out seven epic voyages more than half a century before Christopher Columbus set sail.

The voyagers collected much useful knowledge as well, compiled in books such as Zheng He's 1434 *Treatise on the Barbarian Kingdoms of the Western Oceans*. They also returned with gifts from foreign sovereigns, including a giraffe, whom sycophants insisted was the mythical *qílín* 麒麟, a beast that Confucius said appeared only when enlightened rulers sat on the throne. The Ming and its products enjoyed global prestige: wealthy Egyptians wore tunics of Chinese silk, and Europeans collected Ming porcelain. A blue-and-white Ming bowl appears in the Italian court painter Andrea Mantegna's *Adoration of the Magi* (1500).

Zheng He sailed for the last time in 1433, nine years after Yongle's death in battle against the Mongols. Yongle's twenty-six-year-old grandson, the Xuāndé emperor (r. 1425–1435), commissioned Zheng He's seventh and final voyage. The scholar-officials of the court, ever hostile toward eunuchs, complained about the expense of the voyages and later claimed to have lost essential navigational documents, thwarting future expeditions.[7] By the following century, piracy had returned to the East and South China Seas. While maritime trade continued, there was to be no further exploration of the world.

Xuande ruled wisely and compassionately, even ordering retrials of criminal cases that saw thousands of innocent people released from prison. He was also a talented animal painter, and his ten-year reign is celebrated for the exceptional blue-and-white porcelain and copper-red underglazing produced by the imperial kilns of Jǐngdézhēn in Jiāngxī province under his patronage.

Yet Xuande defied his great-grandfather Hongwu's ban on educating eunuchs. He even established a school for them in the palace, so they could help him with official business. With greater access to wealth, power, and privilege, the number of castrates rose sharply. The majority lived miserable lives, performing menial tasks and sleeping in tiny, austere cells. The cleverer and less scrupulous among them set about "cleaning and sweeping" through the treasury. As overseers of the workshops producing luxury goods for the court and inventories of foreign items of tribute, they enjoyed ample opportunities for self-enrichment. One notorious eunuch, Liú Jǐn (1451–1510), acquired some 240,000 gold ingots, two bushels of gems, 4,162 jade belts, 3,000 gold brooches, and two solid-gold suits of armor. Eventually accused of rebellion, he was sentenced to the "death of a thousand cuts"—being slowly sliced to death.

The ambitious Wáng Zhèn was another infamous Ming eunuch. As the principal tutor of Xuande's successor, the young Zhèngtǒng emperor (r. 1435–1449), he enjoyed his master's trust. By the 1440s, he was widely considered the most powerful man in the realm. He died one of the most hated after urging Zhengtong to lead an ill-considered campaign against the Mongols in 1449. Scholar-officials opposed the campaign. As the emperor led his troops out of the capital, they knelt weeping by the roadside.[8] About fifty miles northwest of Beijing, the Mongols routed the Ming army and captured the emperor. Wang Zhen was killed, either by the Mongols or by his own men—it's unclear.

With Zhengtong captive, his brother took the throne as the Jǐngtài emperor (r. 1449–1457). He was so fond of blue cloisonné that he invited Byzantine cloisonné artisans to Beijing to pass on their art. To this day, cloisonné is known in Chinese as jǐngtàilán 景泰藍, "Jingtai blue," whatever its color.

Jingtai confiscated Wang Zhen's wealth and executed his supporters and relatives. But his reign lasted only eight years. The former emperor, released by the Mongols for a ransom, bided his time until Jingtai fell sick and then deposed him. Jingtai died under mysterious circumstances a month later.

## SCIENTIFIC STAGNATION, CULTURAL EFFLORESCENCE

Like the Song, the Ming was a time of great urban, mercantile, and artistic vitality, with significant technological advances in silk weaving, printing, and publishing, including the invention of movable type. The prince-mathematician Zhū Zǎiyù (1536–1611), invented the "equal temperament scale," a tuning system for musical instruments, in 1584, at least a decade before Europeans devised a similar method.[9]

It was during the Ming that the physician Lǐ Shìzhēn compiled the *Compendium of Materia Medica*, the basis for traditional Chinese medicine. It includes prescriptions for more than eleven thousand compounds using almost two thousand ingredients. One involves the plant from which artemisinin—the malaria drug that chemist Tú Yōuyōu discovered, and for which she won her Nobel Prize in Medicine in 2005—is extracted.

For all this, China, once ahead of the West in science and technology, began to lag behind. In *The Great Inertia*, the theoretical physicist Wen-yuan Qian observes: "No other nation had so many peasant rebellions, was plagued by so many civil wars, and was invaded so often; yet no nation preserved its own characteristic culture so well." Traditional China, he writes, "remained a basically uniform and intolerant politico-ideological environment." Intolerance, he argues, stifled the intellectual questing critical to scientific advance.[10]

The rise of a wealthy and urbane middle class led to a broad demand for the types of luxury products enjoyed by the court, such as cloisonné, lacquerware, filigree, elegant furniture, and ceramics. Potters began signing their stoneware teapots, embroiderers stitched their personal mark into cloth, and jade-carvers etched their names into their creations.[11] These trademarks boosted the worth of an object. It was buyer beware: Zhāng Yìngyú's 1617 *The Book of Swindles, Piànjīng* 騙經, detailed twenty-four categories of scams, frauds, and deceptions that awaited the unwary consumer, including such unusual ones as "A Buddhist Monk Identifies a Cow as His Mother."

Ming ceramics are considered some of the finest ever made. The best came from the artisans and kilns of the ancient pottery center of Jingdezhen, which the Ming placed under direct imperial control.

The continued growth of a literate middle class also saw a flourishing of fiction. A number of China's most famous novels, which combined the formal literary styles of old with vernacular prose, were published during the Ming—under pseudonyms in many cases, as fiction was considered a vulgar form. The *Romance of the Three Kingdoms* was published during this time; its mix of history, legend, and fantasy has supplanted historical truth in the popular imagination ever since, leaving Cao Cao with the taint of villainy and transforming his rivals into models of honor and courage.

Another great Ming novel was the sixteenth-century *Journey to the West*, aka *Monkey*, which fictionalizes and injects supernatural elements into the story of the Tang monk Xuanzang's journey to India to bring back original Buddhist texts. In the novel, a talking pig and the mischievous, havoc-making Sūn Wùkōng—better known in English as the Monkey King—accompany the monk. The Monkey King employs "magic weapons," *fǎbǎo* 法寶, to battle various "cow demons and snake spirits," including the fearsome White-Bone Demon. The novel is an entertaining blend of mythology, Daoism, Buddhism, Confucianism, and satire. The inspiration for almost thirty films, television series, comics, anime, and operas, it is one of China's most successful cultural exports.

Shi Nai'en's *Outlaws of the Marsh* (also known as *Water Margin* and, in Pearl Buck's abridged translation, *All Men Are Brothers*) is set in a milieu known as *jiānghú* 江湖, literally "rivers and lakes." In this metaphorical place, martial artists, political dissidents, fortune-tellers, outlaws, swindlers, and other fringe-dwellers scorn the state's laws but enforce their own strict codes of honor. Rough but righteous heroes, 105 men and

3 women, individually fall afoul of the law and band together to fight a corrupt and oppressive government.

Though the action of *Outlaws of the Marsh* takes place in the Song dynasty, it's a dig at the Ming, which was growing ever more corrupt and oppressive. It introduces some of Chinese fiction's most famous characters—including the tiger-killer Wu Song and his adulterous sister-in-law Pan Jinlian, whom we met in Chapter 6. Pan Jinlian has served ever since as the archetypal "bad woman"—despite having been sold into servitude to a sexually predacious man, then forced into a loveless marriage before believing she found love with the lascivious official Ximen Qing. Beginning in the Song, the effective age of consent for girls was ten years old (fourteen for marriage). For much of China's history, access to the bodies of young women was deemed the natural privilege of wealthy and powerful men, while public opinion condemned women who acted on their own desires, like Pan Jinlian.

*Jīn Píng Méi*, China's best-known erotic novel, sometimes translated as *The Plum in the Golden Vase*, is a kind of fan fiction based on *Outlaws of the Marsh*. It imagines that Pan Jinlian and Ximen Qing get away with her husband's murder, after which Ximen Qing takes her into his household as a concubine. The novel, which revels in the petty cruelties and domestic politics of the patriarchal, polygamous family structure, is sometimes read as an allegory of the Ming, with the corrupt Ximen and his inept principal wife standing in for a ruling house unfit to govern. *Jin Ping Mei* is considered a literary masterpiece, albeit a scandalous one, and was the first Chinese novel to feature female protagonists and a domestic setting.

## A GAME OF THRONES

By 1487, the Ming was on its tenth emperor, Hóngzhì (r. 1487–1505). Hongzhi proved exceptional, and not just because he was the only monogamous emperor in Chinese history. Diligent in his duties, he appointed talented people to his court and encouraged debate. He curtailed the power of the eunuchs, clamped down on corruption, and imposed order on the government's finances.

Unfortunately, his only son, the Zhèngdé emperor (r. 1505–1521), a contemporary of Henry VIII, proved a hedonist and profligate who also enjoyed wearing disguises and breaking into people's homes, and who "hunted" so many young women for his harem that some ultimately starved for lack of grain to feed them all. Liu Jin, the corrupt eunuch with the solid-gold suits of armor, was one of Zhengde's trusted advisers.[12]

Zhengde's reign was plagued by numerous uprisings. Farmers once again struggled to pay corrupt tax collectors, forcing some to sell their daughters, castrate their sons, take dangerous jobs in illegal mines, or turn to banditry. Some of the rural poor made it to the growing coastal cities devoted to maritime trade, which at one point was bringing in half the dynasty's tax revenues.[13] In addition to dock work, there were opportunities in textile, paper, and steel mills.

In 1513, an expedition led by the Portuguese explorer Jorge Álvares arrived in Guangdong. Southerners, used to friendly contact with Arab and Asian traders, welcomed the Europeans. But the Portuguese acted more like pirates, murdering and plundering, until the local authorities expelled the "foreign devils"—a pejorative that appears to have originated with this episode. The bad behavior of the Portuguese soured the Chinese toward other Europeans, who would after this be treated as barbarians in need of control and monitoring.

By the end of the sixteenth century, the Portuguese nonetheless managed to establish a trading post in the tiny coastal territory of Macao, paying what it called rent and the Ming called tribute, for the privilege. The Portuguese were the first major exporters of tea to Europe, calling it by its Cantonese name, *cha*; the Dutch, who began exporting it from Fújiàn province in the early seventeenth century, called it *thee*, based on the Fujianese pronunciation of the same word, which is how we got to "tea."

Zhengde died at twenty-nine, possibly by falling off a boat while drunk. None of his sons survived childhood, so the throne passed to his equally reprobate cousin, the Jiājìng emperor (r. 1520–1566). Jiajing's reign was marked by two main crises.

The Great Rites Controversy erupted when Jiajing refused to follow custom and name Zhengde his "father," maintaining the fiction of an unbroken dynastic line, insisting that his own father be posthumously declared emperor instead. Court officials who opposed this were exiled, beaten, or killed.

The other great drama was personal. Jiajing was reputedly a sexual sadist. One evening in November 1542, palace maids, pushed to their limit, tried to strangle him in his bed. Discovered before they succeeded, they were condemned to death by "slow slicing."

A shaken Jiajing moved into the Lake Palaces of Zhongnanhai in the Imperial City, just west of the Forbidden City, with a thirteen-year-old concubine and his cats, Snow Brow and Tiger. He continued to force himself on teenage virgins and imbibe Daoist immortality potions that, as they contained mercury (along with the menstrual blood of palace women), were the probable cause of his death. In his forty-five years on the throne, Jiajing badly neglected his duties. The upstanding official Hǎi Ruì (1514–1587) remonstrated with him about this, but Jiajing didn't care for critics any more than Hongwu had. He would have had Hai Rui executed, but died first.

Jiajing's son, the Lóngqìng emperor (r. 1567–1572), did his best to sort out the mess left by his father and Zhengde. He sacked corrupt officials, recalled Hai Rui, negotiated a truce with the Mongols, and reduced the burden of taxation on the peasantry. He would have tackled the eunuch problem, too, had he not become besotted with a Turkish beauty presented to him by a clever castrate. Longqing lost interest in state affairs and died of illness at thirty-five, after only six years in power.

Longqing's son and heir, the Wànlì emperor (r. 1572–1620), took the throne at the age of ten. Ably advised, he reformed government administration to make it more efficient and accountable. He also invested in flood control and other public works. The country prospered. Chinese historians call the first decade of his reign (which lasted forty-eight years in total, the longest of any Ming ruler) the "Wanli renaissance."

But the structural problems that made the Ming highly susceptible to corruption remained. Hai Rui suggested skinning embezzlers to discourage graft, but Wanli refused, stating that such extreme measures didn't accord with his "sense of good government." He wanted to name his third son, sired with his favorite concubine, Lady Zheng, his successor. His ministers opposed this. Frustrated with his imperial duties, in a fit of pique, he refused to attend court or meet with his ministers again.

After abandoning his imperial duties in his twenties, Wanli spent the rest of his life feasting to obesity and obsessing over the building of his tomb, where he hoped to spend eternity with Lady Zheng.

Jesuits believed that if they could convert an emperor to Catholicism, all of China would follow. Educated in useful fields such as science, astronomy, and mathematics, they adopted Chinese dress, learned the Chinese language and customs, and sought access to the court. In 1602, the Italian Jesuit Matteo Ricci was granted an audience with Wanli's court. He performed the kowtow, *kētóu* 磕頭—the act of kneeling and knocking one's forehead on the ground in submission—before Wanli's empty throne, and the court invited him to stay. He taught the eunuchs how to wind the European clocks in the imperial collection and gave them harpsichord lessons. He also devised the first system for transcribing Chinese into the Roman alphabet—his Latinate "Pequim" is why Beijing became known as Peking in English and European languages.

By the time Ricci arrived at court, the eunuchs had a stranglehold on government. Burdensome taxes and corruption were sparking numerous rebellions. A six-year war against a Japanese shogun for control of the Korean Peninsula had drained the treasury. At its height, the Ming had "a greater land area, bigger cities (and more big cities), bigger armies, bigger ships, bigger palaces, bigger bells, more literate people, more religious professionals; and it produced more books, ceramic dishes, textiles, and spears than any other state on earth at that time."[14] Its population in 1600, which some contemporary Chinese demographers estimate at more than 150 million, was greater than that of Europe. Yet all the signs of dynastic decline were apparent: corruption, rebellions, and border trouble.

In the 1630s, Lǐ Zìchéng, a shepherd and manual laborer with imperial designs, led a rebel force that rampaged through the countryside, breaching the dikes of the Yellow River and leaving hundreds of thousands dead. In early 1644, he laid siege to the capital. The original copy of the Yongle Encyclopedia was one of many precious documents to go up in flames during the conflict. The last emperor of the Ming, Wanli's grandson Chóngzhēn, killed his wives and daughters to protect them from Li Zicheng's rapacious forces. He then fled to the artificial hill behind the Forbidden City and hanged himself with a silken sash.

Li Zicheng declared himself emperor of a new dynasty. Peasants rose up and killed their landlords, the poor ransacked and torched the homes of the wealthy, servants rioted, soldiers mutinied, and anarchy reigned.[15]

The Ming had built or repaired thousands of miles of Great Walls. But beyond those walls, a formidable enemy had been gathering strength. The chieftain Nurhaci had united disparate

Jurchen tribes, founding the Latter Jin Dynasty, and subjugating the Mongols. He commissioned the creation of a new alphabet based on Mongolian script, into which he had translated the Chinese legal codes, military handbooks, and *Romance of the Three Kingdoms*. His eighth son and successor, Hong Taiji, renamed the Jurchens "Manchus" to underline the break with their tribal past and, in 1636, remade the Jin into the Qing—the "clear" or "pure" dynasty. He divided the Manchus into eight groups, called Banners, their identifying flags either a solid or a bordered color (for example, yellow, or yellow edged with red). The Banners served as a form of military, political, and social organization.

There is a line in a Chinese text from the second century BCE: "If one man defends a pass, ten thousand men cannot force it open." Nearly two hundred miles from Beijing, at the easternmost pass of the Great Walls, the man charged with defending it, the Ming general Wú Sānguì (1612–1678), threw it open to a Manchu army that pledged to help quell Li Zicheng's rebellion. That they did—before declaring Beijing the capital of the Qing dynasty and installing Hong Taiji's son, six-year-old Aisin Gioro Fulin, on the Forbidden City's throne as the Shùnzhì emperor.

# THE MANCHU QING

## The Rocky Road to Modernity

*Manchu men shaved the crown of their heads, growing the rest of their hair long and plaiting it in a "queue." Soon after arriving in Beijing, the child-emperor's regent, his uncle Dorgon, demanded that former officials and soldiers of the Ming do the same, eventually extending the order to all adult males. The choice was stark: get the queue or lose the head. The Qing justified forcing all male subjects to adopt the Manchu queue in Confucian terms: "Now that the country is one family, the ruler is like a father and the people are like sons . . . How can they be different?"[1] The Qing court also commanded their subjects to adopt the Manchu style of dress, with robes that fastened diagonally at the right shoulder and sleeves that tapered to hoof-like cuffs, both symbolic and practical for a people who spent so much time on horseback.*

ABHORRENCE OF THE QUEUE was personal as well as political. A luxuriant head of hair, dressed perhaps in a bun or ponytail, signified virility and elegance in a man. Resistance to the queue—and the Qing—was fiercest in the South. In the end, the South would produce a rebel leader who would first cut his queue and then help to bring down not just the dynasty, but the entire imperial edifice.

The Qing ordered all Chinese men to adopt the Manchu "queue," on pain of execution. This infuriated their Han subjects—shaved heads were for boys, monks, criminals, and castrates.

In 1644, when the Shunzhi emperor first sat on the throne in the Forbidden City, known as the Dragon Throne, the Manchus numbered less than one million in a total population of well over a hundred million. Bannermen established garrisons in the center of cities throughout the empire, from which they terrorized the populace into submission. The ancient town of Yángzhōu, close to Nanjing and an economic and cultural center since the Tang, suffered a particularly ferocious massacre by the Bannermen in 1645, though the commonly cited figure of eight hundred thousand killed is undoubtedly an exaggeration, as the total population was likely to have been less than half that.

One of the most stubborn of the anti-Qing holdouts was an irascible Chinese-Japanese pirate and scholar called Zhèng Chénggōng. European texts usually refer to him as Koxinga, an approximate spelling of the title "Lord of the Imperial Name," granted him by a would-be Ming emperor. Zheng Chenggong fled with his followers to Taiwan in 1661. With the help of the island's indigenous Austronesian population, his men expelled the Dutch colonists who had been there for almost forty years. Zheng Chenggong died the following year, in 1662, at the age of thirty-eight. His followers settled on Taiwan, the ancestors of many of today's Taiwanese. A little over two decades later, the Qing brought Taiwan under its formal administrative control, the first dynasty to do so.

Like the Mongols before them, the Manchus didn't trust the Han. They reserved half of all civil service positions for themselves and attempted to segregate the two populations—with the exception of Han Chinese who had earned Bannerman status by joining the Qing cause before 1644. The Qing divided Beijing up among the Eight Banners, evicting all non-Bannermen Chinese. Many of the city's former Han residents moved to the walled suburbs south of the capital's "Front Gate," Qiánmén. But the Manchu knew they couldn't consolidate their rule or achieve legitimacy without Han Chinese collaboration and cooperation.

In 1662, Shunzhi died of smallpox at twenty-three, passing the throne to his eight-year-old son, the Kāngxī emperor (r. 1662–1722). As a boy, Kangxi diligently studied the Confucian classics. As he grew older, he worked hard to establish himself as a model ruler. He attended to flood control along the Yellow River and repair of the Grand Canal, which the Ming had neglected, and limited the number of eunuchs in the palace, confining them to menial tasks and the guarding of his relatively modest harem of three hundred concubines.

Kangxi, China's longest-ruling emperor, was an "exuberantly curious" man who earned the respect of his fellow Manchu and Han subjects alike.

Kangxi wooed the Han scholar-officials by adhering to Confucian ritual and upholding the system of triennial civil service examinations. He commissioned projects of cultural and historical significance, including a history of the Ming, a Chinese-language dictionary, and the comprehensive *Complete Poems of the Tang* mentioned earlier. He surprised his court by organizing a command performance of *The Peach Blossom Fan*, a popular opera lamenting the fall of the Ming. Its author, Kǒng Shàngrèn, a descendant of Confucius, was astonished by the court's enthusiasm, though he caught some (presumably Han) officials "quietly weeping behind their sleeves."[2]

At home on horseback, brave in battle, and conscientious in performing the shamanistic rites of his people, Kangxi also earned the respect of his fellow Manchus. He fought off border challenges and negotiated a treaty with Moscow, setting the Russo-Qing border along the upper reaches of the Amur River. His troops invaded Lhasa in 1720, installed a new Dalai Lama, and laid down the basis for creeping control over the kingdom of Tibet.

Historian Jonathan Spence writes that Kangxi's "outstanding trait was an exuberant curiosity."[3] His father, Shunzhi, had appointed the young German Jesuit Johann Adam Schall von Bell head of the Imperial Bureau of Astronomy after he accurately predicted a solar eclipse. When he cured Shunzhi's ailing mother using Western medicine, Shunzhi permitted him to build a cathedral on the site of Matteo Ricci's former home in Beijing. By the time Kangxi became emperor, the court hosted several Chinese-speaking Jesuits. Kangxi ordered them to learn Manchu as well, to better converse with him on such topics as cannons, cartography, Euclidean geometry, and windmills. They even taught him to play the spinet, a type of harpsichord.

The Jesuits in China had pragmatically chosen to treat "ancestor worship" as a civil rather than religious ritual. But in 1715, Pope Clement XI issued a papal bull condemning it as "idolatrous and barbaric." Offended by this and the disrespectful behavior of the pope's envoys, Kangxi, despite being well disposed toward individual Jesuits, banned the preaching of Christianity.

Kangxi died in 1722, having reigned for sixty-one years, longer than any other emperor. His son, the Yōngzhèng emperor (r. 1723–1735), also ruled conscientiously, reforming the tax system to make it fairer and cracking down on corruption. While retaining the service of the more useful Jesuits, Yongzheng banned Christianity outright in 1724. He also brutally suppressed worker unrest in the textile industry, wary in general of the south's volatile *jianghu* underworld of itinerant laborers, kung-fu fighters, fortune-tellers, and other potentially subversive elements.

Chinese was Yongzheng's second language, after Manchu. He found it difficult to understand his ministers, who spoke in a variety of dialects and accents. He decreed that they were to use a single system of pronunciation based on the Beijing dialect. This was called *guānhuà* 官話, the "language of the officials," or mandarins—Mandarin Chinese.

The Italian Jesuit Giuseppe Castiglioni, an accomplished painter in the Renaissance tradition, was highly respected by the Qing for his ability to marry Western techniques, such as linear perspective and chiaroscuro, with Chinese aesthetics and traditional palettes. Qiánlóng (r. 1735–1796), Yongzheng's son and successor, commissioned three official portraits from

Castiglione portrayed Qianlong as a mounted archer of the steppes; a ruler on the Dragon Throne in imperial yellow robes; and an incarnation of Mañjuśrī, the bodhisattva central to Tibetan Buddhism, the faith shared by Tibetans and Mongols alike.

Castiglioni, designed to appeal to his fellow Manchus as well as his Han Chinese and Tibetan subjects.

Qianlong's reign is celebrated as one of China's great *shengshi*, golden ages. He almost doubled the size of the realm of the late Ming by conquering the Mongolian homelands and a Central Asian region of some 645,000 square miles (1.67 million sq km) that he called Xinjiang ("new frontier"). It included the Taklimakan Desert, across which ran the Silk Roads. After Qing troops massacred some half a million—eight out of ten—Buddhist Mongols known as Dzungars between 1755 and 1758 (the Dzungar Genocide), Xinjiang's population consisted mainly of the Turkic-speaking, non-nomadic Uyghurs, who had converted to Islam in the fifteenth century. The area remained prone to rebellions, each followed by violent suppression. In 1820, the Qing began sending Han and Manchu settlers to Xinjiang and investing in canals and other agricultural infrastructure there to consolidate its control.

On the central plains, in the areas populated by the Han, Qing rule from Kangxi onward generally brought peace and prosperity. Global demand for Chinese tea, silk, and porcelain, paid for in foreign silver, boosted the nation's coffers and invigorated domestic commerce. The Qing increased economic and social mobility by abolishing a Ming law that bound men to particular occupations from birth. Subsistence farmers could now freely sell their labor in the towns—even if they became a source of amorphous fears about crime and, in a widespread panic in 1768, "soul-stealing" sorcery.

An aesthete and a connoisseur, Qianlong assembled an enormous collection of cultural treasures. Enamored of Wang Xizhi's "Preface to the Orchid Pavilion Poems," he amassed

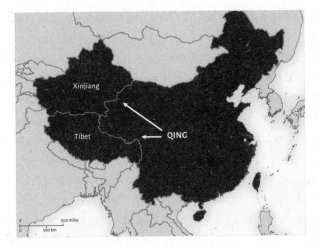

The conquest of Xinjiang and Tibet greatly increased the size of the Qing, which claimed that Han and Tang military outposts on the Silk Roads "proved" that Xinjiang belonged to China.

paintings, carvings, calligraphy, and other objects dedicated to the gathering, eventually building an Orchid Pavilion in the Forbidden City, complete with an artificial stream.

He also lavished attention on the Yuánmíngyuán, the Garden of Perfect Brightness. Established by his grandfather Kangxi and expanded by his father, Yongzheng, the Yuanmingyuan was one of several alternative residences and imperial parklands within riding distance of the capital where the court could relax and hunt. Yongzheng had had audience halls constructed in the Yuanmingyuan so that he could attend to official business without returning to the Forbidden City, which, like most Qing emperors, he found claustrophobic, or as one put it, a warren of "dank ditches with vermillion walls."[4]

Qianlong continued the work of enhancing the eight-hundred-acre parkland, adding artificial hills and waterways, and re-creations of the Song-era literati gardens he'd admired on inspection tours of the South, as well as reimagined scenes from famous paintings and poems.[5] It boasted flowing streams, elegant bridges, pavilions, and audience halls. There were also the Western Pavilions, designed by Castiglioni and other Jesuits: mock rococo buildings of stone and marble, hung with valuable scrolls of Chinese calligraphy and precious French tapestries. Castiglioni also designed a mechanical fountain clock featuring the twelve animals of the Chinese zodiac cast in bronze.

The Yuanmingyuan even featured a miniature township with a shopping street modeled after a southern market. There, Qianlong and his consorts pretended to bargain for goods from eunuch "merchants" while guarding their purses from other eunuchs, who played the part of pickpockets.

Along with more than six hundred elegant wooden structures, the Yuanmingyuan featured the Jesuit-designed Western Pavilions, the marvels of which included a mechanical fountain clock.

## OMINOUS VAPORS

Advances in agriculture, including terraced rice fields and the planting of hardy New World crops such as peanuts, corn, and sweet potatoes on otherwise infertile hilly or sandy ground, meant greater food security for all. General prosperity contributed to a rising population over the course of the eighteenth century, which reached more than three hundred million by 1776. But the large population increased pressure on the food supply. The Qing had retained the Ming taxation system that required farmers, almost 93 percent of the population, to pay taxes in silver rather than in kind. When the price of silver rose, the taxes became insupportable. The bureaucracy, which did not expand in proportion to the population, could not hope to stay on top of the increasingly complex problems faced by the people.[6]

The elite—and the venal—thrived. Héshēn, a handsome officer forty years younger than Qianlong, provoked gossip and scandal on account of his unusually close relationship with the emperor and the astonishing fortune he accumulated. Heshen, who would go on to marry Qianlong's favorite daughter and take some 600 concubines, acquired mansions with a total of some 3,000 rooms; mountains of gold and silver; 14,000 bolts of fine silk; 460 expensive European clocks; and 24 solid-gold beds with gemstone inlays. He was polymorphously corrupt: an influence peddler, extortionist, and embezzler. In 1796 he even stole money intended for the quelling of a major rebellion by the White Lotus Society, an outlawed religious sect. After Qianlong's death in 1799, the court presented Heshen with a silk sash with which to hang himself.

The novel *Dream of the Red Chamber*, or *The Story of the Stone*, by Cáo Xuěqín (c. 1715–1763) captures both the majesty of the

Qing at its height and the sense of a world perched on the edge of decline. Widely considered Chinese literature's finest novel, with many passages of brilliant poetry embedded in its prose, it presents in exquisite detail the lifestyle and worldview of a large, privileged Han Bannerman family brought down by corruption and moral depravity.

The cantankerous scholar Gōng Zìzhēn (1792–1841), who detested foot-binding, foreigners, corruption, and Confucianist clichés alike, wrote of these unsettled times:

> when the wealthy vie with each other in splendor and display while the poor squeeze each other to death; when the poor do not enjoy a moment's rest while the rich are comfortable; when the poor lose more and more while the rich keep piling up treasures . . . All of this will finally congeal in an ominous vapor which will fill the space between heaven and earth with its darkness.[7]

That vapor, and that darkness, would soon come to have a name: opium.

## THE OPIUM WARS

European traders had been trying to get a foothold in China for centuries. As eager as the Europeans were for Chinese tea, silk, and porcelain, the Chinese remained indifferent to European goods. The Qing restricted access to ports, confining foreign merchants to Guangzhou (Canton), from October to March. Foreign traders resented this, as well as having to work with licensed Chinese intermediaries and abide by local law. In 1793, the British sent an experienced diplomat, Lord George

Macartney, to Qianlong's court carrying a letter arguing for greater access to the empire's markets, including a reduction in tariffs, the ability of merchants to live in China year-round, and the stationing of an ambassador in Beijing.

The eighty-year-old Qianlong agreed to receive the Englishman at his imperial hunting lodge at Chéngdé, northeast of Beijing. The protocol of an imperial audience demanded a kowtow. Macartney refused, instead bowing on one knee before Qianlong, just as he did with his own sovereign, King George III. Qianlong received him courteously anyway, but once Macartney left and his letter was translated, Qianlong instructed his ministers to bolster the Qing's coastal defenses, predicting that England, "fiercer and stronger than other countries in the Western Ocean," might "stir up trouble." To Macartney he prefaced his reply by saying that the Qing had everything it needed in abundance: "I set no value on objects strange or ingenious, and have no use for your country's manufactures."[8]

The British East India Company, which enjoyed a British monopoly on East Asian trade, had something for which at least some Chinese had use: opium, grown in British-controlled India. Opium was already cultivated in China, but in small quantities— soldiers and manual laborers relied on it for pain relief, and some of the idle rich smoked it for pleasure. In 1729, the British sold two hundred chests of opium into China, each containing almost sixty kilograms of the drug. In 1790, three years before Macartney's visit, they sold 4,054 chests. That number increased steadily.

Qianlong retired in 1796 in a gesture of filial piety, not wanting his reign to outlast that of his revered grandfather, Kangxi. This left the problem of opium to his successor, Jiāqìng (r. 1796–1820).

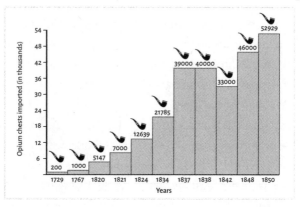

Before the British began smuggling opium into China, addiction had not been a widespread social problem. People smoked it in different styles of pipe, some quite ornate.

In 1815, the British sent another envoy, Lord Amherst, to Beijing. Jiaqing expelled him after another tussle over the kowtow.

Opium addiction began to damage the fabric of Chinese society. The illegal trade fostered corruption, and silver drained from the imperial coffers. Debate raged in the court of Jiaqing and his successor, Dàoguāng (r. 1821–1850), over whether to legalize opium—encouraging domestic production and limiting trade-related corruption—or ban it. In 1838, Daoguang decided on prohibition. In March 1839, the emperor sent the official Lín Zéxú (1785–1850) to Guangzhou, the hub of the opium trade, to implement the ban. By July, Lin had arrested thousands of addicts and confiscated almost twenty-three thousand kilos of opium, as well as seventy thousand pipes.

Lin Zexu demanded that the 350 or so foreign traders in Guangzhou surrender their opium. As tensions rose, he locked them in their warehouses. Chinese soldiers blew horns and banged gongs to increase the pressure on them. It took six weeks, but the foreigners handed over twenty thousand chests. Now in possession of almost 1.4 million kilos of opium, Lin Zexu had it mixed with water, salt, and lime and flushed out to sea.

In response, British warships blockaded the entrance to Guangzhou's harbor, smashed through Chinese defenses, and captured ports including Shanghai and Níngbō, blocking maritime traffic on the Grand Canal and lower Yangtze. This became known as the First Opium War.

Under duress, the Qing signed the Treaty of Nanjing in 1842, which granted the British access to Guangzhou, Shanghai, and three other "treaty ports." It also ceded the island of Hong Kong—"fragrant port," named for the spice trade—to the British in perpetuity. (The British foreign secretary at the time, Lord Palmerston, questioned the wisdom of acquiring "a barren island with hardly a House upon it" that would never become a great "Mart of Trade."[9]) It imposed indemnities on the Qing totaling twenty-one million silver dollars. The United States, France, and other nations piled on with their own demands, including "extraterritoriality"— exemption from local justice for foreigners who committed crimes in China. Chinese law would not apply within "concessions"— those parts of the treaty ports controlled by foreign powers. These agreements were the first of what are called the Unequal Treaties, beginning a century of China's humiliation at the hands of various imperialist powers. They heralded the beginning of the end, not just of the Qing, but of the dynastic system by which China had been ruled for thousands of years.

## REBELS AND RAIDERS

In 1853, the American Baptist missionary Reverend I. J. Roberts recalled:

Some time in 1846, or the year following, two Chinese gentlemen came to my house in Canton professing a desire to
be taught the Christian religion. One of them soon returned
home, but the other continued with us two months or more,
during which time he studied the scriptures and received
instruction, and maintained a blameless deportment.[10]

That "other" was Hóng Xiùquán (1814–1864), who in 1847
declared himself the Chinese brother of Jesus Christ and the
founder of the anti-Manchu *Tàipíng Tiānguó*, Heavenly Kingdom
of Great Peace. He declared it his mission to expel the Manchus, whom he considered to be demons, and turn China into
a Christian land, a "paradise on earth where food, clothes, land,
and money are shared by everyone."[11] A ban on gambling, foot-
binding (which Manchu women never practiced, incidentally),
and prostitution attracted hundreds of thousands of women to
the Taipings' cause, many of whom served in its militias, some
as military commanders. The Taipings, who unplaited their hair,
captured Nanjing in 1853, declaring it their "Heavenly Capital."

Hong Xiuquan invited the reverend to Nanjing in 1856. His
former teacher wrote that he was horrified by Hong's "crazy"
interpretation of Christianity and how the "whole affair" seemed
based on slaughter and looting: "They do nothing but burn,
murder and destroy."[12] Another missionary noted that for all
the empowered women in the militias, Hong and other Taiping
leaders kept large harems, and their soldiers raped women and
girls at will.[13]

The Taiping Rebellion—called a revolution by some contemporary historians for its goal of systemic change—would be
praised by Mao as an exemplary peasant uprising. It was also

one of the deadliest conflicts in world history and the bloodiest of the nineteenth century. By the time Qing forces, helped by British and American soldiers, brought it to an end in 1864, some 20 to 30 million people had lost their lives to violence, disease, or starvation. The casualties dwarfed that of the roughly contemporaneous American Civil War (approximately 750,000) and Crimean War (almost 1 million).

In 1856, with the Taiping Rebellion ongoing and bubonic plague having broken out in the Southwest, Britain and France joined forces against the Qing in the Second Opium War. It's sometimes called the Arrow War, because it began with an incident aboard the British ship *Arrow*. The second series of Unequal Treaties, negotiated in Tianjin in 1858, created ten more treaty ports, allowed foreign navigation of the Yangtze, and opened the hinterland to foreigners, including missionaries. They imposed a further indemnity of six million taels of silver (a tael equaled about 1.4 ounces/40 g) to be paid to Britain and France, and gave Britain, France, the United States, and Russia the right to maintain permanent embassies in Beijing.

Following continued skirmishes, a thirty-nine-member Anglo-French negotiation team arrived in Beijing in the autumn of 1860. The Qing court imprisoned them in the Yuanmingyuan, torturing eighteen of them to death, and "even the liberal use of lime in their coffins could not conceal the fact that they had suffered horribly before expiring."[14] In retaliation, a large Anglo-French force, led by Baron Gros and Lord Elgin (whose father, Thomas Bruce, had stripped the Parthenon of its marble sculptures), marched on Beijing. Assisted by southern Chinese camp followers, they sacked and burned the Yuanmingyuan in an "ardor," according to one British witness, "of insatiate rapacity."[15]

Its hundreds of elegant wooden Chinese buildings were burnt to ashes, and the Western Pavilions collapsed. Captain Charles Gordon of the British Royal Engineers wrote:

> You can scarcely imagine the beauty and magnificence of the places we burnt. It made one's heart sore to burn them; in fact, these palaces were so large, and we were so pressed for time, that we could not plunder them carefully. Quantities of gold ornaments were burnt, considered as brass. It was wretchedly demoralizing work for an army. Everyone was wild for plunder.[16]

What the foreign troops left, locals scooped up. A Chinese-language verse popular at the time captures this moment: "In an old peasant woman's basket lies a Song dynasty book / In a herds-boy's hut a Yuan painting hangs from a hook."[17]

An appalled Victor Hugo described the actions of his country-men as "banditry." Likening the Yuanmingyuan to the Parthenon, the Pyramids, and Notre Dame, he remarked: "We Europeans are the civilized ones, and for us the Chinese are the barbarians. This is what civilization has done to barbarism."[18] The image of the ruins of the Yuanmingyuan is central to the story of the "century of humilia-tion" at the heart of patriotic education on the mainland today.

At the time of the looting of the Yuanmingyuan, the Xián-fēng emperor (r. 1850–1861)—the ninth Qing ruler and the third after Qianlong—was on the throne. The 1860 Convention of Peking granted the British the Kowloon Peninsula, on the mainland opposite Hong Kong Island, in perpetuity. It raised the indemnities by another two million taels of silver. And it legalized the opium trade. The Russians redrew their border with the Qing to their advantage, establishing Vladivostok on what had once been part of the Manchurian homelands.

One year later, at the age of thirty, Xianfeng died, some said of shame.

## ENTER THE EMPRESS DOWAGER

Xianfeng's empress, Cí'ān, had been childless, but her cousin, a concubine, had borne the emperor a son. At the age of five, the boy became Xianfeng's successor, with the reign title Tóngzhì (r. 1861–1875). The concubine formed a joint regency with Ci'an and Tongzhi's sixth uncle, Prince Gōng, to become the Empress Dowager Cíxǐ. Intelligent, ambitious, and forceful, she was the dominant personality in the trinity.

The Empress Dowager Cixi effectively ruled the Qing for almost fifty years, her reign overlapping with that of Queen Victoria. Complex and contradictory, she remains a controversial figure today.

Just two years after the burning of the Yuanmingyuan, a series of rebellions broke out among the Qing's Muslim subjects. These uprisings, which meant the Qing had effectively to reconquer Xinjiang in 1876, tended to be sparked by minor incidents, racial antagonisms, or, in some cases, false rumors that Muslims had aided the Taipings. Over this period, the population of northwestern Gansu and Shaanxi (Shǎnxī) provinces fell by almost twenty million, with people fleeing the violence accounting for some of the drop.

The court quelled the Taiping and Muslim rebellions at great cost and without addressing the popular grievances that fed them. Ongoing incursions and land grabs by Western imperialist powers, meanwhile, damaged Qing prestige, wounded Chinese pride, and depleted the country's finances. A number of scholar-officials, including Lin Zexu, advocated national "self-strengthening" and military and economic modernization. The Qing began to build a modern navy and establish foreign language schools, as well as a foreign office headed by Prince Gong. It regularized an arrangement by which foreigners ran the Chinese Maritime Customs Service, assessing, but not collecting, import and export taxes on behalf of the Qing.

In 1868, after facing a similar challenge from foreign powers, Japan had transformed itself into a constitutional monarchy, with an elected parliament, free public education, modern industry, and an advanced military. Compared to Japan's Meiji Restoration, the self-strengthening reforms of the Tongzhi Restoration were piecemeal at best.

After Tongzhi died childless at the age of eighteen in 1875, Cixi maneuvered his three-year-old cousin onto the throne as the emperor Guāngxù (r. 1875–1908). She continued to reign together with Ci'an "from behind the beaded curtain"—the powers behind the throne.

Newly powerful Japan muscled in on China's traditional spheres of influence, including the kingdom of Ryukyu (Okinawa) and Korea. The French occupied Indochina, further hemming in the Qing—and, within two hours on a single day in August 1884, destroyed or sank all eleven vessels of the Qing's new southern fleet. The French suffered 5 casualties; the Chinese, 521, not counting an additional 51 missing, presumed drowned.[19] In 1887, Portugal acquired the right to "perpetual occupation" of Macao. Seven years later, Japan inflicted a humiliating defeat on the Qing in the Sino-Japanese War (1894–1895), obliterating its northern fleet. The Treaty of Shimonoseki forced the Qing to renounce any claim over Korea, promised Japan two hundred million taels of silver in reparations, and granted Taiwan to Japan in perpetuity.

By 1894, bubonic plague spread from China's Southwest to Guangzhou in the east, where it killed some sixty thousand people. The plague reached Hong Kong and then, via the British, to India and beyond, with an eventual global death toll of fifteen million. The pandemic exacerbated rising anti-Chinese sentiment around the world, including in the United States, which had already banned Chinese immigration, and Australia, which passed its Immigration Restriction Bill (nicknamed the White Australia Policy) in 1901. As would happen again in 2020 with COVID-19, fear of disease combined with prejudice to fuel a virulent racism. In the nineteenth century, this drew, without irony, on an image of the Chinese as sickly opium addicts.

Just a century earlier, Voltaire and other European philosophers had considered China to represent civilization at its best. The racialist logic of imperialism, which justified exploitation and colonization on the basis of supposed white superiority, changed all that—even if nineteenth-century Westerners still treasured their Willow pattern plates.

## A SHORT HISTORY OF REFORM

A group of forward-thinking younger scholars agitated for more comprehensive reforms, including political, educational, and social change, to transform the Qing into a constitutional monarchy and a modern power, again pointing to the model of Japan. Some were avid supporters of women's equality who wanted to ban foot-binding and arranged marriages. By June 1898, they convinced Guangxu, at last ruling in his own right, to launch an ambitious program of reform.

Suspecting that his aunt and her conservative cabal might try to interfere, Guangxu asked Yuán Shìkǎi (1859–1916), a military officer known for his progressive thinking, to help restrain her. Instead, Yuan told Cixi about her nephew's request and, on her orders, detained the emperor in the Lake Palaces adjacent to the Forbidden City. The Hundred Days' Reform, as it became known, was dead. Some reformists managed to flee the country for Japan or Hong Kong. Six were caught and, on September 28, led to an execution ground just outside the city walls (where a Walmart stands today) and beheaded before ten thousand spectators. Cixi resumed power.

Thus, one of the most powerful women China ever produced crushed a movement that would have given Chinese women greater rights than they had ever known. Some contemporary writers claim Cixi was a feminist. The facts don't back the spin. But neither was Cixi the she-monster portrayed in the many misogynistic portrayals of later popular culture.

The Qing, with a population of some four hundred million, fell into terminal crisis, with widespread corruption and failing infrastructure. Foreign powers continued to squeeze the court for more concessions. Britain demanded and obtained a ninety-nine-year lease on 368 square miles (953 sq km) of land adjacent to Kowloon, which it called the New Territories. Cheap textiles and other products flooded into the Chinese market, leaving many farmers and producers struggling in an already collapsing economy. Famine spread.

Missionaries were the only foreigners most Chinese ever came into contact with. They ran schools, medical clinics, and orphanages and campaigned against opium and foot-binding. Some compiled bilingual dictionaries or translated Western scientific texts into Chinese. Some were generous and kind, others arrogant, disrespectful, and racist. Having gained access to the countryside through the Unequal Treaties, they were all tainted by the imperialist project. Rumors swirled that they drank the blood of Chinese children.

A grassroots movement, the Society of the Righteous and Harmonious Fist—the Boxers—arose in 1898 in northeastern Shandong. Its slogan was "Revive the Qing, Destroy the Foreign." Most of its members were poor peasants, including cohorts of girls called Red Lanterns. They practiced martial arts, worshipped Guan Gong, and performed rituals they believed made them impervious to foreign bullets, such as burning paper charms and consuming the ashes. They staged murderous attacks on Chinese Christians—including those whose ancestors had converted to Catholicism in the late Ming—slaughtering 5,700 Catholics in Shānxī province alone. Beginning in 1899, they attacked missionaries as well.[20]

The Boxers are considered anti-imperialist heroes by the CPC, but most of their victims were in fact Chinese. Here is a postcard showing a young Boxer.

On June 5, 1900, after cutting Beijing's railway connection to the treaty port of Tianjin, the Boxers, conspicuous in their red, black, and yellow turbans, rampaged through Beijing. They were so xenophobic that they murdered Chinese people simply for wearing watches or selling Western goods like paraffin lamps, and smashed up rickshaws, a Japanese import. On June 9, they burned down the Peking Racecourse, beloved by the nine-hundred-odd Western residents of Beijing. Days later, they set fire to the Eastern Cathedral, on the site of Schall von Bell's old house, killing a French priest and many Chinese Catholics. They laid siege to the Northern Cathedral, where thousands of converts were sheltering. Following the brutal murder of a Chinese boy by a German diplomat, they blockaded the Legation Quarter, the site of Beijing's foreign diplomatic missions. Sympathetic imperial troops joined the siege.

The siege lasted fifty-five days. During that time, nearly three thousand missiles landed inside the legations, where thousands of Chinese Christians also sheltered, killing more than fifty people and wounding over one hundred. The attack on the British legation accidentally sparked a fire that tore through the nearby Hanlin Library, a repository of China's most priceless historical manuscripts, including ancient copies of the Four Books and Five Classics.[21]

The court was divided. Some considered the Boxers ignorant and reactionary. Others believed they were useful allies against foreign imperialism. After Western troops attacked the Dagu forts near Tianjin, Cixi declared war on the foreign powers, which "have been aggressive towards us, infringed upon our territorial integrity, trampled our people under their feet."[22]

On August 14, 1900, the Eight-Nation Allied Army, consisting of almost twenty thousand Japanese, British, American, French, German, Russian, Italian, and Austro-Hungarian troops, arrived at the walls of Beijing, having marched inland from Tianjin, where they put down the Boxer uprising there, and pummeled their way into the capital. The Empress Dowager, the captive emperor and court in tow, fled to the countryside disguised as a peasant.

The foreign troops who relieved the siege of the legations unleashed a wave of violence on the city, raping, looting, and murdering. Here, American soldiers are relaxing in the Forbidden City.

Let loose on the capital's civilian population, the foreign troops raped, murdered, and plundered, looting the Forbidden City and destroying invaluable imperial archives. Among those they killed was the father of an infant who would grow up to become one of China's most beloved authors, a Manchu who used the pen name of Lao She (1899–1966). Many of the foreign residents joined the troops in plunder.

Tens of thousands died in the conflict, most of them Chinese civilians, including some 20,000 Christian converts murdered by the Boxers (who also destroyed more than four thousand Chinese shops, temples, and residences in one part of Beijing alone). It's believed the allied forces killed about 3,000 Boxers and imperial soldiers. Of the more than 240 non-Chinese casualties, most were missionaries and their families.

The Boxer Protocol, signed by the Qing in September 1901, dealt the dynasty another vicious blow. The long list of demands of this newest Unequal Treaty included indemnities equal to six times the Qing's annual revenue, payable in gold.[23]

In 1904 to 1905, war broke out between Japan and Russia over, in essence, which power had the right to dominate and exploit the resources of northeast China. The Qing could but watch as foreign armies rampaged over fields, flattened villages, and brought death and destruction to their ancestral homelands. Japan won, embarking on a path that would lead to a full-scale invasion of China in 1937.

Toward the end of the nineteenth century, a Qing dynasty official noticed that a traditional malaria remedy of "dragon bones" that he was about to grind into powder bore strange markings. His eventual identification of these as oracle bones led, historian Andrea Bachner writes, to "the birth of modern Chinese archaeology as a science with national implications."

They proved the existence of the Shang dynasty, and "in a time of uncertainty, change and turmoil, they also knit Chinese intellectuals . . . into a kind of imagined community." The idea of an ancient and enduring civilization consoled those worried that China might be "entering terminal decline."[24]

It was toward the end of the Qing that Han Chinese began calling themselves "descendants of the Fiery and Yellow Emperors." The exiled reformer Liáng Qǐchāo (1873–1929) may have been the first to introduce the phrase *mínzú* 民族 from Japanese into the Chinese language. *Minzu* combines the sense of a people, *mín*, with the notion of clan, *zú*, to imply a national ethnic identity.[25] Liang, who also translated the works of Hobbes, Rousseau, and others into Chinese, was an advocate of constitutional monarchy combined with a form of democracy.

A Cantonese anti-Qing activist called Sun Yat-sen (1866–1925), also in exile, believed monarchy incompatible with democracy. At the same time, he felt that with widespread illiteracy and unfamiliarity with democratic processes, China should approach democracy in stages. Sun became an international celebrity in 1896 when Qing officials in London kidnapped him and tried to return him to China. Sun, who founded the Revolutionary Alliance against the Qing in 1905, popularized the phrase *Zhōnghuá mínzú*, which combined the notion of Chinese civilizational glory with Liang Qichao's expression of identity. The dragon, an ancient totem that had become a symbol of imperial authority, and which appeared—blue against an imperial yellow background—on the flag of the Qing, would gradually come to signify that broader civilizational glory and pride.

Among the revolutionaries were radical women's rights pioneers. The most famous was Qiū Jǐn (c. 1876–1907). She unbound her feet, abandoned her arranged marriage, and donned men's clothing to devote herself to the twin causes of promoting women's rights and bringing down the Qing. She was caught and executed in 1907. Her friends included Táng Qúnyīng (1871–1937), a Qing general's daughter and ardent suffragette from Hunan province who trained with Russian anarchists in weapons and bomb-making and was the first female member of Sun's Revolutionary Alliance.

Queue-cutting became a statement of political defiance. Overseas, students and diplomats had suffered mockery because of their queues, and modernizers argued that the hairstyle posed a danger to anyone operating industrial machinery. It also hindered military training and athletics. Sun Yat-sen cut his, as did a teenager from a Hunan farming family by the name of Mao Zedong (1893–1976).

On November 11, 1908, Guangxu died after suffering sudden and violent stomach pains. In 2008, Chinese forensic scientists confirmed a century-old rumor that he had been poisoned. Cixi, who was recovering from a stroke, died four days later. Cixi, Yuan Shikai (who feared that if Cixi died first, Guangxu would take revenge for 1898), and Cixi's favorite eunuch, Lǐ Liányīng, whom Guangxu also detested, remain the three prime suspects in the unsolved murder.[26]

The new emperor, Xuāntǒng, was a three-year-old whose Manchu name was Aisin Gioro Puyi (1906–1967). He bawled throughout his coronation.

In 1911, military uprisings in Guangzhou and then Wǔhàn, a Yangtze port city not far from Shanghai, spelled the end of the Qing. The court announced Puyi's abdication in February 1912. The Republic of China was born, and two millennia of dynastic rule came to an end.

# THE REPUBLIC

## High Hopes and Vicious Betrayals

*Despite the hopes of the revolutionaries, there would be no smooth transition to a modern nation-state. Imperialist powers still occupied key ports and demanded the reparations promised them by the Qing. Military leaders and local power holders, the bane of weak states since the Zhou dynasty, threatened the central authority of the new government from the start. Corruption didn't take long to set in, either. Turbulent and polarizing, the early republican period produced the social, intellectual, cultural, and political ferment that would set the stage for the rise of Chinese communism.*

IN ITS FINAL years, the Qing had appointed a national assembly. The goal was to transition to constitutional monarchy by 1917. After the shock of the October 1911 uprising in Wuhan, the court ordered the assembly to draft a constitution and elect a premier. Its members chose Yuan Shikai, the "progressive" who had once imprisoned an emperor but more recently had led the Qing army in negotiations with the revolutionaries in Wuhan, and helped persuade the new emperor, through his advisers and regent, to abdicate.

Sun Yat-sen was inaugurated provisional president of the Republic of China on January 1, 1912. His Revolutionary Alliance reformed as the Nationalist Party, or Kuomintang (KMT). The capital moved to Nanjing, both to mark a clean break with dynastic tradition and to reduce the power of northern military men such as Yuan Shikai. Especially Yuan Shikai, who wanted the presidency for himself. A government delegation traveled north to dissuade Yuan from making trouble. He showed them how much trouble he could make: soldiers rampaged through Beijing, looting, murdering, setting fires, and wrecking its new telephone exchange. In February, Sun resigned and Yuan got his wish.

Yuan Shikai, the military man who wanted to become emperor, was prone to grandiosity, once arriving at a winter meeting with foreign diplomats on a red-and-gold sled pulled by servants in frock coats and top hats.

In April, the government dragged itself back to Beijing from Nanjing with all the enthusiasm of the Ming court in the time of Yongle. As provisional president, Yuan Shikai established his residence and offices in the Lake Palaces of Zhongnanhai, within the old Imperial City. He built a two-story villa, decorating it with mock Louis XIV mirrors and ornate furniture. A new parliament was to be convened within a year, with the president chosen through national democratic elections.

Tang Qunying had fought for the revolution at the head of an all-female militia. When she learned that only propertied and educated men would be eligible to vote, she stormed the assembly with her followers to demand female suffrage and an explanation of why the KMT had dropped gender equality from its platform. The women smashed windows and kicked guards to the ground. One paper reported that Tang Qunying twisted the beard and boxed the ears of a legislator "with her delicate hands."[1] Although Sun Yat-sen tried to mollify them with vague promises, women wouldn't gain full suffrage until 1947.

Passions ran high as well on the subject of the Chinese language. At the 1913 Conference on the Unification of Pronunciation, advocates for northern dialects clashed with those wanting to create a hybrid between northern and southern dialects, or to choose Shanghainese or Cantonese as the national language. When a northern delegate misheard something said by a Shanghainese as a curse word, he punched the southerner, proving the need for a language everyone could understand. In the end, the advocates for a modified version of the Beijing dialect, like Mandarin, prevailed.[2]

The results of the first elections, announced in January 1913, handed the KMT a clear majority. The party's popular young leader, Sòng Jiàorén (1882–1913), was on the station platform in Shanghai, about to board his train to Beijing, when an assassin armed with a Browning revolver rushed up and shot him. The hunt to discover who ordered the hit came to nothing, as suspects, including some with links to Yuan, met such misadventure as being hacked to death by swordsmen on a train. In May, Yuan Shikai declared the KMT a seditious organization and banned its members from parliament. Troops loyal to the KMT battled those loyal to Yuan.

In 1914, Sun Yat-sen fled into exile again, this time to Japan, to escape the mounting chaos, reorganize the KMT, and lead the resistance.

As the figurehead of the revolution that overthrew the last dynasty, Sun Yat-sen is officially revered in both Taiwan and the PRC.

Yuan Shikai, who was not a Christian, shrewdly requested American Christians to pray for China. President Woodrow Wilson was "so stirred and cheered" by this request that he recognized Yuan's government and forgave Chinese government loan repayments to the United States.[3] Great Britain unhappily followed suit, while demanding autonomy for Tibet, on which it had made complicated claims. The Russians made a similar demand for Mongolia. Yuan dissolved the parliament and suspended the constitution, awarding himself near-absolute powers.

After World War I broke out in Europe, Japan (which fought on the side of the Allies) occupied Germany's concessions in northeastern Shandong province. One year later, Tokyo issued the Twenty-One Demands for wide-ranging economic, political, and military benefits in China, including dispensation to station police in the Northeast, which, since the Russo-Japanese War, it regarded as within its sphere of influence. Nationwide protests and an anti-Japanese boycott forced Yuan Shikai to confront Japan, from which he wrested minor concessions.

On January 1, 1916, Yuan mounted the Dragon Throne as the self-anointed first ruler of the China Empire. His foreign advisers, including the Australian journalist George Morrison, quit in disgust, as did many formerly loyal generals. Protesters took to the streets. Military leaders around the country declared their independence, laying the foundation for what would be known as the Warlord Era. Yuan died humiliated, furious, and uremic six months later, aged fifty-six.

In June 1917, before a new president could put the pieces of Chinese democracy together again, Qing loyalist general Zhāng Xūn (1854–1923), nicknamed "the Pigtailed General" for his queue, staged a coup. He put the eleven-year-old Puyi, who'd been living in the inner court of the Forbidden City all this time, back on the throne.

The republican air force dropped three bombs on the Forbidden City. Only one exploded, injuring one of Puyi's palanquin bearers. After twelve days, Puyi abdicated a second time but was still allowed to live in the palace. The Pigtailed General sought asylum in the Dutch legation. A new, hapless president was installed as the country slid further into chaos and division, and warlords (men with a territorial base and an army to defend it) carved it into virtual fiefdoms. Some warlords were Yuan loyalists. Others were gangsters or opium runners. One, a Christian, baptized his troops with a hose. Another promoted a political program dizzily combining "militarism, nationalism, anarchism, democracy, capitalism, communism, individualism, imperialism, universalism, paternalism and utopianism."[4]

### RENEWAL AND FERMENT

The New Culture Movement arose on the campuses of China's Western-style universities. It advocated democracy, the rule of law, and civil rights, including for women. When its flagship journal, *New Youth*, published a translation of Henrik Ibsen's *A Doll's House* in 1918, Nora became an icon for young women resisting arranged marriages. The English feminist, socialist, and birth control campaigner Dora Black spent ten months in China with her lover and future husband, the philosopher Bertrand Russell, in 1920 to 1921. She was so impressed by the female students she encountered, and their interest in everything from free love and contraception to social reform, she contended that these young "female warriors" were more progressive than the most progressive European women.[5]

*New Youth*'s writers detested the hide-bound orthodoxy of institutionalized Confucianism, judging its "gentlemanly" obsessions with moderation, social hierarchy, and loyalty to authority antipathetic to a modernizing China. The only "gentlemen" who could "save China from the political, moral, academic, and intellectual darkness in which it finds itself," argued Chén Dúxiù (1879–1942), the journal's founder and editor, were "Mr. Science" and "Mr. Democracy."[6] *New Youth* championed the vernacular over archaic literary language based on the Confucian classics, which required a high degree of literacy to comprehend. The philosopher and educator Hu Shih (Hú Shì, 1891–1962) put it simply: "Speak in the language of the time in which you live."[7]

A number of the ideas embraced by the New Culture Movement entered China from Japan. Chinese who had studied in Japan in the late Qing and early Republican period encountered a wealth of European philosophical, political, and other texts in Japanese translation, which made ample use of *kanji*, or Chinese characters, creating ready-made Chinese phrases for words ranging from "police" to "democracy" and "civilization." Among those who retranslated these texts into Chinese was a medical student, Zhōu Shùrén (1881–1936), who put medicine aside to treat what he saw as China's spiritual malaise. Taking the pen name Lǔ Xùn, he wrote scathing critiques of traditional Chinese society and culture, contending, "A writer must attack what strikes him as false with the same intensity as he promotes what he holds to be true. Even more fervently than he embraces what he loves he should embrace what he hates, just as Hercules held the giant Antaeus in a tight embrace in order to break his ribs."[8] "Save the children," the last line of his story "Diary of a Madman," would resurface as a slogan in popular movements through to the student-led protests of 1989.

Lu Xun's most iconic work, the novella *The True Story of Ah Q*, is set at the end of the Qing. Its eponymous scabby antihero is a ne'er-do-well whose chief preoccupation is saving face and whose main talent is self-deception, turning every defeat into a mental victory. He is servile to his superiors, and bullies those even lower on the social scale than himself. Lu Xun wrote that he wanted readers to recognize Ah Q in themselves as well as in the broader society, opening "a road to self-examination."[9]

Mao would later call Lu Xun a sage for the modern era in the way that Confucius was a sage for the old China, saying that he studied the society around him with "both a microscope and a telescope." His enduring influence is hard to overstate—even if the CPC today downplays the humanism and antipathy to dogma and authoritarianism in his writing.

During World War I, some 140,000 Chinese laborers traveled to Europe to aid the Allied war effort, working on the docks, digging trenches, manufacturing ammunition and delivering it to the front, repairing tanks, and building barracks and field hospitals.[10] It was dirty, dangerous work, and thousands lost their lives. Celebrating the Allied victory in 1918, the Chinese people expected that the Allies would remunerate them by returning the former German concessions to China. Had US president Woodrow Wilson not spoken of the equality of nations and the right of national self-determination? The Treaty of Versailles, revealed in April 1919, granted the German concessions in China to Japan instead.

On May 4, 1919, thousands of university students in Beijing, their ranks swelled by ordinary citizens, marched toward Tiananmen Gate and the Legation Quarter. They were as incensed at their government for failing to protect the nation's interests as at the treaty itself. The May Fourth Movement embraced the New Culture Movement to become a broad and lasting push for the interwoven goals of national salvation, political reform, civil rights, cultural renewal, and universal education. The social, literary, and intellectual ferment spread across the country, over newly laid railway lines and roads, and by telegraph, telephone, and a vibrant vernacular press.

The May Fourth protests of 1919 began in Beijing and spread across the country, along with a second anti-Japanese boycott, but Japan refused to relinquish power in Shandong or elsewhere.

The reformists faced resistance from the cultural old guard. A Malaya-born professor of Western literature at Peking University, Gū Hóngmíng (1857–1928), who'd opposed the Hundred Days' Reform two decades earlier, feared that universal literacy would make every "stableboy in Beijing" want to participate in politics, to which Hu Shih replied: "The only way to have democracy is to have democracy."[11]

Society was changing: industrialization had created an urban working class, offering women a path toward financial independence and farmers a way out of rural poverty. Even those most nostalgic for the old ways understood that there was no going back. The literary critic Táo Yòuzēng (1886–1927), pen name "Fetish Tao," wrote wistfully of bound feet that one "wouldn't think of making an antique to order, but why not admire what's already here?"[12]

The times were literally changing—in the 1920s, China switched from its millennia-old lunisolar calendar to the Gregorian one, even if traditional holidays would continue to be celebrated according to the old calendar. Modernity also found expression in fashion. Beijing women created a comfortable style of dress based on Manchu men's robes. The *qípáo* 旗袍, Banner robe, was worn loose and comfortable before Shanghai tailors transformed it into the body-hugging version still worn today. Sun Yat-sen promoted a practical jacket design for men partly inspired by Japanese student uniforms. Called a "Sun Yat-sen suit," *zhōngshān zhuāng* 中山装, in Putonghua, in English it's known as the Mao suit, after its other most famous wearer.

If extraterritoriality protected miscreant foreigners and attracted many a Chinese criminal to the concessions, it also made them a haven for dissidents and revolutionaries. On July 23, 1921, thirteen men, including Mao Zedong, inspired by the Russian Bolshevik revolution of 1917 and convinced that China needed more than gradual solutions and liberal ideas, convened the founding congress of the Communist Party of China in Shanghai's French Concession. At that time, the CPC had fewer than sixty members. They elected Chen Duxiu, the editor of *New Youth*, the party's first secretary-general.

The Soviet Comintern (Communist International) sent advisers. They urged the CPC to form a temporary, strategic

Soong Ching-ling, the wife of Sun Yat-sen and one of the most influential Chinese women of the twentieth century, often wore the *qipao*, a high-collared, side-fastened frock based on Manchu men's robes. It is known in Cantonese as the *cheongsam* 長衫, "long shirt."

alliance with the KMT—a united front—against both the warlords and imperialist aggression. Other Comintern agents persuaded Sun Yat-sen, now leading a Guangzhou-based government in opposition, to allow CPC members to join the KMT. Mao became an alternate member of the KMT Central Executive Committee in 1924. Hu Shih despaired that the "iron-fisted discipline" and intolerance of heterodox views among China's Soviet advisers to both the CPC and KMT was "diametrically opposed" to the liberal spirit of the May Fourth Movement.[13]

In 1924, the Soviet Union helped the KMT establish a military academy in Guangzhou to train members of both parties as officers. The suave and canny Zhōu Ēnlái (1898–1976), a Communist who had studied in France, served as the head of the Whampoa Academy's political department. Its first commandant was Chiang Kai-shek (1887–1975), a committed anti-Communist with vaunting personal ambitions and underworld connections.

Shanghai had become one of the most glamorous, vibrant, and cosmopolitan cities in the world, the "Paris of the East." Chinese artists, filmmakers, and writers flocked there, along with foreign luminaries, including George Bernard Shaw and Rabindranath Tagore. Stateless foreigners, refugees from Russia's Bolshevik revolution, Baghdadi Jews, and others were also drawn to the city's tolerant and freewheeling cultural, political, and intellectual environment, and its opportunities in business and finance. Chinese and foreigners of means went to the races, dined well, lived in Western-style mansions, and danced at clubs where daring young socialites wore bobbed hair and flapper dresses.

But the city's glittering wealth existed alongside teeming, desperate poverty. Hundreds of thousands of internal refugees fleeing warlord violence eked out a living as cooks and servants, rickshaw pullers, dockworkers, and factory and foundry laborers. Working conditions were deplorable, protections negligible. Strikes for better pay and conditions invited swift and brutal retribution by both Chinese and foreign bosses.

In one notorious incident in 1923, a warlord's army pitched in to break a strike, shooting thirty-five workers and beheading their union leader. In another labor dispute in Shanghai on May 30, 1925, a guard shot and killed a worker at a Japanese factory. British police, including Chinese and Sikh constables, fired on protesters, killing eleven and wounding twenty. The May Thirtieth Massacre sparked nationwide anti-foreign demonstrations. There were calls for "triple strikes" by students, workers, and businesses. When students, workers, children, and farmers came together in Guangzhou to support a general strike in Hong Kong against the British, British troops shot and killed fifty-two of them, wounding more than a hundred others.

## CHIANG KAI-SHEK AND THE GREAT BETRAYAL

Sun Yat-sen died of illness in 1925, at the age of fifty-eight. His idealistic young widow, Soong Ching-ling (1893–1981), the middle daughter of self-made Shanghai millionaire Charlie Soong, detested Chiang and his extreme right-wing politics. She observed with dismay how quickly he was consolidating his influence within the KMT, with the backing of conservative industrialists, bankers, and financiers.

On July 1926, Chiang Kai-shek led a Northern Expedition against the warlords at the head of an army consisting of both Communists and Nationalists. By the end of the year, they reached the industrial Yangtze port of Wuhan. The Communists wanted to continue to drive north, toward Beijing. Chiang decided to move east, toward Shanghai, instead. The army split, with Communists and their sympathizers in the KMT remaining in Wuhan.[14]

By then, China boasted nearly five hundred unions representing close to a million workers. In March 1927, the unions of Shanghai called a citywide general strike in aid of the KMT-led forces heading their way.

With the help of Shanghai's ruthless criminal Green Gang and cooperative warlords, Chiang Kai-shek turned without warning on his erstwhile CPC allies, slaughtering unionists and arresting, torturing, and executing anyone, from students to illiterate farmers, suspected of having Communist sympathies.

In Guangzhou, KMT soldiers rounded up hundreds of members of a local "soviet," or revolutionary council, identifying them by the red stains on their necks left by their hand-dyed scarves. To save bullets, the Nationalist soldiers roped the leftists together and pushed them into the Pearl River to drown. Changsha, in Mao's home province of Hunan, was another site of extreme anti-Communist violence. It's estimated that around seventy thousand Communists and sympathizers fell prey to the White Terror of April to December 1927.

In the midst of the thuggery, Chiang achieved social respectability by marrying Soong Ching-ling's younger sister, Soong Mei-ling (1898–2003), to Ching-ling's dismay and to the delight of their conservative older sister Ai-ling (1888–1973) and Ai-ling's husband, H. H. Kung (1881–1967), a wealthy magnate and seventy-fifth-generation direct descendant of Confucius who would later become Chiang's finance minister.

In January, Chiang became generalissimo of the National-ist Army, chair of the KMT's Central Executive Committee, and head of the government in Nanjing. The KMT had embedded itself so securely into the structure of government that the flag of the Republic of China incorporated the party's emblem, the white sun. Chiang relaunched the stalled Northern Expedition without the Communists.

# JAPANESE INVASION AND CIVIL WAR

## The Republic Disintegrates

*Puyi, the last emperor, had lived an odd and useless life, surrounded from childhood by eunuchs and other members of his defunct imperial court. He had never even been outside the Forbidden City when, in 1922, he cut his queue and, inspired by the example of his Oxford-trained tutor, Reginald Johnston, decided to escape to England. When Johnston refused to call him a cab, he gave up on the idea. That year, he married the Manchu noblewoman Gobulo Wanrong (1906–1946). Wanrong came with a missionary school education and a dowry of eighteen sheep, two horses, and forty pieces of satin. On their wedding night, Puyi had an attack of nerves and fled the marital bed. The pair were compatible enough and amused themselves like the kids they were, racing bicycles along the Forbidden City's long corridors. Two years later, a warlord seized Beijing, stripped Puyi of his imperial title, and gave him three hours to vacate the palace. His imperial fantasy life was over—for the time being.*

JAPANESE DIPLOMATS HELPED PUYI and his entourage, which included one concubine, to settle in the Japanese concession in Tianjin. Wanrong, wearied by the ever-present eunuchs and courtiers, who disapproved of her fondness for dancing, tennis, and jazz, disappeared into opium dreams. Puyi played with his dogs, visited foreign men's clubs, and hung out with his cousin, Aisin Gioro Xianyu, aka Eastern Jewel, aka Yoshiko Kawashima—a flamboyant, cross-dressing, bisexual Manchu princess raised in Japan. Unbeknownst to Puyi, Eastern Jewel had lovers in, and spied for, the Kwantung Army, a militarized Japanese security force looking after Japanese railway and other assets in the Northeast.

Aisin Gioro Puyi, the last emperor of the Qing dynasty, became more than just an eccentric footnote to history after the Japanese offered to put him back on the throne in 1931.

On the night of June 3, 1928, the warlord Zhāng Zuòlín (1875–1928) was on a train heading back to his base in the Manchurian heartland. He'd made a deal with the Japanese: he would protect their investments and they would help him fight off challenges from rival warlords. They were now urging him to break off from the Republic of China and rule the Northeast with them instead. He refused. Some officers of the Kwantung Army, acting independently of Tokyo, took matters into their own hands and blew up his train. They figured that his son and heir, "Young Marshal" Zhāng Xuéliáng (1901–2001), a dissolute, womanizing opium addict, would put up less resistance to Japanese occupation. They underestimated him. He threw away the opium pipe and joined forces with the KMT.

Three years later, in September 1931, the Kwantung Army invaded and occupied Manchuria. Knowing, possibly through Eastern Jewel, how furious Puyi was with Chiang Kai-shek for allowing a warlord ally of the KMT to sack the tombs of his Qing ancestors, the Japanese invited him to become emperor again—this time of his ancestral homelands, which they called Manchukuo. He agreed. After the League of Nations, predecessor to the United Nations, condemned the move and declared Manchukuo a puppet state, Japan withdrew from the League.

The following year, Eastern Jewel led a counterinsurgency force to wipe out Chinese resistance to the Japanese occupation in Manchuria.

## A MOUNTING CRISIS

Ignoring popular pleas to focus on the Japanese threat, Chiang continued to attack the Communists. The Blue Shirts Society, a proto-fascist paramilitary organization modeled after

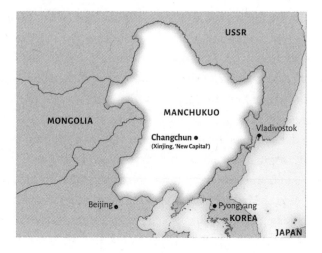

Japanese investments in the Northeast, the homeland of the Manchus, grew steadily after the Russo-Japanese War. Once Japan occupied the area, they renamed it Manchukuo, or "Manchu country."

Mussolini's Blackshirts, disappeared, tortured, and murdered suspected Communist sympathizers. Among them was one of Lu Xun's favorite protégés and four other young writers. In 1931, Lu Xun wrote a poem, "Untitled," with the lines: "I can but stand by, looking on as friends become new ghosts, / I seek an angry poem from among the swords."

On January 28, 1932, following a skirmish between Chinese and Japanese soldiers in Shanghai, the Japanese bombed Shanghai. It was the first "terror bombing," as historian Barbara W. Tuchman has written, of a civilian population in an era "that was to become familiar with it."[1] (The Fascist Condor Legion bombed the Basque town of Gernika—more widely known by the Spanish version of the name, Guernica—five years later, and there would be worse to come.) Chiang's government eventually signed a ceasefire agreement with the Japanese, withdrawing its troops from Shanghai and nearby cities, which it placed under Japanese "protection."

The CPC had established "revolutionary base areas," or soviets, in the countryside, including in eastern Jiangxi and Fujian provinces. There, the Communists mobilized impoverished peasants and rural laborers against local landowners in a process called Land Reform. The poor were invited to abuse the "enemies of the people," verbally and physically, in "struggle sessions" that sometimes ended in murder. The CPC then divided the land among the peasants, earning their gratitude, teaching them "class consciousness" while implicating them in revolutionary violence. As Mao wrote in 1927: "A revolution is not a dinner party, or writing an essay, or painting a picture, or doing embroidery; it cannot be so refined, so leisurely and gentle, so temperate, kind, courteous, restrained and magnanimous. A revolution is an insurrection, an act of violence by which one class overthrows another."[2]

Both the CPC and the KMT employed violence to achieve their ends. But the Communists appeared to be working for the many, whereas the KMT seemed to care only about the elite. The Communists projected an image of rectitude; the KMT exuded the stench of corruption. The Communists also appealed to patriotism, calling on the KMT to fight the Japanese, but the KMT gave the impression of being more interested in attacking the Communists. The country was becoming increasingly polarized.

Some prominent cultural figures, including Lu Xun's brother, the essayist Zhōu Zuòrén (1885–1967); the gentle Buddhist artist-essayist Fēng Zǐkǎi (1898–1975); the cosmopolitan writer, humorist, and translator Lin Yutang (1895–1976); and the bestselling Shanghai novelist Eileen Chang (1920–1995), could not bring themselves to align with either side. But disgust with the KMT's corruption and ineptitude, and outrage at Chiang's reluctance to fight the Japanese, radicalized a great many other intellectuals, artists, and filmmakers, rallying them to the Communist cause. While some, including Hu Shih, sided with the KMT, by the early 1930s it was clear that the KMT was losing the battle for hearts and minds.

Under the guidance of Chiang's wife, Soong Mei-ling, the KMT came up with a novel solution: the New Life Movement, a quaint blend of New Testament Christianity, Confucian rectitude, authoritarianism, and Emily Post–style etiquette, enforced by the Blue Shirts. Its guiding document was written in the formal, semiclassical language that had gone out of fashion with the May Fourth Movement and required a high degree of literacy to understand. Among other things, it urged people to keep their homes well aired and toilets sparkling clean—easy for Soong Mei-ling (and her servants), not so much for subsistence farmers or the urban poor sleeping in overcrowded tenements or on the street. Chiang himself launched the movement with a tone-deaf speech in September 1934, in which he chastised the Chinese people for being "spiritless," rude and vulgar.[3]

### THE LONG MARCH TO YAN'AN

That same year, as the Japanese continued their depredations, the KMT focused on ousting the Communists from their Jiangxi Soviet (revolutionary base area). On October 16, 1934, some one hundred thousand Communists and followers, fighters and peasants, broke through KMT lines to the west, leading their animals and hauling their weapons, supplies, and equipment.

新生活壁掛圖 臺衛生化育兒之民和活習新 一第圖化衛生清

飲食要
清潔

闕衛生習慣行動

Greeted with ridicule and contempt, the New Life Movement, which stressed decorum and good hygiene, demonstrated how out of touch the KMT was with life under its rule. This poster says, "Be hygienic with food and drink."

Among the fighters, only some thirty were women, including Dèng Yǐngchāo (1904–1992), the wife of Zhou Enlai. This military retreat became known as the Long March.

In January 1935, the Long Marchers reached Zūnyì, a town in Gùizhōu province. There, the CPC's leaders thrashed out the question of the party's relationship with Moscow. By the time they left Zunyi, the Comintern was no longer calling the shots. Mao Zedong had advocated for guerrilla warfare and a rural-based revolution against Comintern advice and had weathered three expulsions from the party leadership for his unorthodox ideas. Soon, he would be recognized as the leader of the CPC.[4]

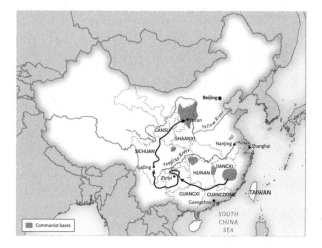

Edgar Snow, the American journalist and author of *Red Star over China*, wrote that the Long March made Hannibal's march over the Alps "look like a holiday excursion."

Ten arduous months later, the Long Marchers arrived at the isolated, impoverished town of Yán'ān, a 210-mile (340 km) hard tramp into the barren hills north of Xi'an.

The Long March began as a retreat under fire. Fortitude, acts of bravery, and survival turned it into legend. Over 358 days, the ragtag army trekked about 6,000 rugged miles (10,000 km) across 11 provinces, in sweltering heat and freezing cold, crossing snowy mountains, fording swift-flowing rivers, tramping through malarial swamps, and fighting off attacks by the KMT, bandits, warlords, and hostile southern tribesman. They'd lost their supply train and nearly all their artillery. Their numbers had shrunk to fewer than 35,000.

Exhausted but triumphant, they settled into spartan cave dwellings, *yáodòng* 窑洞, dug into the loess hills of the mountainous region, to plan their next move.

As news of the Communists' epic journey and survival fil-
tered back east, left-leaning activists, artists, and writers, as
well as foreign journalists, including Americans Edgar Snow
and Agnes Smedley, made the pilgrimage to Yan'an. In her book
*China Correspondent*, Smedley recorded her first impression of
Mao: "I pushed back a padded cotton drape across a door in
a mountain cave, and stepped into a dark cavern. Directly in
the center of this darkness stood a tall candle on a rough-hewn
table. Its glow fell on piles of books and papers and touched
the low earthen ceiling above." She saw a tall man in a padded
greatcoat. "The tall, forbidding figure lumbered towards us and
a high-pitched voice greeted us. Then two hands grasped mine;
they were as long and sensitive as a woman's. . . ." After getting
to know him well, she described Mao as being "as stubborn as
a mule, and a steel rod of pride and determination ran through
his nature. I had the impression that he would wait and watch
for years, but eventually have his way."[5]

The progressive Shanghai journalist Huáng Yánpéi (1878–
1965) also visited Yan'an. He asked Mao how the Communists
planned to handle the question of succession and avoid the
dynastic cycle of decline. Mao replied that they had found
"a new path": democracy.[6]

The Long March gave the CPC a heroic origin story, an
ethos of rural austerity and egalitarianism, and a disciplined
and battle-hardened leadership. In that cave with the candle
and the books, in collaboration with his political secretary
Chén Bódá (1904–1989), Mao produced essays and speeches
that would define the unique ideology of Chinese communism:
Mao Zedong Thought. These important works included "Talks
at the Yan'an Forum on Art and Literature," which laid out the

principle that the purpose of art is to serve the revolution and the "workers, peasants, and soldiers." This document guided cultural policy throughout the Maoist era and remains relevant today.

In 1942, the CPC launched the Yan'an Rectification Movement. Setting the pattern for future "thought reform" movements and ideology-based purges, it demanded that people remold their thinking through a rigorous process of criticism and self-criticism, "struggle," and confession. Or, as one prominent ideologue put it: "Take down your pants, cut off your [bourgeois] tails, and have a wash."[7]

Among the campaign's targets was the writer Wáng Shíwèi (1906–1947), who criticized the Communists for indulging in the hierarchical privilege and arrogant behaviors they'd pledged to eliminate: "There is not one cook here who has the ambition to live on the same footing as his superiors," he wrote.[8] They also punished the feminist writer Dīng Líng for calling out patriarchal attitudes and gender inequality in the CPC. The violence of the attack on Wang, Ding, and other writers in Yan'an signaled the CPC's renunciation of the humanistic, cosmopolitan, and individualistic elements of the May Fourth legacy. In 1947, while evacuating Yan'an under KMT attack in the civil war, they beheaded Wang, unwilling either to take him or leave him behind. (Forty-four years later, the CPC conceded that his execution had been a "mistake.")

Mao met his fourth wife, Jiāng Qīng (1914–1991), a Shanghai film actress, in Yan'an. He'd refused to consummate his first, arranged marriage. In 1930, a KMT-aligned warlord tortured and executed his second wife, the twenty-two-year-old Yáng Kāihuì (1901–1930), a fellow Communist and mother of his first three children. She had refused to betray Mao or renounce the revolution, even though Mao had deserted her two years earlier for Hè Zǐzhēn (1910–1984), his third wife. A brave and committed guerrilla fighter, He Zizhen bore Mao six children, most of whom didn't survive or were lost in the confusion of war. Mao divorced He in Yan'an to marry Jiang Qing.

In the cities, students and others continued to agitate for Chiang Kai-shek to focus on the fight against the Japanese, who were encroaching further and further south. Chiang, who considered the Japanese invasion a "superficial wound" compared with the "cancer" that was Communism, rebuffed the Communists' offer to form a second united front, against the Japanese.

## THIS MEANS WAR

In October 1936, Mao Zedong and Zhou Enlai contacted the "Young Marshal," Zhang Xueliang, with a proposal. Zhang, who had Chiang's trust, concocted a story to get him to fly to Xi'an. There, in what became known as the Xi'an Incident, he and the Nationalist general Yáng Hǔchéng (1893–1949) took the generalissimo captive at Huaqing Pools, the ancient hot springs resort where the voluptuous Yang Guifei once bathed under the gaze of a besotted Tang emperor. The ambushed Chiang unhappily agreed to a second united front—he would later put Zhang Xueliang under house arrest and have Yang Hucheng executed.

On July 7, 1937, the Japanese instigated a military incident at the seven-century-old Marco Polo Bridge, some 10 miles (16 km) west of Beijing. This marked the Japanese invasion of China proper (south of the Great Walls). One conventional way of referring to the war with Japan in China, "the eight-year war of resistance," dates from that incident.

In August, Japanese tanks were rolling up Qianmen Street in Beijing. The Nationalists left the city to the Japanese, who made it their base for operations in north China. By November, Shanghai, Guangzhou, and Hànkŏu were in Japanese hands. The Nationalist government decamped for Chongqing, abandoning Nanjing to the Japanese. There, over six weeks, Japanese troops slaughtered residents; gang-raped women and girls, some to death; and committed countless other atrocities, including bayoneting infants. The death toll of civilians and prisoners of war is estimated in the hundreds of thousands. The Rape of Nanjing, or Nanjing Massacre, still evokes strong emotions in China, where its memory is kept alive in history texts, books, films, and a dedicated museum.

The other most notorious Japanese war crimes occurred in a secret center for "germ warfare research" in Manchuria. There, members of Unit 731 of the Imperial Japanese Army carried out medical experiments similar to those of the Nazi doctor Josef Mengele in the concentration camps of Europe. They infected Chinese and Russians with anthrax and typhoid, and carried out vivisections on pregnant women. Some three thousand people died as a result. The suffering was incalculable.[9] After the war, the United States offered the perpetrators immunity from prosecution in exchange for their research data.[10]

In 1940, the Japanese established a puppet Reorganized National Government in Nanjing. The president was the fascist-friendly Wāng Jīngwèi (1883–1944), one of Sun Yatsen's original comrades in the republican revolution and, after Sun's death, Chiang Kai-shek's chief rival for the leadership of the KMT. Wang is universally reviled as the most notorious of all those who collaborated with the Japanese, the equivalent of Vichy France's Philippe Pétain or the Norwegian Vidkun Quisling.

On December 8, 1941, Japanese military forces invaded Hong Kong. Hours later, Japan attacked Pearl Harbor. With the United States now at war, Chiang's government joined the Allied war effort against the Axis powers. It would take decades (and a desire for rapprochement) before the CPC conceded that KMT troops had made any significant contribution to the anti-Japanese fight. It's safe to say that the Nationalists fought the majority of pitched battles while the Communists specialized in the sabotage and guerrilla warfare that frustrated Japan's ambition to control China's vast hinterland.

By the end of the war, the Nationalists had lost much of their US allies' goodwill. Even the fervently anti-Communist publisher Henry Luce ran an article in *Life* magazine slamming the KMT as "dominated by a corrupt political clique that combines some of the worst features of Tammany Hall and the Spanish Inquisition."[11]

A physicist from Jiangsu, Chien-Shiung Wu (1912–1997), joined the Manhattan Project in 1944, making several key contributions to the creation of the world's first atom bombs. On August 6 and 9, 1945, the United States used them on Hiroshima and Nagasaki, in the world's most extreme terror bombing of a civilian population to date. The war ended with Japan's surrender on September 2, 1945.

Taiwan, under Japanese rule since the Sino-Japanese War, returned to Chinese sovereignty. US president Franklin D. Roosevelt wanted the British to give Hong Kong back to China as well, but he died months before the war's end, and the British resumed control. Puyi, the disgraced puppet emperor of Manchukuo, tried

As a university student, Chien-Shiung Wu protested KMT inaction against the Japanese invasion. After gaining her PhD in physics at Stanford University, she helped create the bombs that brought it to an end.

to flee to Japan, but the Soviets captured him and sent him to Siberia. The papers reported the arrest of a "beauty in male costume"; Eastern Jewel was executed for treason three years later.

Chiang Kai-shek's government had financed itself during the war by printing money, and now China suffered from hyperinflation, mass unemployment, and food shortages. Despite the urgency of these challenges, Chiang Kai-shek remained focused on eradicating the Communists. The country barely had enough time to mourn its war dead—nearly four million soldiers and some twenty million civilians—before it was plunged into civil war.

The Red Army, one million strong at the time of the Japanese surrender, renamed itself the People's Liberation Army (PLA). Its soldiers had strict orders not to molest women, trample crops, or take even "a needle or thread" from the people without permission. Any Communist soldier caught looting was shot. The PLA presented an appealing contrast with the ill-disciplined and desperate Nationalist troops, some of whom were involved in black-market war profiteering and many of whom had to be roped together during marches to keep them from deserting. (Hundreds of thousands did so anyway.) The KMT funded the war effort by printing even more money and selling off the country's gold reserves, plunging the country ever deeper into financial crisis. The PLA continued the process of Land Reform wherever they had control, dispossessing and punishing the landlords and other local power holders who were the KMT's main supporters in the countryside.

Preoccupied with civil war, the Nationalists neglected to pay attention to events in Taiwan. After half a century of Japanese colonial rule, most Taiwanese had celebrated the return of sovereignty to China in 1945. But the Nationalist officials sent to govern the island proved despotic, corrupt, and unscrupulous. Tensions were running high when, on February 28, 1947, an official pistol-whipped a widow suspected of selling contraband cigarettes. An angry crowd gathered to protest, and another officer shot and killed a man. The protests grew, and the response, which included the imposition of martial law, was even more brutal: it's estimated that Nationalist forces went on to kill up to twenty-eight thousand people out of a total population at the time of less than ten million.[12] The February 28 Incident, as it's known, planted the seeds of the Taiwanese independence movement.

Over the course of the anti-Japanese war, the United States had loaned Chiang's government hundreds of millions of dollars and provided military equipment, advisers, and air support through the American Volunteer Group, the "Flying Tigers." Despite ample testimony from their own people on the ground that Chiang was unpopular and corrupt, the US political establishment was terrified by the global ambitions of the Soviet Union and fixated on the possibility of China becoming a "Slavic Manchukuo." In 1947, US President Harry S. Truman ended the longstanding American policy of non-intervention in other nations' civil conflicts. Two years later, when it was clear that the Communists were winning, Truman's secretary of state, Dean Acheson, conceded: "The unfortunate but inescapable fact is that the ominous result of the civil war in China was beyond the control of the government of the United States."[13]

Statistics on the casualties of China's civil war vary. One PRC report claimed that almost 264,000 PLA soldiers and 1.7 million KMT soldiers lost their lives or were injured. There's no reliable data on civilian deaths.

Having won the support of the peasantry, the CPC courted liberal intellectuals, members of minority democratic parties, professionals, and businesspeople through a campaign called the United Front, recruiting them to advise the party via the Chinese People's Political Consultative Conference (CPPCC). Using the term for Monkey's "magic weapons" in *Journey to the West*, Mao called the United Front one of the party's *fabao* that would see it to victory. On September 21, 1949, he told the CPPCC that China had "stood up." Although Chiang had not surrendered, less than two weeks later, on October 1, 1949, Mao, aged fifty-five, stood among comrades and allies, including Soong Ching-ling, on the rostrum of the Tiananmen Gate and proclaimed the birth of the People's Republic of China.

Although Mao would mount the rostrum of Tiananmen many times after October 1, 1949, he never visited the Forbidden City, and contemplated demolishing it.

In December 1949, Chiang retreated to Taiwan with Soong Mei-ling, some two million troops and followers, six hundred thousand treasures from the Palace Museum, and Zhang Xue-liang, still under house arrest. The Nationalists offered passage to many cultural and intellectual luminaries. Hu Shih went; most stayed.

Chiang intended to use the island as a base from which to "recover the mainland." Like Zheng Chenggong, the would-be Ming restorationist three centuries earlier, he would never make it back. The Communists had won.

# THE MAO YEARS

## Continuous Revolution

*Even history changed in 1949, which became known officially as the year of Liberation. Traditional historians described cycles of dynastic renewal and decay, with Heaven awarding its mandate to the virtuous founders of a dynasty and stripping it from their corrupt descendants. Marxists envisioned history as a progression toward communism. China's past didn't fit into Marx's schema, which drew on European experience and included a prerevolutionary stage of capitalism, so CPC ideologues adapted it to Chinese realities. Most people began simply to speak of history as having two eras: Pre-Liberation and Post-Liberation. Chinese historiography retained its didactic, moral tone, but its archetypal heroes changed. Out went the sage rulers and scholar-officials and in came the rebels and revolutionaries. The CPC's list of villains began long and would grow to include some of its original heroes.*

*Yet New China never fully shook off ancient historical patterns or preoccupations, including the fear that corruption or succession crises could bring down a regime, or the notion that a leader could lose the Mandate of Heaven.*

THE CPC SETTLED INTO Zhongnanhai, where Khublai Khan built his palace, the Ming emperor Jiajing went to sulk, the Qing emperor Guangxu had been sequestered, and both Yuan Shikai and the Japanese occupation had made their headquarters. A large stone screen was erected inside the "New China" gate that Yuan Shikai had opened in the Imperial City wall west of Tiananmen. On the screen was written in Mao's distinctive calligraphy, in gold characters on a red background: *Serve the People*.

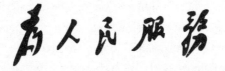

"Serve the people" in Mao's writing. In CPC rhetoric, "the people," *rénmín* 人民, signifies the presumed great majority of citizens who support the revolution and CPC.

The Communists initially confronted challenges similar to those faced by most dynasties from the Qin onward. One was rebuilding a war-torn economy. With no experience in industrialization, they turned to the Soviet Union for assistance. On a visit to Moscow in 1949, Mao secured a loan equal to three hundred million dollars from Stalin, who also pledged to help develop Chinese industry and strengthen its navy.

The Agrarian Reform Law of 1950 extended the policy of land reform nationally, putting all arable land under state ownership and dividing it among those who farmed it. To battle entrenched corruption, the CPC called on its citizens to inform on others for such crimes as wasting state resources, stealing state property, and economic espionage.

Then there was the question of pacifying the borders.

## TROUBLE IN THE BORDERLANDS

During the civil war, Uyghur separatists had proclaimed the founding of the East Turkestan Republic in the northern part of Xinjiang. With the help of the Soviet Union, the army put all of Xinjiang under Beijing's control. It became an "autonomous region," theoretically self-governing.

Tibet, for some fifty years, had been under shifting, piecemeal rule by semicolonial British administrators, its own theocratic rulers, warlords, and the KMT. The events that the PRC dubs a "peaceful liberation," advocates of Tibetan independence call an "invasion," and some independent scholars name the "annexation" took place between 1949 and 1951. Forced to the negotiating table, the Tibetan government signed a Seventeen-Point Agreement with Beijing that promised the Tibetans religious freedom and self-governance as another "autonomous region" within the PRC.

The PLA also captured Hainan Island from remnant KMT troops. Throughout the 1950s, the PLA would engage in skirmishes of greater or lesser seriousness with the Nationalist Army, including mutual bombardment between coastal Fujian province and the Nationalist-held islands of Jīnmén and Mǎzǔ (aka Kinmen/Quemoy and Matsu), which lay not far offshore.

As if to stress the importance of national unity, the Communists abolished the time zones established in the Republican era. All clocks, from the east coast to the city of Urumqi, nearly 2,000 miles (3,000 km) away in Xinjiang, were set to Beijing time.

At the end of World War II, the United States arbitrarily divided the Korean Peninsula along the 38th parallel, stationing troops in the South. In 1950, the North Korean leader Kim Il-sung informed Mao that he planned to reunify Korea.

He wanted the PRC's backing if the Americans entered the fight. Mao cautiously committed to step in if the parallel was crossed.[1] As he told Stalin, he believed China needed "three to five years of peace" to return the economy to "prewar levels" and "stabilize the country in general."

Kim attacked the South on June 25, 1950, armed with Russian tanks; United Nations and American troops pushed him back across the parallel. The conflict might have ended there, but Truman wanted regime change. Michael Pembroke observes in *Korea: Where the American Century Began*, "as has happened so often since, Washington's ideological and military enthusiasm ensured a wider and more substantial conflagration."[2]

After the Americans crossed the 38th parallel, Mao sent in some three million "volunteers"—so-called to avoid having to declare war on the United States. In what is officially known as the War to Resist American Aggression and Aid Korea, Chinese and North Koreans fought the stunned Americans back down below the parallel. Representatives of the United Nations, the PRC, and the North Korean armies signed an armistice in 1953.

About one out of ten Koreans died in the conflict; the majority of the three million or so casualties were civilians. Mao's eldest son with Yang Kaihui, Máo Ànyīng (1922–1950), was one of an estimated four hundred thousand Chinese fighters who lost their lives in Korea. Many hundreds of thousands more were wounded.[3]

The war fueled American fears of the "Red menace" already whipped up by the infamous Republican senator Joseph McCarthy, whose anti-Communist witch hunts had seen the blacklisting of prominent figures in American public life on the basis of false claims that they were infiltrators or spies for the Soviet Union. The war also helped to create an insular and paranoid North Korea

In 1953, Mao was shaken by the death of Stalin, mourning him as "the greatest genius of the present age." The relationship between the PRC and the Soviet Union began to deteriorate after that.

that would pose myriad diplomatic and practical conundrums for China to the present day. Mao embraced isolationism, calling it a virtue ("self-reliance") after falling out with the post-Stalin leadership of the Soviet Union at the end of the decade.

The Communists constructed a new system of government inspired by the Soviet Union. They established parallel bureaucracies, one belonging to the CPC, the other to the state. This system continues today.

The general secretary presides over the CPC, which makes policies. The National People's Congress (NPC) passes them into law. Its head, the head of state, is the chairman, sometimes called the president in English. The CPC leads and controls the army as well.

The State Council supervises the implementation of policy and law. The CPC's Propaganda Department disseminates information about policies and laws and oversees campaigns to indoctrinate and persuade. There is dual leadership at all levels of government—a city has both a mayor and a CPC secretary, for example. The CPC guides the state and chooses leading comrades for the top posts in government—hence the albeit imperfect shorthand "party-state."

Anyone who works for the party or state at any level may be called a "cadre," *gànbù*. Cadres are divided into hierarchical classes that determine their privileges and rights. Despite an official ethos of egalitarianism, from the start, status was precisely defined, and determined everything from access to special provisions of food and the quality of one's "Mao suit" to the size and placement of photos published in the press.[4]

The national party, congressional, and advisory bodies, as well as national federations, such as of writers or women, have equivalents at regional levels. The center dictates, the regions follow—in theory, at least. As a popular saying goes, "Above they have policies, below they have ways of getting around policies." (A traditional version of this is "Heaven is high and the emperor far away."[5])

### FLOWERS BLOOM AND WILT

A century of invasion, war, and political instability had left society in disarray. Disease was rife and health care all but nonexistent. Even in the capital, sanitation was rudimentary. Eight out of ten people were functionally illiterate.

Within its first three years in power, the party-state built new public schools, began simplifying the writing system, and increased the number of medical clinics on the mainland from 800 to almost 30,000, doubling hospital beds over the same period to 160,300.[6] It launched campaigns to eradicate smallpox, plague, cholera, and STDs. Drug addicts went to rehabilitation, dealers to the execution grounds. Prostitutes were rounded up and retrained, in some cases as nurses, while pimps were shot.

With Mao's 1942 speech on the function of art and literature as a guide, the CPC mobilized artists, writers, actors, and film-makers to propagate its policies. Film and stage were considered key to communicating the CPC's message to a semi-literate population. Later, there would be established systems for cultural supervision and censorship, but in 1951, a lack of clarity about what the CPC expected saw a dozen new films no sooner completed than banned.[7]

Before 1949, film audiences were small and urban. Now mobile film projection teams took screens into even the smallest villages. Troupes of actors and entertainers spread the CPC's message beyond the cities. Popular works included Lao She's *Dragon Beard Ditch*, about the socialist transformation of a poor Beijing neighborhood—a work that earned its author the honorific "the people's artist."

The CPC assigned all citizens a "class status" based on occupation, political history, and family background. To be classified a "poor peasant," "revolutionary cadre," or "family of a revolutionary martyr" brought benefits, including assumed political reliability. The worst categories included "landowner," "capitalist," and "historical counterrevolutionary." Between 1950 and 1953, the state executed up to two million accused "counterrevolutionaries," including remnant KMT supporters.[8]

Class status determined all, from access to higher education to marriage prospects. It was inscribed in a person's *dàng'àn*, the secret dossier that followed them throughout life, containing reports by schoolteachers, employers, and even informers. There was some flexibility: capitalists could become "red capitalists," for instance, by donating significant assets—factories or businesses—to the state. Less cooperative business owners had their property confiscated. By 1956, the state would wholly or partly own all mainland enterprises and businesses.[9] Banking was also nationalized. The new national currency was the People's Currency, rénmínbì 人民币 (RMB). Its basic unit was the yuan, made up of one hundred fēn.

The PRC launched its first Soviet-style economic Five-Year Plan in 1953. That year, according to the first major post-1949 census, 89 percent of the mainland's population of 583 million lived in the countryside, where the second stage of Land Reform, collectivization, was underway, consolidating the land distributed to the peasants into agricultural cooperatives of two hundred to three hundred rural households each. Between 1954 and 1958, the size of the collectives grew to become People's Communes. Mao scoffed that anyone worried about the speed of change was like an old woman with bound feet, "tottering along" and complaining that others were going too fast.[10]

Agricultural collectives were responsible for water conservation, irrigation, education, health care, and social welfare. They paid wages, including in collective-run factories, according to a system of "work points," each of which was worth about twenty to twenty-five fen.[11] Government and party cadres were paid according to their rank. In 1952, annual per capita gross domestic product was RMB119, the equivalent of $54; by 1956, it was RMB166.

At first, men earned more than women for the same jobs. Following collectivization in Little Fort Village in Guizhou, few of the village's twenty-three women bothered coming out to work. The head of women's affairs in the village, Yì Huáxiān, explained to the male chief that with men earning 7 points a day and women 2.5, women had little incentive to do so. After equal pay was instituted, all the women went to work, and productivity increased threefold. Learning of this in 1955, Mao ordered that all counties and collectives implement equal pay, adding: "Women hold up half the sky."[12]

The CPC banned foot-binding, concubinage, and arranged marriages, and promised women economic, social, educational, and political equality. Yet the CPC's Eighth Politburo, elected by the Central Committee in September 1956, didn't include one woman among its twenty-three members and alternative members.

妇女能顶半边天

The text reads, "Women hold up half the sky." Despite CPC promotion of gender equality, less than 30 percent of CPC members in 2019 were women, and as of 2021, none have ever sat on the powerful Politburo Standing Committee.

Intellectuals (*zhīshi fènzǐ* 知识分子, "elements with knowledge") were a prime target for "thought education." Mao had distrusted and resented intellectuals ever since working as an assistant librarian in Peking University, where his thick Hunan accent and rustic manners drew condescension. Some members of the intelligentsia stayed after 1949 because they believed in the Communist cause; others, because they figured the Communists couldn't be worse than the Nationalists, or they had no other choice. The CPC demanded that all cleanse themselves of old ways of thinking. The process of "washing"—involving forced self-examination and self-criticism under CPC supervision—would soon become all too familiar.

In 1955, the veteran Communist literary theorist Hú Fēng (1902–1985), a friend of Lu Xun, complained in a long article about the "five daggers plunged into a writer's head": Marxism, populism, politics, thought reform, and an officially ordained style of expression. Accused of "ideological deviationism" and "counterrevolutionary conspiracy," he was jailed on charges of secretly working for the United States and the KMT.

The following year, evoking the intellectual vibrancy of the Warring States period, Mao invited public criticism of the CPC. What was it doing wrong? What could it do better? He called for "one hundred flowers to bloom and one hundred schools of thought to contend."

With the Hu Feng affair fresh in the public memory, few spoke out at first. Eventually, millions did. Some protested the harshness of the cleansing campaigns. Others remarked that despite the CPC's egalitarian rhetoric, it was already displaying signs of corruption and privilege.

According to Mao's personal physician, by mid-1957 Mao was taken aback by the avalanche of criticism and spent days stewing in bed, ill, "depressed," and "furious," before emerging to claim it had all been a plot to "tempt the snake out of its hole."[13] Mao, who had also been alarmed by the anti-Soviet Hungarian Uprising and Nikita Khruschev's denunciation of Stalin the previous year, published an essay, "On the Correct Handling of Contradictions Among the People." It stated that although the "days of national disunity and chaos" were gone, there remained some "contradictions" between and among different classes of people that needed addressing:

> Our state is a people's democratic dictatorship led by the working class and based on the worker-peasant alliance. What is this dictatorship for? Its first function is internal, namely, to suppress the reactionary classes and elements and those exploiters who resist the socialist revolution, to suppress those who try to wreck our socialist construction, or in other words, to resolve the contradictions between ourselves and the internal enemy.[14]

The Anti-Rightist Campaign, run by fellow Long Marcher Deng Xiaoping, caught about one million people in its dragnet, many of them for speaking out the year before.[15] Approximately four hundred thousand "Rightist elements" were sent off to labor camps, where they were subjected to grueling physical work in punishing conditions, along with intensive political indoctrination. Many died. In his memoir of his time in a labor camp, *Grass Soup*, the writer Zhāng Xiánliàng (1936–2014) described feeling as though a "sharp knife had sliced through the middle of my existence." One half had landed in "this barren wasteland." As for the other, "I wasn't even sure if I had ever been whole before."[16]

### THE GREAT LEAP TO FAMINE

In 1958, Mao decided that China was ready take a "great leap forward" into Communism. The CPC mouthpiece, *People's Daily*, called on the country to "go all out" and "aim higher" to double agricultural and industrial production in 1958, and double it again in 1959. The PRC would "surpass Britain and catch up with America." Farmers were to plant crops "dense and deep." All property was nationalized—even water buffalos.

"People must conquer nature," Mao declared. Across the nation, citizens ripped the metal frames from their windows, took the woks from their kitchens, and threw whatever other metal they could find into improvised smelters to make steel, felling forests to feed the smelters. To eliminate pests such as sparrows (which ate grain), everyone banged pots and pans to scare the birds from landing until, exhausted, the birds dropped from the sky. The "backyard furnaces" produced millions of tons of useless scrap metal. Without sparrows to keep insects in check, and crops planted too densely, harvests failed. It wasn't long before food began to run out.

Local cadres, under pressure to meet unrealistic quotas, confiscated farmers' seed grain and raided the emergency granaries while official media churned out surreal accounts of triumph: "Rice Production in Huánjiāng County, Guangxi, Reaches Six and a Half Tons Per Acre," the *People's Daily* boasted on September 18, 1958.[17] In mid-July 1959, Péng Déhuái (1898–1974), a Long March veteran and the defense minister, wrote to Mao warning of "winds of exaggeration." "Putting politics in command," he argued, was "no substitute for economic principles."[18]

At a meeting of the CPC leadership on Lúshān mountain in Jiangxi, Mao, convinced that Peng Dehuai was plotting his overthrow, accused him of being a "counterrevolutionary." If the army stood by Peng, Mao threatened to raise a new Red Army of peasants and overthrow the government. His words shattered the illusion of collective leadership. Mao placed Peng Dehuai under house arrest and made Lín Biāo (1907–1971), who'd led the PLA into Beijing in 1949, the new minister of defense.

Agricultural production and distribution collapsed. The withdrawal of Soviet aid in 1959 added to the troubles, as did natural disasters. As famine spread, reports of cannibalism emerged from many parts of the countryside. Even in relatively privileged cities, people scraped bark off the trees to eat. Over a three-year period from the start of the Great Leap, tens of millions perished. Deforestation and overplanting, as well as the campaigns against "pests," severely harmed the natural environment.

The famine hit Tibet hard as a result of misguided directives that saw barley production and yak herds decline. The region fell into turmoil in 1959. Over the eight years after the signing of the 1951 Seventeen-Point Agreement, the central government had built hospitals, schools, roads, and bridges and, following the Dalai Lama's advice, curtailed the power of the *dzongpon*, regional administrators whose taxes and cruel punishments had tormented the poor. Then, in 1955, Mao startled the Dalai Lama at an otherwise cordial meeting by calling religion a "poison."[19] It wasn't long before Tibetan insurgents were once more skirmishing with the PLA.

Tensions were running high when, in March 1959, PLA commanders in Lhasa invited the Dalai Lama to their headquarters, stipulating that he was to come alone. Fearing a kidnap plot, some three hundred thousand Tibetans surrounded the Dalai Lama's residence, the Norbulinka Palace, to protect him. The Dalai Lama fled to India and the Chinese military shelled Norbulinka, killing the thousands still camped outside. Hundreds of thousands of Tibetans lost their lives between 1959 and 1961, either from famine or in the Tibetan Uprising, as it is known outside the PRC, where it is called the Tibetan Regional Turmoil.

Nothing, though, would stop celebrations of the PRC's tenth anniversary in 1959. The CPC mobilized ten thousand "volunteers" to build Ten Great Constructions in Beijing within ten months. These included the Great Hall of the People—home of the National People's Congress—and the Museum of Revolutionary History, built on opposing flanks of Tiananmen Square. The square had been expanded to become, at 4.7 million square feet (440,000 sq m), the biggest public space in the world. It was paved with numbered flagstones for choreographing large-scale assemblies and parades. In its center stood an obelisk, the Monument to the People's Heroes, decorated with friezes commemorating Lin Zexu's destruction of opium, the Taiping Rebellion, and the May Fourth Movement. Mao's portrait—an evolving series—had overlooked the square from Tiananmen Gate since 1949. Now, the CPC commissioned a mural for the Great Hall that would take as its theme Mao's poem "Snow," a riposte to Su Dongpo's melancholic meditation on Red Cliff:

> *This land so rich in beauty*
> *Has made countless heroes bow in homage.*
> *But alas! Qin Shihuang and Han Wudi*
> *Were lacking in literary grace,*
> *And Tang Taizong and Song Taizu*
> *Had little poetry in their souls;*
> *And Genghis Khan,*
> *Proud Son of Heaven for a day,*
> *Knew only shooting eagles, bow outstretched*
> *All are past and gone!*
> *For truly great men*
> *Look to this age alone.*[20]

As part of the celebrations, the government pardoned Puyi, the last emperor, who'd been confined in a center for war criminals since 1950. There he'd tended a vegetable garden as Prisoner 981. Now, Puyi became a gardener in the capital's botanical gardens, and an ornamental plant in the flowerbed of CPC propaganda. In the autobiography he wrote with the help of the novelist Lao She, the former emperor called the voter's card he was issued in 1960 "the most valuable thing" he'd ever owned.

## THE RINGING ARROWS FLY

Peng Dehuai wasn't the only critic of the Great Leap or the developing personality cult around Mao. Beijing's deputy mayor, Wú Hán (1909–1969), was a Ming historian. A few years earlier, he'd organized the excavation of Wanli's tomb to see if the Ming court had respected the emperor's desire to be buried with his beloved Lady Zheng. (It hadn't.) Mao invited Wu Han to write about Hai Rui, the principled Ming official, to emphasize that he'd fought for the good of the people against an entrenched bureaucracy. Wu Han, thinking of Peng Dehuai, wrote instead about how Hai Rui reprimanded an emperor for refusing to listen to advice and wasting resources while the people starved.[21] He also wrote a play on a similar theme, Hai Rui Dismissed from Office.

With tens of millions dead and hundreds of millions malnourished, there was no more pretending: the Great Leap Forward had been ruinous. With Mao's grudging approval, the CPC leadership—including Deng Xiaoping and President Liú Sháoqí (1898–1969)—reduced the size of the agricultural communes and gave peasants scope to grow their own food and sell the surplus at local markets. Liu Shaoqi said that the nation's suffering had been "three parts natural disasters, seven parts man-made catastrophe."[22]

In 1962, China and India fought a brief border war. The United States, in the midst of the Cuban missile crisis, offered India its support. Mao was not reassured by Soviet protestations of "unbreakable fraternal friendship"; they'd recently sold arms to India.[23] The CPC, worried that Moscow might launch a nuclear attack, mobilized the citizenry to dig bomb shelters in cities including Beijing and Shanghai and ordered the construction of a top-secret military-industrial complex—the Third Front—in the hinterlands.

China needed to achieve technological self-reliance. In 1960, a team led by Xià Péisù (1923–2014), who held a PhD from the University of Edinburgh, built China's first homegrown computer, the "107"; she is known as the Mother of Chinese Computer Science. Qián Xuésēn (1911–2009), the Father of Chinese Rocketry, had been named first director of the Jet Propulsion Laboratory at Caltech when he fell victim to persecution in the anti-Communist witch hunts of the McCarthy era. He returned to China and spearheaded the work that led to the PRC exploding its first atomic bomb in 1964.

Mao fulminated against Soviet perfidy and "revisionism" in verse seeded with allusions to Tang literature, including to a poem by the Confucianist Han Yu:

> Gnats that talk glibly of uprooting an oak,
> Ants vaunting of their Superpower on the
> Locust Tree!
> The west wind is scattering sere leaves
> Over the ramparts of Chang'an—
> Let fly the Ringing Arrow![24]

He was also preparing to let fly the ringing arrow *within* the ramparts of Chang'an. In 1963, he launched the Socialist Education Movement, sometimes called the Four Cleanups campaign, to address the problem of "reactionary" elements within the CPC and the bureaucracy. Although it resulted in the persecution of more than five million people and the deaths of many tens of thousands, it was but a prelude to a bigger storm: the Great Proletarian Cultural Revolution. Mao believed that revolution had to be ongoing, both to purge "revisionists" and "capitalist roaders"—people who pretended to be socialists while pushing a Soviet or capitalist agenda—from the CPC's ranks and to battle-harden a new generation of revolutionary successors.

In late 1965, a radical writer in his early thirties, Yáo Wényuán (1931–2005), penned a scathing attack on Wu Han's play about Hai Rui, calling it a "poisonous weed." Mao ordered all state media to reprint Yao's essay. When the Cultural Revolution began the following year, Wu Han became one of its first targets, and Yao Wenyuan one of its guiding lights. Along with Mao's wife, Jiang Qing, and two other extreme-left ideologues, he was part of a group later called the "Gang of Four."

In May 1966, Mao called on the masses to attack the counter-revolutionaries and capitalist roaders (including Deng Xiaoping) in the party, whose attacks on him, he claimed, were undermining the revolution. On May 25, the secretary of Peking University's philosophy department, Niè Yuánzǐ (1921–2019), put up an inflammatory poster in large characters denouncing "bourgeois reactionaries" on campus:

*Resolutely, thoroughly, totally and completely wipe
out all ghosts and monsters and all Khrushchevian
Counter-Revolutionary Revisionists and carry the
socialist revolution through to the end. Defend the
Party's Central Committee! Defend Mao Zedong
Thought! Defend the Dictatorship of the Proletariat!*

Mao praised her "big character poster" in an article titled "Bombard the Headquarters!"

A group of students at an elite middle school in Beijing met at the ruins of the Yuanmingyuan, vowing to protect Mao and the revolution with their lives. They called themselves the Red Guards. On June 1, the *People's Daily*, using language from the Ming-era novel *Journey to the West*, called for the elimination of "all Cow Demons and Snake Spirits." Mao urged the young to attack the "class enemies" and "revisionists" among their teachers and school administrators. The Great Proletarian Cultural Revolution was on.[25]

The first teacher to die at the hands of Red Guards was the vice principal at an elite girls' school. Two weeks later, at a Red Guard rally in Tiananmen Square, a member of the group that attacked her, a girl called Sòng Bīnbīn (b. 1949), pinned a Red Guard armband on Mao. Noting that "Binbin" meant "refined and polite," Mao suggested she change her name to Yàowǔ, "be militant." This was seen as an endorsement of the violence, which quickly escalated. Some students even wrote "Long Live the Red Terror" in their teachers' blood on a wall near the Forbidden City. Along with punishing alleged counterrevolutionaries, capitalist roaders, and Soviet-sympathizing "revisionists," the Red Guards, some as young as twelve and others university students, persecuted anyone with connections to Taiwan or the KMT. American combat troops had entered Vietnam the year before, and Mao feared that the United States was plotting with the KMT to attack the mainland.

In August and September 1966, Red Guards killed or drove to suicide nearly 1,800 people in Beijing alone.[26] The writer Lao She's body was found floating in a lake a day after he experienced a brutal "struggle session" at the imperial college founded

Song Binbin pinned a Red Guard armband on Mao on August 18, 1966, at the first of eight Red Guard rallies in Tiananmen Square, each a million strong.

by Khublai Khan. The struggle session against Wu Han took place in front of ten thousand spectators in the Workers' Stadium; he later died from a prison beating. Deng Xiaoping was "struggled," stripped of his posts, and exiled to the countryside for "reeducation"; his son Dèng Pǔfāng (b. 1944) was made paraplegic when Red Guards either forced him to jump or threw him from a window at Peking University, breaking his back. (He later became the PRC's first advocate for the disabled.) Eric

Gordon, a British journalist under house arrest in Beijing, likened the constant "roar" of the struggle sessions to the "moaning of a gigantic animal crouching over the city."[27]

Mao and fellow ideologues, including Chen Boda and Lin Biao, whipped up political hysteria at eight Red Guard rallies in Tiananmen Square between August and November 1966. Students flocked to Beijing from around the country to attend. In thrall to the cult of personality, they and others around China danced the Loyalty Dance to Mao, carried Little Red Books of his writings, and sang songs with titles like "Sailing the Seas Depends on the Helmsman."

Mao and Lin Biao called on the Red Guards to destroy the Four Olds: old ways of thinking, customs, culture, and habits. "We set out," one Red Guard later recalled, "like an army of Monkey Kings eager to make havoc under Heaven."[28] Across the country they smashed up mosques, churches, Daoist and Buddhist temples, and religious statuary, including of the Yellow Emperor, and tortured the faithful. They vandalized the tombs of the Jesuits Matteo Ricci and Schall von Bell, the Ming emperor Wanli, and even the Jiajing emperor's cat Snow Brow. They attacked women for wearing makeup and *qipao*, and destroyed everything from Ming-style furniture to translations of Western novels. They changed street and place names to revolutionary slogans, creating great confusion with multiple "Oppose Imperialism" or "Liberation" streets in the same city. Saner voices prevailed over proposals to rewire traffic signals so that red signaled go. The CPC had decried Chiang Kai-shek's removal of some of the Forbidden City's greatest treasures to Taiwan; it's hard to say how many would have survived had they remained.

Premier Zhou Enlai, while supporting Mao, used his authority to safeguard a number of valuable heritage sites, including, belatedly, the Forbidden City and Shanghai's Jade Buddha Temple. Although Zhou was able to save the Dalai Lama's Potala palace in Lhasa, Red Guards, some of them ethnic Tibetans, blew up a number of temples that had survived the violence of the 1950s. They fought pitched battles inside others, including Lhasa's sacred Jokhang, home to a Buddha statue brought to Tibet by Princess Wencheng. Red Guards reportedly destroyed 4,922 of Beijing's 6,843 cataloged historical relics.[29]

Red Guards also ransacked and trashed people's homes. Terrified, many people preemptively burned or destroyed invaluable books, scrolls, and other artwork, as well as personal diaries and letters. The writer and scholar Yáng Jiàng (1911–2016) had almost finished her translation of Cervantes's epic *Don Quixote* when Red Guards raided her house and took the manuscript. After the Cultural Revolution it was found in a pile of scrap paper and returned to her. She finished it and in 1986 was awarded a medal from Spain's King Juan Carlos.

The point of destroying the Four Olds was to make way for a new, revolutionary culture, epitomized by the Revolutionary Model Operas, *yàngbǎnxì* 样板戏, a genre that also included ballet and symphonic work. The brainchild of Jiang Qing, they celebrated Land Reform (*The Red Detachment of Women*), the anti-Japanese struggle (*Shājiābāng*), PLA heroics in the civil war (*Taking Tiger Mountain by Strategy*), and the defeat of counterrevolutionary saboteurs (*On the Docks*), to name a few.

Across the nation, unstable coalitions of cadres, soldiers, workers, and students called revolutionary committees took over from local governments as the country fell into

The ballet *The Red Detachment of Women* told a story of Land Reform. The Revolutionary Model Operas continued the project begun in the late Qing to "modernize" Chinese culture.

near-anarchy. Red Guard groups, armed by the military on Mao's orders, fought pitched battles over who was more loyal to Chairman Mao with Molotov cocktails, machine guns, spears, and tanks. In August 1967, a single conflict at Beijing's Xidan involved three thousand armed combatants and hundreds of casualties. Corpses rotted on university campuses, and streets ran with blood. Red Guards enjoyed free train and bus passes to propagate the Cultural Revolution throughout the nation (while, as it turned out, unwittingly spreading cerebrospinal meningitis in an epidemic that would claim 160,000 lives).[30]

In Portuguese-ruled Macao, Maoists put on Red Guard armbands, ransacked the city hall, and tore the arm off a statue of the original "foreign devil," explorer Jorge Álvares. Clashes with colonial police in December 1966 left eight dead and hundreds wounded. With mainland Red Guards massing on the border, the governor apologized for the actions of the police. (After the Portuguese dictatorship fell in 1974, Lisbon offered to hand Macao back to Beijing. Beijing declined; it wasn't ready to receive it.)

Hong Kong between 1958 and 1965 saw wages rise and workers' lives improve. Yet from 1966, wage growth lagged behind inflation. As anti-colonial sentiment grew, demonstrations against an increase in the price of tickets for the Star Ferry, the main cross-harbor transport, became violent riots. After the Cultural Revolution broke out on the mainland, unrelated labor disputes in Hong Kong turned political, with unionists brandishing copies of the Little Red Book.[31] Leftist radicals plastered the Bank of China headquarters with anti-imperialist slogans such as "Hang [British Governor] David Trench." The bank blasted anti-British propaganda; the British responded with high-decibel jazz and the Beatles. The leftists rioted, laid siege to Government House, planted more than a thousand bombs across the colony, and firebombed the car of an anti-Communist journalist, killing him and his cousin. In all, fifty-one people, including two children, were killed in the violence.[32]

In 1968, following intense factional fighting in Guangzhou, hundreds of bloated corpses, many trussed and bearing gunshot wounds or signs of torture, floated into Hong Kong waters from the Pearl River, further hardening anti-Communist sentiment in a territory that had for decades served as a place, as the Hong Kong journalist Lee Yee later put it, for "fleeing the Qin."[33]

By the end of 1968, Mao's enemies in the CPC were silenced. Intellectuals who survived the purges were sent off for "reeducation."

The Red Guards had served their purpose. It was now necessary, Mao said, for urban youth to go to the countryside and "learn from the poor and middle-level peasants." In 1969, the CPC declared the Cultural Revolution over.

In 1970, Mao held a rambling conversation with US journalist Edgar Snow, whose sympathetic portrait of the Communists in Yan'an, *Red Star over China*, had introduced the CPC and its revolutionary aspirations to the world. At the end of their chat, as he saw the American out, Mao likened himself to a "monk holding an umbrella." Snow misunderstood the phrase as the poignant lament of an isolated man. In fact, it was a cryptic pun: "no hair, no sky," *wúfà wútiān* 无发无天, is a near homonym for "no law, no Heaven," *wúfǎ wútiān* 无法无天—he was telling the American that he was an absolute ruler.

## EVERYTHING CHANGES

In 1968, the Soviets invaded Czechoslovakia and declared the Brezhnev Doctrine, which could theoretically sanction a Soviet invasion of China on the grounds of ideological deviation. The following year, the armies of the Communist giants fought a seven-month undeclared war along their eastern border with Hēilóngjiāng and western border with Xinjiang, with at least a hundred casualties.

Mao, now in his seventies, had named his minister of defense and "closest comrade-in-arms," Lin Biao, as his successor. But Lin, who was in his sixties, was in ill health. Who would succeed the successor? Mao reportedly favored a left-wing ideologue in his wife's circle, while Lin advocated for his son Lín Lìguǒ, a "super genius" (in his father's estimation), a Beatles fan, and, according to numerous later accounts, a serial sexual abuser.[34] In 1971, Lin Biao and his family, including Lin Liguo, disappeared. Weeks later, the CPC announced to a shocked public that Lin Biao had been plotting to kill Mao, and he and his family had died while fleeing to the Soviet Union when their plane crashed in Outer Mongolia. Many Chinese who lived through the Cultural Revolution described this as the moment when disillusion set in. As with the assassination of US president John F. Kennedy, there are many speculative alternative histories and conspiracy theories surrounding these events.

In 1971, the PRC took over the China seat at the United Nations from Taiwan. The following year, Japan and Australia normalized relations with Beijing, and US president Richard Nixon, a long-term anti-Communist, visited China to meet with Mao. Nixon agreed to support the One China policy, which acknowledged, as the official communique put it, "there is but one China and Taiwan is part of China." This paved the way to normalization of Sino-American relations. For the first time in years, PRC citizens began to study English, beginning with phrases such as "Long live Chairman Mao!" Under Zhou Enlai's patronage, Deng Xiaoping returned to power as deputy premier to help organize a political and economic recovery in 1973.

In 1972, the CPC launched the "Criticize Lin Biao, Criticize Confucius" campaign. It obliquely targeted Zhou Enlai as the "Duke of Zhou," the ruler idolized by Confucius. But if Zhou's moderation of some of the Cultural Revolution's excesses enraged the hard-left ideologues around Mao and Jiang Qing, it endeared him to many ordinary citizens. His death on January 8, 1976, prompted a massive public outpouring of grief.

On April 5, the day of the traditional Qingming festival, on which one tidies the graves of one's ancestors, young people swarmed onto Beijing's Tiananmen Square bearing white paper flowers (white is the Chinese color of mourning), poems, and posters, many of which denounced the ancient tyrant Qin Shihuang and the "White-Boned Demon": Chairman Mao and Jiang Qing. Similar demonstrations occurred in Guangzhou, Shanghai, Wuhan, and elsewhere. In Beijing, after police ordered people to leave the square at the end of the day, conflict broke out, and the square was cleared by force. The CPC denounced the "Tiananmen Incident" as "a counterrevolutionary riot." Those arrested were sent to prison or labor camps. Deng Xiaoping, named an instigator, dropped from sight a second time. Huá Guófēng (1921–2008), a guerrilla fighter and Mao loyalist, was promoted to premier of the State Council and vice-chairman of the CPC, making him Mao's heir apparent.

## THE END OF THE OLD GUARD

In 1975, Chiang Kai-shek succumbed to illness in Taiwan, aged eighty-seven. His son, Chiang Ching-kuo (1910–1988), succeeded him as president, retaining martial law. "Young Marshal" Zhang Xueliang, now in his seventies, remained under house arrest. The notorious offshore prison on Green Island was full of political prisoners. Among them was the writer Bó Yáng (1920–2008), charged with "being a Communist agent and attacking national leaders" for translating an American cartoon in which Popeye and his son land on an island and argue over who gets to be president. "Free China," as the Republic of China in Taiwan likes to call itself, was not so free.

The two sides had kept the civil war hot for decades with the alternate-day shelling of Jinmen Island and the nearest part of the mainland by the PLA and KMT troops. In later years, the bombs were filled with propaganda leaflets. Only with the normalization of Sino-American relations in 1979 would the bombardment cease.

On July 28, 1976, a massive earthquake devastated Tangshan, an industrial city about 95 miles (150 km) southeast of Beijing, killing approximately a quarter of a million people, about one in three of the city's residents. The aftershocks were felt in Beijing. Some whispered that the earthquake was a sign that Mao had lost the Mandate of Heaven.

Mao died on September 9, 1976, aged eighty-two. "I'm Marx plus Qin Shihuang," he once remarked. He also had a touch of the first Ming emperor, Hongwu—hypersensitive to criticism, insistent on centralizing power, and inclined to ruthless purges of intellectuals and former allies.

Hua Guofeng succeeded Mao as CPC chairman. On the night of October 6, he arrested Jiang Qing, Yao Wenyuan, and the other two members of the Gang of Four, accusing them of taking the nation to the brink of a second civil war. As ordinary people joined in the denunciations of the Gang of Four, many held up five fingers—one for Mao. Jiang Qing inevitably drew comparisons to the Tang's Wu Zetian and the Qing Empress Dowager Cixi, though "White-Boned Demon" also stuck.

In 1977, despite his express wish to be cremated, Mao's preserved body was installed in a mausoleum on Tiananmen Square, where it remains today.

## THE REFORM ERA

### Prosperity and Its Discontents

*In 1978, the CPC declared that the events in Tiananmen Square in 1976 had not been counterrevolutionary but "completely revolutionary." By reversing its verdict on the "Tiananmen Incident," the CPC seemed to be giving the people permission to express decades of pent-up emotions and silenced thoughts. In a scene replicated in cities around the country, a wall at the Xīdān intersection in central Beijing was transformed into "Democracy Wall," featuring poems, laments, accusations, manifestos, and petitions for justice. It drew crowds of thousands daily.*

FROM THE LATE 1970S, *Samizdat* (unofficial, self-published) journals, including *Beijing Spring*, *Exploration*, and the art and poetry journal *Today*, gave many young people their first encounter with heterodox political ideas, art, and literature. The former Red Guard Běi Dǎo (b. 1949) penned one of the most iconic poems of his generation, "The Answer":

> *Let me tell you, world,*
> *I—do—not—believe!*
> *If a thousand challengers lie beneath your feet,*
> *Count me as number thousand and one.*[1]

Democracy Wall helped Deng Xiaoping demonstrate to more recalcitrant members of the CPC leadership that the Chinese people were done with Maoist ideology. In December 1978, the Third Plenary session of the Eleventh Central Committee of the CPC formally endorsed the principle of collective leadership. Hua Guofeng remained CPC chairman, but Deng and his allies called the shots.

Many of the most extreme Cultural Revolution activists went to prison. A number of their surviving victims among the CPC leadership returned to power, including Xí Zhòngxūn (1913–2002), a veteran of the anti-Japanese and civil wars, whom Mao once likened to the legendary Three Kingdoms strategist Zhuge Liang. His son, Xi Jinping (b. 1953), then a university student, would soon begin his own political career.

## ALL MICE-CATCHING CATS ARE GOOD CATS

Deng wanted the PRC to be a "modern, powerful socialist country" by the end of the twentieth century. This required modernizing agriculture, industry, defense, and science and technology. The Four Modernizations, first proposed by Zhou Enlai in 1954 (with "communications and transport" instead of "science and technology"), reflected reformist goals dating back to the late Qing.

Mao had wanted to take a leap straight into communism. Deng rewound the clock to what he called the primary stage of socialism. This allowed the CPC to introduce market mechanisms into the PRC's centralized command economy and create the hybrid system of "socialism with Chinese characteristics." Mao tried to force reality to fit his vision; Deng preferred to see what worked and let the vision catch up. Catchphrases of the early Reform Era included "Seek truth from facts," "It doesn't matter if the cat is black or white so long as it catches mice," and "Cross the river by feeling for the stones."[2]

Deng Xiaoping survived the Long March and several purges by his own CPC colleagues to become the chief architect of the Reform Era.

The state dismantled the People's Communes and introduced the "responsibility system," whereby individual farmers or groups of farmers were contracted to deliver produce. By raising the prices it paid them while lowering those on fertilizers and other agricultural necessities, the state helped rural areas out of poverty while keeping food costs in the cities stable. Deng shifted industry from the hinterland to the coastal regions, which offered abundant labor and access to ports, and transitioned it to the production of consumer goods.

Bringing science and technology into the modern age required investment in education and research. In 1977, the government reinstated the university entrance examination system, opening up places to students based on merit rather than class status. With a university education the key to placement in a good job, and spaces for less than 5 percent of the nearly six million candidates, competition was fierce.

Defense was the most controversial of the Four Modernizations. Mao's theories of guerrilla warfare and "human wave" tactics had seen the Communists through the anti-Japanese resistance, civil war, and conflict in Korea. His ethos of egalitarianism was integral to the PLA's image, even if it never quite matched the reality. The idea of transforming the PLA into a modern, professional fighting force, complete with formal ranks, seemed a betrayal.

Deng was as ruthless as he was pragmatic. In 1978, Vietnam invaded Cambodia, ousting the Chinese-backed Khmer Rouge, and signed a mutual defense treaty with the Soviet Union. Early the following year, Deng visited the United States to celebrate the normalization of Sino-American relations, the first Chinese Communist leader to set foot on American soil. While there, he remarked of Vietnam: "When little kids are naughty, they should get spanked."[3] In mid-February, following his return, the PLA attacked Vietnam, citing, among other reasons, a dispute over islands in the South China Sea (still ongoing today). Both sides claimed victory in the short but bloody war. Thousands of Chinese casualties, and breakdowns in outdated field communications and the chain of command, made the point: China's military had to modernize.

## LOOSE ENDS AND NEW BEGINNINGS

The Democracy Wall movement became an irritant to the CPC. When Deng told the nation to "liberate" its thinking, he did not mean to embrace Western concepts of liberal democracy and human rights, which the CPC argues are best served by improving people's economic circumstances. In March 1979, Deng announced the Four Basic Principles, immutable and nonnegotiable: adherence to the Socialist road, the dictatorship of the proletariat, the leadership of the CPC, and Marxism–Leninism–Mao Zedong Thought.

Wèi Jīngshēng (b. 1950), an electrician and former Red Guard, had argued in an essay posted on Democracy Wall that without "the Fifth Modernization," democracy, the others were meaningless. The Chinese people didn't need gods, emperors, or another "autocratic tyrant," he wrote. "We want to be masters of our own destiny."[4] In November 1980, an unrepentant Jiang Qing faced court with the other members of the Gang of Four. "I was Chairman Mao's dog," she insisted during the nationally televised trial. "I bit whoever he asked me to bite."

The court handed down a death sentence, commuted to life imprisonment. Ten years later, diagnosed with cancer, she hanged herself. Her suicide note, scrawled on a People's Daily, reportedly read: "Chairman, I love you! Your student and warrior is coming to see you!"[5]

In 1981, the CPC officially acknowledged: "The 'cultural revolution,' which lasted from May 1966 to October 1976, was responsible for the most severe setback and the heaviest losses suffered by the Party, the state and the people since the founding of the People's Republic."

A popular misconception is that the resolution declared Mao's legacy to have been 70 percent good and 30 percent bad. It did not. It did concede Mao's responsibility for launching and leading the Cultural Revolution, and that he had made serious errors, but called these secondary to his accomplishments and said he remained the Chinese people's "respected and beloved great leader and teacher."[6]

The party proceeded to purge its ranks of tens of millions of recalcitrant "leftists" and rehabilitated the reputation of most of the victims of the Cultural Revolution and the Anti-Rightist campaign—including, posthumously, deputy mayor Wu Han and author Lao She. Beginning in 1979, the Department of Propaganda began the work of dismantling the Mao cult, including taking down statues and issuing instructions for the disposing of "loyalty" products such as badges and porcelain busts.[7]

The PRC adopted its fourth constitution, endorsing Putonghua as the national language and specifying a two-term limit for the presidency (chairman or head of state) to enforce the principle of collective leadership. Hua Guofeng stepped down in 1981, the last CPC leader to be called "chairman." The following year, Hú Yàobāng (1915–1989), a Long Marcher and reformist ally of Deng, became the party's first general secretary. Deng Xiaoping, the most powerful man in the PRC from 1978 until his death in 1997, only ever held one top leadership post: chairman of the Central Military Commission.

Having officially closed the book on its past, the CPC told the population to "look to the future," *xiàng qián kàn*, which, as was popularly noted, sounded exactly like "look to money."[8]

Nine out of ten of the mainland's 981 million people survived on or under the World Bank's "extreme poverty" line of $2 a day. Identifying unfettered population growth as an obstacle to prosperity, the CPC introduced a one-child policy in 1980. Because many cadres retained a Maoist mindset—conducting every campaign as if it were a war—there were countless forced abortions and sterilizations, especially in the countryside, now home to 80 percent of the population. There was also a rise in female infanticide, as many rural families clung to the traditional view that sons were more valuable than daughters, resulting in a serious gender imbalance. In cities, where living conditions were cramped and education levels higher, the policy encountered less resistance.

As the central government loosened its grip on the economy, citizens enjoyed more opportunities to raise their living standards in collective ventures or as "individual entrepreneurs." Sino-foreign joint ventures sprang up in sectors from cigarette manufacturing to hotel management. A handful of Special Economic Zones, including the once-modest county seat of Shenzhen, near the Hong Kong border, served as testing grounds for ambitious market-based economic reforms. Recognizing the need for clarity on intellectual and other property rights, the PRC introduced its first civil code in 1986. Another aspect of the "demilitarization" of Chinese society was a moderate relaxation of the ban on religion and the revival of traditional holidays and customs—including in Tibet and Xinjiang.

Deng Xiaoping, *Time*'s 1978 Man of the Year, received the accolade again in 1985. Many in the West had convinced themselves that the man Mao had accused of being a "capitalist roader" was both a capitalist and a democrat at heart. International trade and investment, scholarly and cultural exchange, and global goodwill all contributed to China's rising prosperity and international status over the course of the 1980s.

## STRAIT TALK AND A TICKING CLOCK

In September 1981, the CPC offered Taiwan a Nine-Point Plan for "peaceful reunification." It reiterated earlier proposals for mail and phone links and cross-strait travel and promised that Taiwan would retain its army and capitalist lifestyle under a "one country, two systems" formula. If the island resisted reunification, Beijing wouldn't rule out the use of force. Should it declare independence, that would mean war—there could only be one China.

President Chiang Ching-kuo responded: "No meeting, no discussion, no compromise." He was still planning to "recover the mainland" and free its citizens from Communist slavery, he said. Taiwan, despite its martial law, repressive politics, and unhealed historical wounds, prided itself on having one of Asia's fastest-growing "tiger economies," alongside Hong Kong, Singapore, and South Korea. In 1981, annual per capita gross domestic product on the mainland was $197; on Taiwan, it was $2,692. If many bristled under the KMT's autocratic rule, few preferred the alternative. A cartoon expressed the widespread reaction to the PRC's offer of financial aid: a man on an old bicycle in a shabby Mao suit waves a handful of Chinese *yuan* at a well-dressed man in an expensive sedan.

When one of Taiwan's better-known singer-songwriters, Hóu Déjiàn (b. 1956), defied Taiwan's sedition laws to travel to China in 1983, the mainland propaganda machine went into overdrive, lauding his return to "drink the milk of the motherland." On

Taiwan, people surmised he was escaping debts or his marriage, had been tricked, was kidnapped, or had simply lost the plot.

Meanwhile, the clock was ticking for Hong Kong. The Unequal Treaties of the nineteenth century had ceded Hong Kong Island and Kowloon to Britain in perpetuity. Yet Britain's ninety-nine-year lease on the New Territories—92 percent of Hong Kong's land and home to half its population—would run out in 1997. A Sino-British agreement signed on December 19, 1984, elaborated the "one country, two systems" formula: Hong Kong would retain its way of life, legal system, and "high degree of autonomy" for at least fifty years from 1997. The new constitution for post-handover Hong Kong—the Basic Law—indicated that the chief executive and legislative council would be elected by universal suffrage but didn't attach a date to the promise.

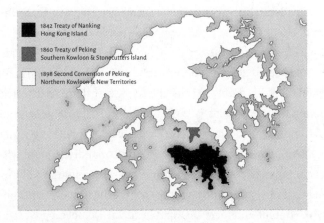

1842 Treaty of Nanking
Hong Kong Island

1860 Treaty of Peking
Southern Kowloon & Stonecutters Island

1898 Second Convention of Peking
Northern Kowloon & New Territories

At the start of Sino-British negotiations over Hong Kong's future in 1982, Deng Xiaoping insisted that China would recover sovereignty over all Hong Kong in 1997. Only the details were negotiable.

## CULTURAL FEVER

On the mainland, the winding back of state subsidies for publishers, film studios, and other cultural enterprises had the unintended consequence of liberating cultural production from Maoist strictures. In 1970, during the Cultural Revolution, mainland readers had a choice of 42 newspapers, 21 magazines, and fewer than 5,000 new book titles; by 1985, those figures were 698, 4,705, and 45,602 respectively. Sensationalist accounts of such topics as life in Mao's bodyguard and sexual awakenings emerged alongside pioneering works of feminism, environmentalism, historical investigation, and cultural self-reflection that echoed some of the concerns of the May Fourth Movement. Many Western books were published in translation—Nietzsche, Sartre, and Kafka all found new and enthusiastic fans.

Readers also encountered a number of writers from Taiwan, Hong Kong, and the republican era for the first time. *The Ugly Chinaman* by the former Green Island prisoner Bo Yang stirred heated debate and comparisons to Lu Xun, before being banned. Many embraced the cheeky, satirical urban fiction of young writers such as Wáng Shuò (b. 1958). A new generation of filmmakers, including Chen Kaige (b. 1952) and Zhang Yimou (b. 1950), broke post-1949 cinema's propagandistic mold with open-ended narratives and naturalistic representations of Chinese life. Artists and poets continued the bold experimentation with content and form that had begun at Democracy Wall. By the middle of the decade, China even had its first homegrown rock star, Cuī Jiàn (b. 1961). People used the phrase "cultural fever," *wénhuà rè* 文化热, to describe the 1980s explosion of creativity and intellectual exploration.

The CPC greeted these developments with a volatile mix of tolerance, enthusiasm, displeasure, and fury. Deng oversaw several ideological campaigns targeting "excessive individualism," "humanism," "bourgeois liberalism," and "spiritual pollution" (also referred to as "spiritual opium," code for Western influences). As each campaign petered out, there was another detonation of cultural and intellectual energy.

In late 1986, inspired by astrophysicist and university vice president Fāng Lìzhī's (1936–2012) lectures on the social responsibility of intellectuals, students in Shanghai, Beijing, and more than half a dozen other cities demonstrated for greater freedoms. General secretary Hu Yaobang argued against Deng's order to expel Fang and other outspoken individuals from the CPC—and lost his own post as a result.

## THE IRON HOUSE

Lu Xun once explained how he came to write his story "Diary of a Madman." A friend had asked him to submit something to *New Youth*. He demurred:

> Imagine an iron house with no windows, and absolutely indestructible. Inside, many people are sleeping, and soon they will die of suffocation. But they will die in their sleep and won't experience sorrow over their death. Let's say you shout at them to wake up, arousing the few light sleepers, condemning them to inconsolable agony before they die— are you sure you're doing the right thing?[9]

His friend replied that if enough sleepers awoke, they might be able break out of the house.

On January 6, 1989, Fang Lizhi wrote an open letter to Deng Xiaoping, urging the CPC to celebrate the fortieth anniversary of the PRC, the seventieth of the May Fourth Movement, and the bicentenary of the French Revolution by releasing all political prisoners, including the Democracy Wall activist Wei Jingsheng.[10] The letter inspired numerous similar petitions, including from members of the original May Fourth generation and the poet Bei Dao. On February 22, officials stated that these appeals "contravened the principles of legality."[11]

Hu Yaobang died on April 15, 1989. Over the next few days, university students began to gather in Tiananmen Square, placing banners at the Monument to the People's Heroes, including one that read "The one who shouldn't have died is dead; the ones who should be dead are still alive."[12] The snowballing protests initially focused on corruption, with slogans like "Sell the [Mercedes] Benzes and save the nation." On April 26, the *People's Daily* accused "an extremely small number" of people with "ulterior purposes" of conspiring to "plunge the whole country into chaos and sabotage to negate the leadership of the Communist Party of China and the socialist system."

The following morning, tens of thousands of defiant students flooded into the streets and marched in a swelling parade toward the square, igniting a popular, nationwide movement demanding democracy, accountability, and freedom of speech.

Over the next month, students occupied Tiananmen Square. In early May, they undertook a mass hunger strike that galvanized even broader public support. The protests disrupted a visit by Mikhail Gorbachev on May 15, the first meeting between the leaders of the PRC and Soviet Union since the Sino-Soviet split thirty years earlier. Deng was furious. After Deng imposed martial law on the capital, citizens of all ages poured onto the streets to block the army from getting to the students in the square.

The movement had begun to lose steam when, on June 2, the singer-songwriter Hou Dejian and the university lecturer and acerbic cultural critic Liu Xiaobo—the one who said that the "stray dog" Confucius would have become a "guard dog" had he found an owner—began a hunger strike in the square with two friends. When the order came for the PLA to clear the square "with extreme prejudice," there were still tens of thousands on the approach roads, and thousands in the square itself. Citizens tried to block the army's advance. Beginning late on the night of June 3, the soldiers opened fire with live ammunition.

No one knows what happened to the anonymous man who stood up to a row of tanks on June 4 in Beijing before disappearing in the crowd.

Although Hou and Liu helped to negotiate the evacuation of the students from the square, it's estimated that the army killed around a thousand people in Beijing and hundreds more in other cities. Untold thousands were wounded.[13] Testimonies published abroad told of young women shot point-blank by soldiers, and hospitals with bodies piled up in the corridors. Despite the Western media shorthand of the "Tiananmen Massacre," the killings in Beijing largely occurred on the approach roads to the square. Official accounts described those killed as "rioters" and dwelled on the deaths of PLA soldiers who were beaten or burned to death by Molotov cocktails thrown into armored vehicles, their bodies then strung like gruesome trophies from the pedestrian overpasses.

Many student leaders fled abroad with the help of Hong Kong supporters. Within days, Liu Xiaobo was under arrest, along with many others. Hou Dejian took temporary refuge in the Australian embassy, and Fang Lizhi went into exile in the United States. In the months that followed, police continued to make arrests, and schools and work units punished those who'd participated in the protests. Party, government, and army officials who had expressed sympathy for them were fired or demoted. The cultural and intellectual renaissance of the 1980s was over, and so was the West's love affair with Deng.

The events of 1989 had a profound impact on Hong Kong. Millions of the territory's residents had rallied in support of democracy in the PRC. They would hold mass vigils of commemoration every June 4 thereafter, until security laws introduced in the territory in 2020 criminalized such gatherings.

Chiang Ching-kuo had lifted martial law on Taiwan in 1987, one year before his death. In 1989, the island enjoyed a free press and Taiwanese could travel to the mainland. Scarifying reports of the June 3 to 4 violence in Beijing from Taiwanese journalists and other eyewitnesses hardened popular sentiment there against reunification.

## THE NEW WORLD ORDER

Lao She's play *Teahouse*, about life in Beijing from the late Qing through to the revolution, enjoyed a revival in 1990. In a scene from the civil war, the teahouse owner berates the police for beating up anti-KMT student protesters, prompting pointed applause from Beijing audiences. But the streets were quiet. The CPC leaders had successfully suppressed outward signs of dissent and preserved the party's power in the face of an unprecedented popular challenge and international condemnation.

The fall of the Berlin Wall in late 1989 and the crumbling of the Soviet Union alarmed CPC hardliners, who saw a slippery slope from private property and market forces to demands for multiparty democracy. Believing the reforms had gone too far, they demanded to know: was the PRC "surnamed socialism or capitalism"?[14]

China's leaders were CPC general secretary Jiāng Zémín (b. 1926) and Premier Lǐ Péng (1928–2019). With his legacy under threat, Deng Xiaoping, officially retired, embarked on a "southern inspection tour," a *nánxún* 南巡 (the same word used to describe the southern tours of the Kangxi and Qianlong emperors). Deng visited the Special Economic Zones, Guangzhou and Shanghai. There, he declared that if the reforms benefited "the development of socialist productive forces," "increased a socialist country's overall national strength," and "raised the living standard of the people," the PRC's surname was socialist.

Deng's *nanxun* quashed uncertainty about the future of reform and kickstarted the economic revival of the 1990s. The party-state would manage the people not through class struggle but "stability maintenance" (stricter policing), "harmony" (social unity through ideological indoctrination and censorship), "patriotic education" (harnessing the force of nationalism), and the building of a "socialist market economy."

The central message of patriotic education was that in 1949, the CPC had ended the "one hundred years of humiliation" that began with the Opium Wars. The image of the ruins of the Yuanmingyuan's Western Palaces was used to reinforce the message that only the CPC could protect and advance China against a hostile world. If their parents were raised on class struggle, and their older siblings tempted by dreams of democracy, the post-Tiananmen generations were weaned on an aggrieved nationalism and the promise of economic opportunity.

The age of the "iron rice bowl"—guaranteed lifetime employment, housing, medical care, and education for one's children—was over. The CPC allowed private enterprise to take over many industries and services previously monopolized by the state, lifted some price controls, and made it easier to invest and conduct business for PRC and non-PRC citizens alike. In the Mao era, nearly all travel, including domestic, was restricted to official business; in the mid-1990s, domestic tourism kicked off with the introduction of the two-day weekend and an increase in public holidays.

The benefits of the reforms did not flow equally. The scaling down of state-owned enterprises led to a surge in urban unemployment. The coastal fringe left the hinterland behind, and rural areas struggled while cities prospered. By 1993, sixty-two million people had left their villages to work in factories and mines and on construction sites, as well as for the burgeoning middle class as renovators, cleaners, cooks, and nannies. But without official urban residence permits, *hùkǒu* 戶口, they couldn't enroll their children in public schools or access social welfare in the cities where they worked.

In 1996, the last imperial eunuch, Sūn Yàotíng, whose family castrated him shortly before the fall of the Qing, passed away at the age of ninety-four. As an old man, he still wept at the memory of how, in 1966, terrified of the Red Guards, his family had destroyed his "precious."

Deng Xiaoping died in 1997, just months before the handover of Hong Kong from Britain that he'd hoped to live to see. (Macao returned to Chinese sovereignty on the eve of the new millennium.) As the old guard was dying off, a new guard was rising through the ranks. Xi Jinping was now a member of the CPC's Central Committee.

## GUESS WHO'S BACK

Lu Xun remarked that there were two ways to attack original genius: suppression and exaltation. In 1994, the CPC, which once condemned Confucius, hosted an international symposium to celebrate the 2,545th anniversary of his birth. His attachment to social stability, moderation, and respect for authority now suited the party's purposes. Its newfound reverence reflected its broader desire to be seen as the rightful inheritor and guardian of traditional Chinese culture.

The thinker's image was useful as well. In 2004, the world's first Confucius Institute opened in Seoul, South Korea. Run by the Ministry of Education, Confucius Institutes promote PRC soft power through language teaching and cultural activities. They have since been evicted from a number of universities in the United States, Canada, and the European Union, accused of interfering with academic discussion on subjects including

Tibet, Taiwan, and Tiananmen. Official Chinese media blamed the closures on anti-China sentiment and the West's "fear or ignorance of other cultures, perhaps both."[15]

One day in 2011, the people of Beijing woke to discover a 31-foot-tall (9.5 m) statue of Confucius in Tiananmen Square in front of the National Museum. Neo-Maoists exploded in online outrage at the honoring of this "slave-owning sorcerer." The statue disappeared as suddenly as it had appeared—banished to the museum's courtyard. The neo-Maoists rejoiced.[16] Other citizens joked that Confucius had failed to get a *hukou* for the capital. Two and a half thousand years after his death, the old sage was as controversial as ever.

Under Mao, the CPC had condemned all religion as spiritual "opium" or superstition. Following the collapse of Maoism, there had been a great upsurge of interest in religion and spirituality. The Reform Era permitted the practice of religion under prescribed conditions—for example, Catholics could worship in "patriotic" churches that didn't recognize the authority of the pope.

In Xinjiang, the 1990s saw a revival of Islamic cultural and religious practices. Xinjiang represents about one sixth of the PRC's territory and one fifth of its reserves of oil, natural gas, and coal. The dissolution of the Soviet Union and rise of the Central Asian states Kazakhstan, Kyrgyzstan, and Tajikistan on Xinjiang's borders prompted the Standing Committee of the Politburo to convene in 1996 to discuss potential threats to the region's stability, including the rise of Uyghur separatism.

As in Tibet, the CPC steadily built up its security and military presence in Xinjiang while accelerating Han migration to the region. Between 1949 and 2020, the percentage of Han in the Xinjiang population would go from under 7 to 40.[17] The state also poured some one hundred billion yuan into Xinjiang's economic development, though many Uyghurs (like Tibetans) complained that the Han reaped most of the benefits.

Across the mainland, a fad arose for *qìgōng* 气功, an ancient form of healing and exercise involving the cultivation of *qi*. Some *qigong* masters, expounding Daoist-influenced philosophies, developed large, cultish followings. Such were the origins of many a rebellion in dynastic times. In the mid-1990s, the CPC placed all *qigong* groups under supervision.

One group resisted. Led by the self-proclaimed healer Lǐ Hóngzhì (b. 1951), the Fǎlúngōng combined Buddhist and Daoist notions of compassion with racialist ideas, homophobia, and the conviction that extraterrestrials were hollowing out humanity spiritually for nefarious purposes. The CPC denounced Falungong as "feudal superstition." Li Hongzhi moved to the United States, but Falungong continued to grow. In 1999, when the CPC had just over sixty-three million members, Falungong claimed seventy million adherents. In April, ten thousand of them surrounded Zhongnanhai, the CPC headquarters, in a silent protest. The shocked leadership deemed this the most serious political incident since 1989 and banned the group.

Falungong has since accused the CPC of serious human rights abuses, including the harvesting of organs from their imprisoned members. The sect promotes its cause abroad through US-based media outlets including the right-wing *Epoch Times*, New Tang Dynasty Television, and the traveling extravaganza Shen Yun, which combines quasi-traditional cultural performances with anti-Communist agitprop.

## COMING OUT AND CLAMPING DOWN

Access to the internet grew from the mid-1990s, along with a multilayered system of surveillance, control, and censorship nicknamed the Great Firewall of China. The CPC kept a tight rein on political expression online and off and a wary eye on religion, while relaxing its once-extensive supervision of people's private lives. Homosexuality was finally decriminalized in 1997, and in 2001, the Chinese Psychiatric Association removed it from the official list of mental disorders. But there are still reports of forced conversion therapy, and prejudice remains—some school textbooks continue to disparage homosexuality as a "social problem" of the West, the result of the "spiritual hollowness" of capitalism.[18] Yet younger generations tend to be more accepting of "comrades," *tóngzhì* 同志, a common slang for gay individuals that galls the CPC.

In the first year of the new century, the PRC joined the World Trade Organization, and Beijing won its bid for the 2008 Olympics. In 2002, China and the Association of Southeast Asian Nations (ASEAN) committed to handling disputes over mutually claimed islands, reefs, and shoals in the South China Sea in a "constructive manner." As the days, hours, minutes, and seconds till the Olympics ticked down on a giant clock in Tiananmen Square, Western commentators (as they had done in the early eighties) excitedly heralded a new age of openness, capitalism, and democratization. Some spoke of the Olympics as the PRC's "coming out" party.

Per capita gross domestic product, measured in US dollars, was $156 in 1978, passed $1,000 in 2001, and reached $3,832 in 2009.[19] By then, the PRC would boast the largest urban population on Earth—some six hundred million people, many of whom could aspire to middle-class goals such as home ownership and overseas travel. The some 40 percent of the population who were under thirty had only known rising living standards and expanding opportunities. Yet problems such as worsening inequality between rural and urban areas remained, and despite rising incomes, higher prices kept actual poverty above the level official statistics suggested. Rapid development had also seen a rise in unsafe and exploitative work, as well as forced, sometimes illegal, acquisitions of homes and farmland by developers. The environmental costs of the economic miracle were becoming apparent, with escalating air, soil, and water pollution. As with the return of prostitution, drug addiction, the keeping of mistresses (a modern form of concubinage), human trafficking, and venereal disease, official corruption played a part.

What's more, as Chen Guidi and Wu Chuntao note in their book *Will the Boat Sink the Water?*—a bestseller in China before being banned—between 1990 and 2000, the burden of taxation on the peasants increased fivefold. In 2000, it averaged 146 yuan per capita, six times that imposed on higher-earning urban residents. Rural dwellers were also subject to up to ninety-three categories of additional fees, including levies to fund village Communist Youth League activities.[20] The English title of the book is a riff on a line from the Tang Taizong emperor, who likened the peasantry to water and the state to a boat: "Water holds up the boat; water may also sink the boat."[21]

In 2002 and 2003 respectively, Hú Jǐntāo (b. 1942), a hydropower engineer who'd risen to prominence through the Communist Youth League, and Wēn Jiābǎo (b. 1942), a geo-mechanical engineer and former protégé of Hu Yaobang, became CPC general secretary and state chairman. Wen Jiabao reduced the burden of taxation on farmers and oversaw popular policies to address inequality of access to health and education. Hu Jintao pledged to foster a conflict-free "harmonious socialist society," suppressing dissent and clamping down on the nascent civil society of human-rights lawyers and activists and nongovernmental organizations working in such areas as the environment and workers' rights. Yet in 2005 alone, in some of the last statistics published on the subject by the Ministry of Public Security, some eighty-seven thousand protests, or "mass incidents," erupted nationwide, a tenfold increase over the previous decade.[22]

The global financial crisis of 2007 to 2008 came as a gift to CPC propagandists, who argued that it exposed the failures of the capitalist system. The PRC's year of Olympic pride, though, revealed stresses within its own system. Cycles of unrest and suppression rocked both Xinjiang and Tibet.

In May 2008, a magnitude-eight earthquake devastated Sichuan province. Around ninety thousand people died—including more than five thousand children, many of them trapped in school buildings that crumbled, people said, like tofu. The one-child policy meant that few had siblings; the neologism *shīdú* 失独 ("to lose the only one") expressed the inconsolable grief of losing an only child. It became evident that the instability of the "tofu buildings" was due to officials illegally siphoning off construction funds.

State corruption was also present in the tainted-milk scandal of July 2008, when hundreds of thousands, including fifty-four thousand infants, suffered kidney damage caused by milk powder adulterated with melamine. Melamine raises the protein count and commercial value of watered-down milk. Less than twenty years after students had called on the CPC to "sell the Benzes and save the nation," corruption had only worsened.

The futuristic "Bird's Nest" stadium, home of the 2008 Beijing Olympics, was codesigned by Ai Weiwei. The artist later fell afoul of the regime, partly for investigating children's deaths in the Sichuan earthquake, and went into exile in 2015.

The CPC censored reports on these and other matters and bristled at criticism from abroad. Nothing would be allowed to spoil its grand celebration. On August 8, 2008, the opening ceremony, directed by filmmaker Zhang Yimou, featured chanting Confucians and marching Terracotta Warriors, Zheng He's fleet, the Four Great Inventions, an exuberant fireworks display, and more, enacted by thousands of performers moving and drumming and dancing in perfect synchronization—a grand spectacle of unity and national pride.

The historian Sima Qian wrote, "The refusal of one decent man outweighs the acquiescence of the multitude."[23] The cultural critic turned democracy activist Liu Xiaobo had been in and out of prison and labor camps since 1989. Now he helped draft Charter 08, named in homage to the dissident Czech Charter 77. Signed by more than three hundred intellectuals, activists, and officials and released in December 2008, it called "not for ameliorative reform of the current political system but for an end to some of its essential features, including one-party rule, and their replacement with a system based on human rights and democracy."[24]

Liu Xiaobo was arrested and, in 2009, sentenced to eleven years in prison for "inciting subversion of state power." In 2010 he was awarded the Nobel Peace Prize in abstentia. He would die of liver cancer while still in custody in 2017.

The economy was continuing to grow and, in 2010, surpassed Japan as the world's second-largest. But anger at corruption was on the rise, too. Internet access—513 million users by 2011, almost half on the microblogging site Weibo—made it harder for the CPC to conceal malfeasance. On July 23, 2011, two high-speed trains collided near the eastern city of Wēnzhōu. Six carriages derailed, two plunging some 130 feet (40 m) to the ground from a viaduct. Dozens died, and many were injured. A student on the train sent out a distress call on Weibo that drew international media attention. Other microbloggers posted videos of workers burying derailed carriages under the viaduct, raising accusations that the authorities were literally covering up evidence. Official media briefly reported on the accident; the *People's Daily* even editorialized against striving for a "blood-stained GDP." Then, abruptly, all media coverage ceased, and a new campaign was launched against online "rumor-mongering."[25]

The most sensational case of corruption involved Bó Xīlái (b. 1949), a Politburo member whose father, Bó Yībō, had made the Long March alongside Xi Jinping's father. Suave and charismatic, Bo was the party secretary of the southwestern municipality of Chongqing and an enthusiastic promoter of retro-revolutionary "red" culture. His anti-corruption campaign took down his own public security bureau chief, whose wife provided investigators with photographs of her husband in bed with underage prostitutes and the location of his illicit fortune (buried under their goldfish pond).[26] After Bo's wife, Gǔ Kāilái, murdered a British business associate in 2011 for allegedly balking at her request to help move the couple's own considerable ill-gotten wealth overseas, both Bo and Gu were put away for life.

On October 11, 2012, Mò Yán (b. 1955), a former PLA soldier, became the first mainland-based Chinese author to win the Nobel Prize for Literature. Speaking on receipt of the prize in Stockholm, he likened censorship in the PRC to the "necessary checks" of airport security. Several weeks later, *The New York Times* website fell afoul of those "necessary checks" for revealing that Wen Jiabao's family had accumulated a fortune worth at least $2.7 billion.[27] The following month, Hu Jintao warned that the scourge of corruption, if left unchecked, could "cause the collapse of the Party and the fall of the state."[28]

In 2012, the Chinese sociologist Sūn Lìpíng (b. 1955) suggested the PRC faced four possible paths. One was a return to Mao-style egalitarian populism, reducing inequality and corruption but risking the violence and irrationality of the Mao era. Another was to deepen the reforms—further privatizing the economy regardless of increased inequality. The third was to maintain the status quo. The fourth was to pursue reform while applying notions of fairness, justice, and universal values.[29]

In November that year, the CPC named Xi Jinping its new general secretary and chair of the Central Military Commission. The following March, the National People's Congress would confirm him as president of the PRC. The CPC had chosen its path, and it would soon look a little bit like the first.

# THE NEW ERA OF XI JINPING

## Rise of the Wolf Warriors

*In 1980, when pushing to limit the state's top leadership posts to two consecutive five-year terms, Deng Xiaoping stated that no one should be allowed to hold high office indefinitely. By 2012, there had been two unbroken leadership cycles of ten years each. Then, in 2018, the National People's Congress, following the CPC's instructions, abolished the two-term limit. Xi, like Mao before him, and emperors before that, could potentially rule for life; the hard-won system for orderly succession was broken. Censors scrambled to scrub comments such as "We're back in the Qing dynasty" from the Chinese internet.*

ONE OF XI'S FIRST ACTS upon becoming general secretary was to launch the most ambitious campaign against corruption in decades, sweeping up "tigers" (high officials) and "flies" (low-ranked officials) in its dragnet. It won wide public support. State media promoted Xi as approachable, egalitarian, and down to earth, with breathless, frequent reports on "Daddy" (or Big Uncle) Xi, Xí Dàdà 习大大, going about daily life—having a "people's breakfast" of inexpensive pork buns in an ordinary and crowded Beijing restaurant, for example.

Xi introduced the "China Dream" of national rejuvenation, in which a prosperous China would take its rightful place in the world. When early in 2013 a popular southern newspaper editorialized that the China Dream should also include constitutionalism—meaning that even the CPC was beholden to law—it was forced to replace the offending editorial with one titled "We Are Closer to Our Dream than Ever."[1] The CPC forbade universities from teaching "Western values" such as civil society and universal rights, or "historical errors" such as the Anti-Rightist Campaign and the Cultural Revolution, condemning crucial episodes in modern Chinese history to what Orwell called "memory holes."

In 2016, the CPC declared Xi Jinping a "core leader," an accolade previously given Mao, Deng, and Jiang Zemin. It implies

In 2012, Xi Jinping became the first head of party and state to be born after 1949. Not since Mao had there been such a cult of personality.

rightful dominance, making it hard for others to argue against his decisions. The CPC revised its constitution to adopt "Xi Jinping Thought on Socialism with Chinese Characteristics for a New Era" as its "guiding ideology." By then, Xi had accumulated so many official titles, including commander-in-chief of the PLA's new Joint Operations Command Center, that he earned the nickname "Chairman of Everything."[2] If this recalls Hongwu, the Ming emperor who insisted on centralizing power into his own hands, Xi envisions himself ushering in a Golden Age like that of Qianlong—prosperous, culturally efflorescent, and militarily powerful.

In 2020, the CPC claimed to have eliminated "absolute poverty" in China. Hundreds of millions of Chinese citizens, some 59 percent of the population, fit the definition of middle class, with a net worth between $10,000 and $100,000. There were 799 US-dollar billionaires—173 more than in the United States—as well as 4.45 million millionaires. Inconceivable in Mao's day, a number of these entrepreneurs were CPC members. The CPC membership had grown to ninety-two million. Representing 6.6 percent of the population, party members were better educated, on average, than the general population, and they covered every profession and field. Some 80 percent of them were born in the 1980s and 1990s.[3] Mao would not recognize the party he helped found, with its new "party-masses service centers" offering exercise classes, karaoke, and speed-dating alongside lectures on Xi Jinping Thought and bureaucratic services.

The China Dream is also of a world united by a PRC-led Community of Shared Destiny for Mankind.[4] This concept, according to Geremie Barmé, provides "substance and diplomatic architecture" to the Qin-era notion of "all under heaven," founded on "a belief that China can be a moral, political and economic great power."[5] The trillion-dollar global aid, infrastructure, and investment program the Belt and Road Initiative (BRI) is Xi's idea for knitting that larger "shared community" together, while referencing both the Silk Roads and the maritime voyages of Ming general Zheng He. It also aims to boost the PRC's soft power and global influence in a time of American decline through educational, scientific, and cultural exchange. The foreign relations slogan of the Mao era was "we have friends all over the world," which for the New Era could easily be "we have clients all over the world." The BRI also promotes an alternative, authoritarian-friendly China Model, or Beijing Consensus, for development, prioritizing prosperity and stability over political freedom and choice.

Mao had wanted to be the leader of the developing world. Deng Xiaoping insisted that, in the international arena, China should "hide its capabilities and bide its time." Xi, by contrast, declared that China must "always be the builder of world peace, the contributor to global development, and the defender of the international order." When the international order doesn't suit its interests, as in a 2016 Hague ruling against PRC claims to islands, reefs, and shoals in the South China Sea,[6] Beijing simply refuses to abide by it. If China had "stood up," *zhànqǐlái* 站起来, under Mao, and "prospered up," *fùqǐlái* 富起来, under Deng, Xi proclaimed that under him, it would "power up," *qiángqǐlái* 强起来.

## WOLF WARRIORS AND TECHNO-LEGALISM

The Rambo-esque 2017 action film *Wolf Warrior II*, about a rogue Chinese special ops soldier in Africa who defeats evil American mercenaries, modified the words of a Western Han general for its tagline: "We will execute whoever insults the mighty Han, no matter how far away they are" becomes "We will execute whoever insults our China, no matter how far away they are!"[7]

*Wolf Warrior II* became the highest-grossing film in mainland history. It has lent its name to the aggressive and aggrieved nationalism of the New Era.

There had been notable explosions of nationalistic anger during the Reform Era. Some were aimed at Japan over attempts to whitewash its invasion of China. In 1999, anti-US sentiment erupted over NATO's bombing—which it claimed was accidental—of the Chinese embassy in Belgrade during an air campaign against Yugoslav atrocities in Kosovo, which resulted in three Chinese deaths. Protesters besieged the US embassy in Beijing and attacked its consulates in Chéngdū and Guangzhou. After four days, state media broadcast President

Clinton's apology and police halted the demonstrations. The CPC, typically, allowed patriotic demonstrators enough leeway to make their point before asserting control.

The Wolf Warriors of the New Era, steeped in the mood of resentment and exceptionalism fostered by decades of patriotic education, enjoy relative impunity in an otherwise controlled and censored space. Mainly operating online, they troll, dox, and incite violence against anyone, Chinese or not, whom they believe has insulted "Our China." "We have made no real progress," mused the scholar of diplomatic history and retired member of the Chinese Academy of Social Science Zī Zhōngyún (b. 1930) in 2020. "Empress Dowager Cixi is still at the helm at the Court in Beijing; below her, the roiling masses of Boxer patriotic thugs thrive as ever." As for "the men and women of conscience and rationality who strain to be heard," she said, they "have repeatedly been censored, silenced and shut down."[8]

The CPC considers the Boxers heroes of anti-imperialism. In a widely read article published in 2006, historian Yuán Wěishí (b. 1931) lamented that students were being taught to venerate a violent and ignorant mob. He decried that while they were taught about the burning of the Yuanmingyuan, they weren't told about the torture of members of the Anglo-French delegation that was the immediate motive for the devastation. The elimination of politically inconvenient aspects of history from textbooks, he argued, fosters an inflamed and irrational nationalism that damages China's ability to act responsibly on the world stage. Officials accused Yuan of "hurting the feelings of the Chinese people." The publication was shuttered until it printed a retraction. In the New Era, it's unlikely such a piece would see print in the first place. The self-reflexive spirit of May

Fourth isn't dead, but the CPC appears determined to bury it; May Fourth in the New Era is celebrated purely as a patriotic, anti-imperialist movement.

In a speech to CPC leaders in 2018, Xi addressed the problem of the "dynastic cycle." In Yan'an, Mao had suggested to the journalist Huang Yanpei that it could be overcome through democracy—following this through in his own way. Xi said that what condemned dynasties was corruption and division; what was needed was discipline, unity, and greater adherence to ideology.[9]

In 2019, the CPC released an app, *Xuéxí qiángguó* 学习强国, which can mean either "study and strengthen the nation" or "study Xi and strengthen the nation." A gamified, digital Little Red Book, political study session, and pocket *dang'an* (personal file) in one, the app lets users earn points while mastering Xi Jinping Thought. The CPC required its members and many government workers to spend time on the app every day, with real-world consequences depending on how well they applied themselves.

The app, part of a broader digitalization of propaganda, fits in with other social credit systems that follow Legalist principles of reward and punishment and are being rolled out in stages and across different platforms around the country. Approved behavior such as donating to charity, caring for the elderly, or volunteering to help in a harvest might be rewarded with a hotel upgrade, a better job, or faster internet speeds. Failing to show up for a restaurant booking, not paying a debt, displaying tattoos, or spreading political "rumors" could result, depending on the seriousness of the offense, in being banned from train or plane travel, or even being denied a good job or subjected to public shaming on giant digital billboards.

To help citizens parse the intricacies of Xi Jinping Thought, the *People's Daily* published a helpful guide in the form of a mind map.

Social credit is part of a larger system of data collection and other forms of technological and human surveillance that, by 2020, made the PRC citizenry one of the most monitored on Earth. Some cities boast more than a hundred CCTV cameras per thousand residents.[10] The PRC's Skynet Project, *tiānwǎng* 天网, integrates big data, biodata, facial recognition, and human systems of surveillance and control, and takes its name from a line in Laozi's *Dao De Jing*: "Nothing escapes heaven's vast net."[11]

In mid-2020, the net was cast even wider with the announcement of a new "rectification" campaign to purge the PRC's legal and security apparatuses of corrupt and "disloyal" elements. The Ministry of Justice described it as a "self-revolution of scraping bones to rid the poison, and a cleansing." The State Council, meanwhile, issued regulations banning government and party cadres from expressing any ideas that deviated from the party line, even in private conversation, or reading or viewing unauthorized materials in their free time, bringing to mind the Qin chancellor Li Si's banning of old books and songs.[12] Scholars were buried by other means. For example, Xǔ Zhāngrùn (b. 1962), professor of law at the prestigious Tsinghua University and one of Xi's sharpest critics, lost his job, his pension fund, and his freedom to publish, while being forbidden access to any form of financial support; others have been arrested, in a system that all but guarantees a prison sentence (99 percent of those charged with a crime receive a guilty verdict in the PRC's courts). Not since the Cultural Revolution has the CPC attempted such totalitarian control over people's lives.

Xi has named the biggest threats to China as invasion, subversion, and division.[13] He also likes to quote a passage by the Song dynasty neo-Confucian official Su Shi (aka the poet Su

Dongpo): "Of all the disasters under heaven, the most damaging is that of the appearance of social stability when elements of instability lurk beneath the surface. To passively observe such a disaster without acting to defeat it will let it develop to the point of no return."[14]

## ELEMENTS OF INSTABILITY

The annual meetings of the National People's Congress and the CPPCC feature a parade of Tibetans, Uyghurs, and others in colorful traditional costumes. But state ethnic policy has become increasingly and coercively assimilatory, promoting a "Chinese" nationality that supersedes ethnicity. The prioritization of Putonghua over indigenous languages in schools, ever-increasing levels of Han migration to "autonomous" regions, suppression of religious practices, and rising levels of policing, surveillance, and control have left Xinjiang, Tibet, and other regions with a native majority non-Han population, like Inner Mongolia, simmering with discontent.

In Xinjiang, following a series of violent incidents between Uyghurs and Hans, and several isolated terrorist attacks by advocates of Uyghur independence, the Chinese government ramped up its military presence, policing, and surveillance in the region. From 2017, the state began interning reportedly a million or more Uyghurs, Kazakhs, and other Muslims, some for growing a beard, owning a Qur'an (Koran), or having too many children, in what became hundreds of detention camps. Accounts by survivors or relatives of detainees that reach the West describe torture, starvation, the removal of children, hard labor, and gratuitous cruelty such as the forced consumption of pork and alcohol, and other measures that human rights advocates claim amount to cultural genocide.[15] Thousands of mosques and shrines have been destroyed or converted into bars or shops. Beijing describes the camps as both "de-radicalization" centers and vocational training schools. It refutes all accusations of abuse and argues that Xinjiang's high per capita gross domestic product (in 2018, three times that of India) is evidence of "human rights protection."

In the decade beginning in 2009, more than a hundred Tibetans self-immolated in protest at policies including the separation of children from their families. The Dalai Lama has also used the term "cultural genocide." In 2020, new regulations forbade the flying of prayer flags, a popular religious practice that made for one of the most striking features of the Tibetan landscape.

These stories are still unfolding; their roots lie too deep in history for simple resolution.

The CPC under Xi has also sought to crush other kinds of religious practice. By 2018, the Kaifeng Jewish community, which once borrowed the words of Yue Fei's tattoo to proclaim its loyalty to China, had dwindled to about five hundred people, mostly nonobservant. Government agents raided the few remaining Jewish community centers, ripping down Hebrew texts and throwing dirt into mikvahs (ritual baths).[16] A common thread in the attacks on practicing Muslims, Jews, Tibetan Buddhists, members of "non-patriotic" (unsanctioned) Christian and Catholic churches, as well as the Falungong, is real or perceived links to foreign powers, states, or organizations.

Taiwan is another "element of instability." In 2020, President Tsai Ing-wen (b. 1956), of the island's anti-reunification Democratic Progressive Party, won her second term by a landslide. Surveys revealed that a record 83.2 percent of the population identified as Taiwanese, only 5.3 percent as Chinese, and 6.7 percent as both (the rest declined to answer).[17] Under Xi, the PRC has pressured countries, international organizations, airlines, and corporations to isolate Taiwan or accede to its view that it is an integral part of China, and repeated long-standing threats to take the island by force.

In Hong Kong, increasing violations of the "one country, two systems" rule, including the cross-border kidnapping of independent publishers and booksellers, sparked a series of protest movements. In 2019, these culminated in the biggest demonstrations in the territory's history, after chief executive Carrie Lam proposed an extradition law that would allow Hong Kong citizens who had violated Chinese law—by agitating for democracy, for example—to be sent to the mainland for trial. Protest slogans including "Reclaim Hong Kong, revolution of our times!" and calls for a "triple strike" by students, workers, and businesses—the term used by anti-imperialist activists in the early twentieth century—infuriated the CPC, which blamed the unrest on foreign agitators.[18] Over the seven months of protest, police used both nonlethal and live ammunition, tear gas, pepper spray, and water cannons on protesters, some of whom responded with Molotov cocktails and bricks. Hong Kong had not seen such violence since the riots of 1967. Lam ultimately withdrew the extradition bill but refused the protesters' other demands, including an independent investigation into police brutality. In local council elections at the end of the year, the only elections for which there is universal suffrage, the pro-democracy opposition swept the polls.

In 2020, the National People's Congress passed a national security law for Hong Kong that outlawed "subversion," nullified the guarantees of legislative and judicial autonomy in the Basic Law, and authorized mainland secret police to operate in Hong Kong. There were mass arrests of pro-democracy activists and raids on independent media. The principle of "one country, two systems" was, for all intents and purposes, dead.

On the mainland, the New Era signaled the end of tolerance for the nascent civil society that developed in the 1980s and 1990s around issues such as feminism, workers' rights, and the recognition of LGBTQI+ communities—even as Taiwan became the first place in Asia to legalize same-sex marriage in 2019. In the days leading up to International Women's Day in 2015, Beijing police arrested five women planning to demonstrate against sexual harassment. The detaining of the "Feminist Five" marked the first suppression of women's rights activism in the history of the PRC. Feminism, *nǚquán* 女权, joined the authorities' ever-expanding list of censored words, followed not long after by #MeToo, despite (or because of) high-profile cases of sexual harassment. In the World Economic Forum's 2019 Gender Gap Index, the PRC ranked 106 out of 153 countries, after falling in the rankings for eleven years in a row.[19]

Workers' rights are a sensitive issue for a party that attained power as the voice of the working classes. In 2018, China's booming economy began to slow, with growth falling under 7 percent for the first time since 1990. Layoffs, reduced hours, and unpaid wages provoked thousands of strikes and demonstrations, which were quickly suppressed. When members of campus Marxist societies joined the fight for workplace rights, police arrested students as well, some of whom sang "The Internationale" as they were carted away.

Mao had urged young people to rebel. From 1960, every high school literature class read Sima Qian's biography of Chén Shèng, the anti-Qin rebel who had "only to wave his arms for the whole empire to answer like an echo." In 2019, textbooks replaced this story with a passage about Zhōu Yàfū (c. 199–143 BCE), a Han dynasty general famous for adhering to rules and regulations.[20]

The year 2020 marked the thirty-seventh year in the traditional sixty-year calendrical cycle. *Gēngzǐ* years, 庚子, as they're called, are associated with disaster and hardship. Previous ones include 1840, the year of the First Opium War; 1900, the year of the Boxer uprising; and 1960, the height of China's great famine.

The COVID-19 pandemic, which may have begun in a Wuhan seafood market, led to a series of rolling crises for Beijing in 2020. The young Wuhan doctor Lǐ Wénliàng (1985–2020) tried to warn colleagues about the disease but was pressured into silence by police, eventually succumbing to COVID-19 himself. After his death, the people of Wuhan leaned out their windows and shouted his name into the night. The whistleblower argued on his deathbed that "a healthy society should have more than one voice."

His colleague Aì Fēn, head of emergency at Wuhan Central Hospital, who alerted other medics about the disease, was also castigated by hospital officials and ordered not to spread "rumors"; later, she said in an interview that if she'd known what was to come, she'd have spoken out regardless of the consequences.[21] In frantic damage-control mode, the CPC removed the interview from the Chinese internet and claimed Li Wenliang as a loyal party member and "martyr," laying the blame for his silencing at the feet of local authorities.

To get Dr. Ai Fen's words past the censors, netizens translated them into emojis (left), Morse code, Klingon—and even oracle bone script (right).

As the pandemic spread, resulting in millions of infections and deaths and damaging economies globally, anti-Chinese racism and anti-CPC sentiment spread with it. Questions about when PRC officials became aware of the virus led to scrutiny of the PRC's responsibilities as a global power. The pugnacious response from online Wolf Warriors and some diplomats to even measured criticism undid years of efforts by the PRC to promote itself as a stable and benign actor on the world stage. As 2020 drew to a close, there was international apprehension about the coming of a new Cold War—or worse.

By framing all criticism, whether from within or outside of the mainland, as "anti-China," the CPC claims to stand for Chinese people everywhere in a hostile world. Within the CPC, however, cracks in Xi's support were showing. In mid-2020, Cài Xiá (b. 1952), a retired political science professor from the

Central Party School, a key training institute for party cadres, accused Xi of having "single-handedly killed a party and a country," acting like a "mafia boss," and turning the CPC into a "political zombie."[22] From exile in the United States, she claimed that 70 percent of CPC members wanted to follow the older path of reform and opening up that had brought such remarkable changes to China over the previous decades.

Perhaps she's right. Or maybe the Wolf Warrior patriots, permanently enraged over the "century of humiliation" and knowing little of the self-inflicted wounds of the Maoist era or Tiananmen Square, represent majority opinion, as they, and the official press, claim. Then again, maybe when the voices of the dissidents, iconoclasts, eccentrics, wits, free spirits, and "friends with arguments" who have enlivened Chinese society and culture for so long are silenced by censorship, fear, or imprisonment, they only appear to.

The present is full of echoes, premonitions, and reverberations from the past. Does the New Era herald the rise of a unifying autocracy to outdo that of Qin Shihuang in severity and longevity? Or will it produce a China that realizes Hongwu's dream of corruption-free governance, as well as an expansive and prosperous realm, with a glorious civilization to make Qianlong proud?

Or might this new era, as so many old ones before it, be cut short by the contemporary equivalent of palace intrigues and popular rebellions?

China's human, cultural, and economic potential is limitless. The CPC under Xi Jinping's leadership believes that the PRC can fulfill this potential without relaxing—and while even tightening—its control over Chinese society, culture, and intellectual life, and suppressing minority cultures and populations.

But historically, China has flourished most in times distinguished by their diversity and openness, such as the Tang dynasty. And what we think of as Chinese civilization is the product of myriad interactions and exchanges between the Han and the peoples and cultures of Central Asia, the Far Southwest, the Northeast, and beyond.

The PRC's economy and technology industries may well overtake those of the United States, and militarily, the PRC is certain to keep flexing its muscles in the East and South China Seas and the Taiwan Strait in ways that will challenge, if not reshape, the world order. Yet the PRC may struggle to see its soft power—the power of attraction—match its hard power.

The only way to learn from history is to learn history. Disparate voices and competing narratives inevitably inhabit a history as long as China's. The CPC prefers to keep it simple, using history to bolster its claim to be the legitimate rulers of this ancient nation. But as the Song dynasty historian Sima Guang wrote: "Listen to all sides if you want to be enlightened; rely on one if you would stay in the dark." And there's nowhere darker than inside an iron house.

The New Era of Xi Jinping is, so far, a blink of the historical eye. Conjectures on how long it will last or what will come next, I leave to those who can find answers in the *I Ching*. But if the future is unknowable, history can at least make it less surprising.

# Acknowledgments

This book is dedicated to Professor Lea Williams of Brown University, whose introductory course on East Asian history hooked me on the study of China in 1973, and whose insistence that I study the Chinese language changed my life.

My next great mentor, occasional collaborator, one-time husband, and lifelong friend, Geremie R. Barmé, has, ever since our first meeting in Hong Kong in 1981, guided my understanding of Chinese history, including how its sources, themes, concepts, and even personalities have echoed down the ages. In particular, his theory of New Sinology, which stresses the role of language, culture, and history in a multidisciplinary approach that engages with past and present debates and discussion across the Chinese world, deeply influences my own approach. His books and other writings, including on the chinaheritage.net website and its predecessor, chinaheritagequarterly.org, have been invaluable resources for this book. I am so grateful for the time he has taken to read a draft and comment on it.

David Brophy, Gloria Davies, Jaime FlorCruz, Olivier Krischer, Melissa Macauley, Antony Dapiran, and Qin Yang have all taken time out of their busy lives to read some or all of this book in manuscript and offer invaluable advice. The writer Xue Yiwei went above and beyond with his detailed comments on my draft, as did Jeffrey Wasserstrom, himself a model popular historian of China. The book is infinitely better for all their expert oversight. I kowtow to them all. I alone am responsible for any errors and any views expressed herein.

The Australian Centre on China in the World at the Australian National University, where I'm an associate and editorial consultant, has provided me, a freelance writer, with an academic base and colleagues. These include is Dr. Chen Mengxue, who helped answer many demographic and other questions that had me stumped.

Jade Muratore was my right-hand woman on this project. I don't know what I would have done without her sharp editorial eye, knack for research and fact-checking, resourcefulness at sourcing illustrations, and ability to read my handwriting. She takes credit, too, for inserting "mammoth extinction" into the timeline. Em Jaay double-checked all the diacritics for names and Chinese expressions. Thank you to Guo Jian as well.

I stood on the shoulders of giants to write this. I turned time and again to the work of Professor Jonathan D. Spence of Yale University, and to Jacques Gernet's *A History of Chinese Civilization*, as well as the magnificent five-volume *The Chinese Classics*, annotated and translated by James Legge for the Hong Kong University Press. Ray Hwang's *1587: A Year of No Significance*, and Ha Jin's more recent, magnificent biography of the Tang poet Li Bai, *The Banished Immortal*, are among the many great works from which I drew inspiration and knowledge.

For the English translations of classic texts, I relied as much as possible on great translators such as Legge, Professor John Minford, and the late Simon Leys (Pierre Ryckmans). I thank all of the authors and translators who have given permission for me to quote from their work here. Where the translator isn't credited in the notes, the translation is my own.

Publisher Chris Feik didn't know that writing a book like

this had been my dream for more than forty years when he approached me to do it. Julia Carlomagno, my fabulous editor at Black Inc., made every step of the Long March to publication by my side; I owe more than I can express to her thoughtful comments, criticism, and guidance. I'm indebted to everyone at Black Inc., including designer Akiko Chan, proofreader Jo Rosenberg, publicist Sallie Butler, and rights manager Erin Sandiford, who made this book happen despite Melbourne's pandemic lockdowns. I am deeply grateful to Matthew Lore, Anna Bliss, Melinda Kennedy, Zach Pace, Jeanne Tao, and the rest of the team at The Experiment for helping to make the American edition shine hard.

Gaby Naher of Left Bank Literary has been the best and most steadfast of literary agents.

I live and work on the land of the Gadigal people, over which sovereignty has never been ceded. I also wrote some of this book on sovereign Darug and Gundungurra land, at the Varuna Writer's House. I'm grateful to the Eleanor Dark Foundation for maintaining Varuna, an oasis for writers, full of calm and care. Josemi furnishes my other oasis.

Generations of Chinese thinkers and poets, artists and inventors have deeply enriched the world and inspire me always. I'll leave you with this poem, written almost one thousand years ago by Su Dongpo:

> *May we all live long,*
> *May we all share,*
> *Though myriad miles apart*
> *The same fair moon.*[1]
> 但願人長久
> 千里共嬋娟

# Notes

**INTRODUCTION**

1. "Beijing Says 400 Million Chinese Cannot Speak Mandarin," *BBC News*, September 6, 2013. Original Ministry of Education press release in Chinese: old.moe.gov.cn//publicfiles/business/htmlfiles/moe/s8316/201409/174957 .html.
2. Confucius, *The Analects of Confucius* (trans. Simon Leys), p. xxvi.
3. Juan González de Mendoza, *Historia del gran Reino de la China*, 1585.
4. In Chinese: 當局稱迷旁觀見審

**CHAPTER 1: ORIGINS**

1. See Minna Haapanen, "The Royal Consort Fu Hao of the Shang," in Kenneth J. Hammond (ed.), *The Human Tradition in Premodern China*, Scholarly Resources, Wilmington, 2002, pp. 1–13.
2. Book Nine, Odes of Wei, Ode 6, Verse 3, *Book of Odes* (trans. the author).

**CHAPTER 2: THE ZHOU**

1. Sun Tzu [Sunzi], *The Art of War* (trans. Ralph D. Sawyer with Mei-chün Sawyer), p. 129.
2. Confucius, *The Analects of Confucius* (trans. Simon Leys), p. 67.
3. Ibid., p. 89.
4. Ibid., p. 76.
5. Ibid., p. 12.
6. Arthur Waley, *Three Ways of Thought in Ancient China*, p. 14.
7. Liu Xiaobo, *No Enemies, No Hatred: Selected Essays and Poems* (ed. Perry Link, Tienchi Martin-Liao, and Liu Xia; trans. Thomas E. Moran), Harvard University Press, Cambridge, 2012, p. 192.
8. Simon Leys, "Foreword," in Confucius, *The Analects of Confucius* (trans. Simon Leys), p. xvi.
9. Director Ang Lee used Mencius's formulation 飲食男女 for the Chinese title of his 1994 film *Eat Drink Man Woman*.
10. Mencius, *The Chinese Classics Volume 2* (trans. James Legge), Hong Kong University Press, Hong Kong, 1960, p. 318.
11. Ibid., p. 167.
12. Laozi, quoted in "A Personal Tribute to C. P. FitzGerald" (trans. Wang Ling), in Donald Leslie et al. (eds.), *Essays on the Sources for Chinese History*, Australian National University Press, 1973, p. 1.
13. In Chinese: 道可道非常道
14. Laozi, *Tao Te Ching* (trans. John Minford), p. 317.

15. Bai Juyi, quoted in "Tao Te Ching—A New Translation of a Chinese Classic," *China Heritage*, Wairarapa Academy for New Sinology, November 20, 2018.

16. Waley, *Three Ways of Thought in Ancient China*, p. 14.

17. Unknown, *I Ching* (trans. John Minford), pp. xi, xiii.

18. Waley, *Three Ways of Thought in Ancient China*, p. 159.

19. Zha Jianying, "China's Heart of Darkness—Prince Han Fei & Chairman Xi Jinping (Prologue)," *China Heritage*, July 14, 2020.

## CHAPTER 3: THE QIN

1. Geremie Barmé, "China's Season of Major Political Anniversaries," lecture, Asia Society, New York, November 13, 2019.

2. Sima Qian, *Records of the Historian* (trans. Yang Hsien-yi and Gladys Yang), Commercial Press, Hong Kong, 1974, pp. 170–72, 177–78.

3. In Chinese: 焚書坑儒

4. In Chinese: 秦始皇算什么? 他只坑了四百六十八个儒, 我们坑了四万六千个儒 ... 你骂我们是秦始皇, 不对, 我们超过了秦始皇一百倍; 骂我们是秦始皇, 是独裁者, 我们一概承认.

5. Yangyang Cheng, "A Birthday Letter to the People's Republic," *China File*, September 28, 2019.

6. Quoted in C. P. Fitzgerald, *China: A Short Cultural History* (third edition), Praeger Publishers, New York, 1972, p. 150.

## CHAPTER 4: THE HAN

1. In Chinese: 牝雞司晨

2. "Evoking Past Glories in the Desert," *China Daily*, April 28, 2003.

3. Sima Qian quoted in Bret Hinsch, *Passions of the Cut Sleeve: The Male Homosexual Tradition in China*, Berkeley, University of California Press, 1990, p. 36.

4. See Jeremiah Jenne, "Long Road to Abolition: Legal, Social and Cultural Barriers to Ending China's Forced Labor Tradition," *World of Chinese*, November 27, 2016.

5. Sima Qian (trans. Wang Ling) quoted in Wm. Theodore de Bary and Richard Lufrano (eds.), *Sources of Chinese Tradition: Volume 2*, Columbia University Press, New York and Chichester, 1999, p. 234.

6. Wang Mang quoted in Mark Elvin, *The Pattern of the Chinese Past*, Stanford University Press, Palo Alto, 1973, p. 31.

7. See Mike Dash, "Emperor Wang Mang: China's First Socialist?," *Smithsonian Magazine*, December 9, 2011.

8. *Chronicles of Huayang* (trans. Chen Mengxue).

9. Ban Zhao, *Lessons for Women* (trans. USC US-China Institute), USC US-China Institute, 2020.

10. Cao Cao, "Graveyard Song" (trans. John Frodsham) in John Minford and Joseph Lau (eds.), *Classical Chinese Literature, Volume 1*, p. 419.

**CHAPTER 5: THE GREAT DISUNITY**

1.  In Chinese: 先主每入，衷心常凛凛. From *Records of the Three Kingdoms*, vol. 37.

2.  Zhuge Liang, "On Deploying the Army" (trans. Robert Joe Cutter), in John Minford and Joseph Lau (eds.), *Classical Chinese Literature, Volume 1*, p. 594.

3.  Cao Cao, "The Empty City" (trans. John Minford) in ibid., p. 553, footnote 20.

4.  See Rafe de Crespigny, "The Three Kingdoms and Western Jin: A History of China in the Third Century AD," *East Asian History*, no. 1, June 1991, Australian National University, Canberra, p. 34.

5.  Liu Ling (trans. Richard B. Mather) in John Minford and Joseph Lau (eds.), *Classical Chinese Literature, Volume 1*, p. 669.

6.  Ji Kang, letter to Shan Tao, in "Portraits of Individualists" (trans. Geremie Barmé), Geremie Barmé and Linda Jaivin, *New Ghosts, Old Dreams*, pp. 194–95.

7.  James Millward, "Mulan: More Hun than Han," *Los Angeles Review of Books China Channel*, September 25, 2020.

8.  See Jacques Gernet, *A History of Chinese Civilization* (trans. J. R. Foster), p. 180.

9.  Wang Xizhi, "Preface to the Orchid Pavilion Poems" (trans. H. C. Chang), in John Minford and Joseph Lau (eds.), *Classical Chinese Literature, Volume 1*, p. 479.

10. Pierre Ryckmans, "The Chinese Attitude Towards the Past," lecture, Australian National University, Canberra, July 16, 1986.

**CHAPTER 6: THE TANG**

1.  See Qi Dongfang, "The Elegance of Tang Women," in Cao Yin (ed.), *Treasures from the Silk Road Capital*, Art Gallery of New South Wales, Sydney, 2016, pp. 99–100.

2.  See Dong Guodong, *Population History of China, Volume 2: Sui, Tang, and Wudai*, Fudan University Press, Shanghai, 2002, p. 181.

3.  Taizong (trans. Geremie Barmé) in "Rudd Rewrites the Rules of Engagement," *Sydney Morning Herald*, April 12, 2008.

4.  Lin Yutang, *Lady Wu: A True Story*, William Heinemann, London, 1957, p. ix.

5.  Han Yu in Wm. Theodore de Bary, Wing-tsit Chan, and Burton Watson (eds.), *Sources of Chinese Tradition*, Columbia University Press, New York, 1960, p. 373.

6.  Confucius, *The Analects of Confucius* (trans. Simon Leys), p. 27.

7.  François Cheng, *Chinese Poetic Writing* (trans. Donald A. Riggs and Jerome P. Seaton), Indiana University Press, Bloomington, 1982, pp. 10–11.

8.  In Chinese: 天生我才必有用

9.  Xue Tao, "Ten Poems of Separation" (trans. Jeanne Larsen), in John Minford and Joseph Lau (eds.), *Classical Chinese Literature, Volume 1*, p. 968.

10. Li Bai (trans. Ha Jin) in Ha Jin, *The Banished Immortal*, p. 176.

11. Bai Juyi (trans. Herbert Giles) in John Minford and Joseph Lau (eds.), *Classical Chinese Literature, Volume 1*, pp. 885–86.

12. Du Fu, "Road to Pengya" (trans. Burton Watson), in Wm. Theodore de Bary and Richard Lufrano (eds.), *Sources of Chinese Tradition: Volume 1*, p. 786.

13. Jacques Gernet, *A History of Chinese Civilization*, pp. 248–51.
14. Wei Zhuang, "The Lament of the Lady Qin" (trans. Lionel Giles), in John Minford and Joseph Lau (eds.), *Classical Chinese Literature, Volume I*, p. 936.

## CHAPTER 7: THE SONG

1. See C. P. Fitzgerald, *China: A Short Cultural History*, pp. 380–82.
2. Kent Deng, "China's Population Expansion and Its Causes During the Qing Period, 1644–1911," London School of Economics Economic History Working Papers No. 219, London, 2015, p. 4.
3. Lin Yutang, *The Gay Genius*, John Day Company, New York, 1947; reprinted in John Meskill (ed.), *Wang An-shih: Practical Reformer?: Problems in Asian Civilizations*, DC Heath and Company, Lexington, 1963, p. 62.
4. See Lu Zhidan, *Mao Zedong Critiques Historical Figures, Volume 2*, Beijing Book Company, Beijing, 2016.
5. Étienne Balazs, *Chinese Civilization and Bureaucracy*, Yale University Press, New Haven, 1964, pp. 88–90.
6. See Jacques Gernet, *A History of Chinese Civilization*, pp. 288–89.
7. Ibid., p. 341.
8. In Chinese: 生當作人傑，死亦為鬼雄; see Alex Colville, "Li Qingzhao, Poet, 'The Most Talented Woman in History,'" *SupChina*, April 6, 2020.
9. Su Dongpo in John Minford and Joseph Lau (eds.), *Classical Chinese Literature, Volume I*, p. 699.
10. Su Dongpo, "Memories of the Past at Red Cliff," in Yang Xianyi and Gladys Yang (eds.), *Poetry and Prose of the Tang and Song*, Panda Books, Beijing, 1984, p. 255.
11. See Mark Elvin, *The Pattern of the Chinese Past*, Stanford University Press, Palo Alto, 1973, p. 87.

## CHAPTER 8: THE MONGOL YUAN

1. See Timothy Brook, "The Great Khan and His Portraitist" in *Great State*.
2. Marco Polo quoted in Colonel Sir Henry Yule (ed.), *The Book of Ser Marco Polo, the Venetian: Concerning the Kingdoms and Marvels of the East, Volume 1*, John Murray, London, 1903, p. 2.
3. Étienne Balazs, *Chinese Civilization and Bureaucracy*, p. 84.
4. Wu Zimu quoted in ibid., p. 91.
5. Jacques Gernet, *A History of Chinese Civilization*, pp. 376–79.
6. Ibid., pp. 376–79.
7. Genghis Khan quoted in René Grousset, *Conquerer of the World: The Life of Chingis-khan*, Viking Press, New York, 1966, p. 287.

## CHAPTER 9: THE MING

1. Jacques Gernet, *A History of Chinese Civilization*, p. 391.
2. Kenneth J. Hammond, "The Eunuch Wang Zhen and the Ming Dynasty," *The Human Tradition in Premodern China*, Rowman & Littlefield, Maryland, 2002, p. 146.

3. See Duncan M. Campbell, "The Huntington Library's Volume of the Yongle Encyclopedia: A Bibliographical and Historical Note," *East Asian History*, Australian Centre for China in the World, Australian National University, 2020.

4. Ibid.

5. See Ian Johnson, "A Radical Realist View of Tibetan Buddhism at the Rubin," *New York Review of Books*, July 13, 2019.

6. See Julia Lovell, "Beauty and Bloodbaths in the Ming Dynasty," *Guardian*, September 20, 2014.

7. See C. P. Fitzgerald, *China: A Short Cultural History*, p. 474.

8. Kenneth J. Hammond, "The Eunuch Wang Zhen and the Ming Dynasty," p. 153.

9. Jacques Gernet, *A History of Chinese Civilization*, p. 441.

10. Wen-yuan Qian, *The Great Inertia: Scientific Stagnation in Traditional China*, Croom Helm, London, 1985, pp. 90, 25.

11. Nancy Berliner (ed.), *Beyond the Screen: Chinese Furniture of the 16th and 17th Centuries*, Museum of Fine Arts, Boston, 1996, p. 32.

12. C. P. Fitzgerald, *China: A Short Cultural History*, p. 470.

13. Jacques Gernet, *A History of Chinese Civilization*, pp. 425–26.

14. Craig Clunas quoted in Julia Lovell, "Beauty and Bloodbaths in the Ming Dynasty."

15. Jonathan D. Spence, *The Search for Modern China*, pp. 44–45.

## CHAPTER 10: THE MANCHU QING

1. Dorgon quoted in Michael R. Godley, "The End of the Queue: Hair as Symbol in Chinese History," *China Heritage Quarterly*, no. 27, September 2011, chinaheritagequarterly.org/features.php?searchterm=027_queue .inc&issue=027.

2. Kong Shangren quoted in Jonathan D. Spence, *The Search for Modern China*, p. 64.

3. Jonathan D. Spence, *Emperor of China*, p. xviii.

4. Geremie R. Barmé, *The Forbidden City*, p. xiii.

5. Geremie Barmé, "The Garden of Perfect Brightness: A Life in Ruins," The Fifty-Seventh George Ernest Morrison Lecture in Ethnology 1996, Australian National University, Canberra, 1996, p. 125.

6. See Jeffrey Wasserstrom and Maura Elizabeth Cunningham, *China in the 21st Century*, p. 33.

7. Gong Zizhen quoted in Jonathan D. Spence, *The Search for Modern China*, pp. 145–46.

8. See Henrietta Harrison, "The Qianlong Emperor's Letter to George III and the Early-Twentieth-Century Origins of Ideas About Traditional China's Foreign Relations," *American Historical Review*, vol. 122, no. 3, June 2017, pp. 680–701.

9. Quoted in Jeffrey Wasserstrom, *Vigil: Hong Kong on the Brink*, Columbia Global Reports, New York, 2020, p. 18.

10. "A Letter from the American Baptist Missionary Rev. I J Roberts," quoted in Prescott Clarke and J. S. Gregory (eds.), *Western Reports on the Taiping*, Australia National University Press, Canberra, 1982, p. 19.

11. *Departed but Not Forgotten*, Women of China, Beijing, 1984, p. 142.

12. Reverend I. J. Roberts quoted in Li Chien-nung, *Political History of China 1840–1928*, Van Nostrand, New York, 1956, p. 81.

13. See Peter Gilbert and Jim Tate, *China, Part 1: Early Western Contacts to 1911*, Australian National University Press, Canberra, p. 55.

14. Geremie Barmé, "The Garden of Perfect Brightness," p. 131.

15. Ibid., p. 132.

16. Charles Gordon quoted in Young-tsu Wong, *A Paradise Lost: The Imperial Garden Yuanming Yuan*, University of Hawai'i Press, Honolulu, 2001, p. 149.

17. In Chinese: 老嫗筐中宋本書，牧童壁上元人畫；quoted in Geremie Barmé, "The Garden of Perfect Brightness," p. 137.

18. Victor Hugo, "The Sack of the Summer Palace," letter to Captain Butler, November 25, 1861.

19. Jonathan D. Spence, *The Search for Modern China*, p. 221.

20. See Jie Liu, "China's Views of History: The Prospect of Changing Self-Image," *Journal of Contemporary East Asia Studies*, vol. 2, no. 1, 2013, pp. 55–76.

21. Donald G. Cheng et al., "Loss of a Recorded Heritage: Destruction of Chinese Books in the Peking Siege of 1900," *Library Trends*, vol. 55, no. 3, 2007, p. 435.

22. Jonathan D. Spence, *The Search for Modern China*, p. 233.

23. See Jie Liu, "China's Views of History," p. 62.

24. Andrea Bachner, "1899: Oracle Bones, That Dangerous Supplement," in David Der-wei Wang (ed.), *A New Literary History of Modern China*, Belknap Press/Harvard University Press, Cambridge, 2017.

25. See Lee Yee, "China, the Man-Child of Asia: Hong Kong Apostasy," *China Heritage*, September 26, 2019.

26. Lin Qi, "The Poisoned Palace—Mystery of Last Emperor's Death," *China Daily*, November 21, 2008.

## CHAPTER 11: THE REPUBLIC

1. *Shenzhou Daily*, August 27, 1912, quoted in Yuxin Ma, *Women Journalists and Feminism in China, 1898–1937*, Cambria Press, 2010, New York, p. 115.

2. See David Moser, *A Billion Voices*, Penguin, Melbourne, 2016, introduction, passim.

3. See Jonathan D. Spence, *The Search for Modern China*, p. 282.

4. Yan Xishan quoted in ibid., p. 289.

5. Zheng Wang, *Women in the Chinese Enlightenment: Oral and Textual Histories*, University of California Press, California, 1999, p. 98.

6. Chen Duxiu quoted in Eric Fish, "1919 to 2019: A Century of Youth Protest and Ideological Conflict Around May 4," *SupChina*, May 1, 2019.

7. In Chinese: 是什麼時代的人，說什麼時代的話. From an essay published in *New Youth*, edition 4, vol. 4, 1918 (trans. Victor Mair); republished online in "Hu Shih and Chinese Language Reform," *Language Log*, February 4, 2017.

8. Translated by Gloria Davies, *Lu Xun's Revolution*, Harvard University Press, Cambridge, 2013, p. 232.

9. Translated by Theodore D. Huters in Leo Ou-fan Lee (ed.), *Lu Xun and His Legacy*, University of California Press, California, 1985, p. 132.

10. Different sources give different figures. This comes from *Over There: The Pictorial Chronicle of Chinese Laborer Corps in the Great War*, Shandong Pictorial Publishing House, Shandong, p. 2.

11. Translated in "Remarks by Deputy National Security Advisor Matt Pottinger to the Miller Center at the University of Virginia," White House, Washington, DC, May 4, 2020.

12. Translation in Dorothy Ko, *Cinderella's Sisters: A Revisionist History of Footbinding*, University of California Press, California, 2005, p. 77. Wording adjusted by the author.

13. Hu Shih, translated in Geremie Barmé and Linda Jaivin, *New Ghosts, Old Dreams*, p. 344.

14. See Tien-Wei Wu, "A Review of the Wuhan Debacle: The Kuomintang-Communist Split of 1927," *Journal of Asian Studies*, vol. 29, no. 1, 1969, pp. 125–43.

## CHAPTER 12: JAPANESE INVASION AND CIVIL WAR

1. Barbara W. Tuchman, *Sand Against the Wind: Stilwell and the American Experience in China, 1911–45*, London, Macmillan, 1971, Chapter 5.

2. Mao Zedong, "Report on an Investigation of the Peasant Movement in Hunan," March 1927, *Selected Works, Volume I*, Pergamon, Oxford, 2014, p. 28.

3. Chiang Kai-shek, "Essentials of the New Life Movement," speech, 1934, quoted in Wm. Theodore de Bary and Richard Lufrano (eds.), *Sources of Chinese History: Volume 2*, pp. 341–44.

4. See Edward E. Rice, *Mao's Way*, University of California Press, California, 1972, pp. 84–86.

5. Agnes Smedley, *Battle Hymn of China*, Victor Gollancz Ltd., London, 1944, pp. 121–22.

6. Mao Zedong quoted in Yang Jintao, "A Spirited Conversation Between Mao Zedong and Huang Yanpei: The Only Escape from the Nation-Dooming Dynastic Cycle Is 'Democracy,'" *People's Daily*, October 24, 2013 (in Chinese).

7. In Chinese: 脫褲子，割尾巴，洗澡

8. Wang Shiwei quoted in Simon Leys, "Bureaucrats," *Chinese Shadows*, Penguin, London, 1978, p. 125.

9. See Jonathan Watts, "Japan Guilty of Germ Warfare Against Thousands of Chinese," *Guardian*, August 28, 2002.

10. See Nicholas D. Kristof, "Unmasking Horror—A Special Report: Japan Confronting Gruesome War Atrocity," *The New York Times*, March 17, 1995.

11. James L. Baughman, *Henry R. Luce and the Rise of the American News Media*, John Hopkins University Press, Maryland, 2001, p. 143.

12. For official figures, see Nicholas D. Kristof, "Taipei Journal: The Horror of 2-28: Taiwan Rips Open the Past," *The New York Times*, April 3, 1992.

13. Dean Acheson, "United States Position on China, August 1949," introduction to *United States Relations with China, With Special Reference to the Period 1944–1949, US State Department*, 1949.

## CHAPTER 13: THE MAO YEARS

1. See Michael Pembroke, *Korea: Where the American Century Began*, Hardie Grant Books, Melbourne and London, 2018, pp. 69–70.

2. Ibid., p. xvi.

3. Minnie Chan, "China's Korean War Veterans Still Waiting for Answers, 60 Years On," *South China Morning Post*, July 28, 2013.

4. See Simon Leys, "Bureaucrats," passim.

5. In Chinese: 上有政策 下有对策 . Traditional version: 天高皇帝遠.

6. *China: Facts and Figures*, Foreign Language Press, Beijing, 1985, p. 153.

7. See Paul Clark, *Chinese Cinema: Culture and Politics Since 1949*, Cambridge University Press, Cambridge, 1987, p. 44.

8. Frank Dikötter, *The Tragedy of Liberation: A History of the Chinese Revolution, 1945–57*, Bloomsbury Publishing, London, 2013, p. 100.

9. Jonathan D. Spence, *The Search for Modern China*, p. 547.

10. Mao Zedong, "On the Co-Operative Transformation of Agriculture," July 31, 1955.

11. See Charles Hoffman, *Work Incentive Practices and Policies in the People's Republic of China*, State University of New York Press, New York, 1968.

12. In Chinese: 妇女能顶半边天

13. In Chinese: 引蛇出洞. Li Zhisui, *The Private Life of Chairman Mao* (trans. Tai Hung-chao), Random House, New York, 1994, pp. 201–2.

14. Mao Zedong, "On the Correct Handling of Contradictions Among the People," February 27, 1957.

15. See Christine Vidal, "The 1957–1958 Anti-Rightist Campaign in China: History and Memory (1978–2014)," C.C.J. Occasional Papers, no. 4, April 25, 2016.

16. Zhang Xianliang, *Grass Soup* (trans. Martha Avery), Secker & Warburg, London, 1994, p. 3.

17. Quoted in Yu Hua, "Revolution," in *China in Ten Words* (trans. Allan H. Barr), Duckworth Overlook, London.

18. Translation from Edward E. Rice, *Mao's Way*, p. 171.

19. Michael Harris Goodman, *The Last Dalai Lama*, Sidgwick & Jackson, London, 1986, p. 213.

20. Mao Zedong (trans. Geremie Barmé) in Geremie Barmé, "For Truly Great Men Look to This Age Alone," *China Heritage*, 27 January 2018.

21. See Jonathan D. Spence, *The Search for Modern China*, pp. 599–600.

22. In Chinese: 三分天灾七分人祸

23. See "Soviet Memorandum on the Sino-Indian Border Issue," Wilson Center Digital Archive, October 22, 1962.

24. Mao Zedong, *Reverberations: A New Translation of Complete Poems by Mao Tse-tung with Notes* (trans. Nancy T. Lin), Joint Publishing Co., Hong Kong, 1980, p. 77.

25. In Chinese: 无产阶级文化大革命

26. *Beijing Daily*, December 20, 1980, quoted in Youqin Wang, "Student Attacks Against Teachers: The Revolution of 1966," *Issues & Studies*, vol. 37, no. 2, March–April 2001.

27. Eric Gordon quoted in Roderick MacFarquhar and Michael Schoenhals, *Mao's Last Revolution*, Harvard University Press, 2009, p. 62.

28. Gao Yuan, *Born Red: A Chronicle of the Cultural Revolution*, p. 92.

29. Wang Jun quoted in Michael Meyer, *The Last Days of Old Beijing*, New York, Walker & Company, 2008, p. 288.

30. See Fan Ka Wai, "Epidemic Cerebrospinal Meningitis During the Cultural Revolution," *Extrême-Orient, Extrême-Occident*, 37, 2014.

31. See Benjamin Leung and Stephen Chiu, "A Social History of Industrial Strikes and the Labour Movement in Hong Kong 1946–1989," Social Sciences Research Centre Occasional Paper 3, Department of Sociology, University of Hong Kong, 1991, passim.

32. See Christopher DeWolf, "1967: When the Bank of China Building Became a Giant Propaganda Machine," *Zolima City Mag*, August 8, 2018.

33. Lee Yee quoted in Geremie Barmé, "The Double Ninth in 2019—Settling Scores, Fleeing the Qin and Eating Crabs," *China Heritage*, October 7, 2019.

34. See Song Yongyi, "The Successor's Successor: A Key Issue Dividing Mao Zedong and Lin Biao," *Modern China Studies*, vol. 23, no. 2, 2016.

## CHAPTER 14: THE REFORM ERA

1. Bei Dao, "The Answer" (trans. Bonnie S. McDougall), in *The August Sleepwalker*, New Directions Publishing Corporation, New York, 1990.

2. In Chinese: 实事求是 ("seek truth . . ."); 不管黑猫白猫，能捉老鼠的就是好猫˜ ("It doesn't matter . . ."); 摸着石头过河 ("Cross the river . . .").

3. In Chinese: 小朋友不听话，该打打屁股喽

4. Wei Jingsheng, "The Fifth Modernisation: Democracy," quoted in Wm. Theodore de Bary and Richard Lufrano (eds.), *Sources of Chinese History: Volume 2*, pp. 497–500.

5. "Jiang Qing's Last Words: Chairman, I Love You!," *Xinhua Net*, May 13, 2015 (in Chinese).

6. "Resolution on Certain Questions in the History of Our Party Since the Founding of the People's Republic of China" (trans. Wilson Center Digital Archive), Wilson Center Digital Archive, June 27, 1981.

7. Various documents from the Central Department of Propaganda, in Geremie Barmé, "Documenting the Demise," *Shades of Mao: The Posthumous Cult of the Great Leader*, M.E. Sharpe, Armonk, 1996, pp. 128–34.

8. In Chinese: 向前看 ("Look to the future"), 向钱看 ("Look to money")

9. Lu Xun, *Call to Arms* (in Chinese), from preface, Zhejiang Wenyi Chubanshe, 2018.

10. For complete text, see Geremie Barmé and Linda Jaivin, *New Ghosts, Old Dreams*, p. 24.

11. Ibid., p. 26.

12. In Chinese: 不该死的死了 该死的却没有死

13. Louisa Lim, *The People's Republic of Amnesia*, pp. 7–8: "Early Chinese report was 241, Red Cross estimated 2,600, which was corroborated by the Swiss ambassador who reported 2,700."

14. In Chinese: 姓社还是姓资

15. See "Confucius Teaches Culture," editorial, *China Daily*, 25 June 2014.

16. Reuters Life, "Controversial Confucius Statue Vanishes from Tiananmen," *Christian Science Monitor*, April 25, 2011.

17. See Amy H. Liu and Kevin Peters, "The Hanification of Xinjiang, China: The Economic Effects of the Great Leap West," in *Studies in Ethnicity and Nationalism*, vol. 17, no. 2, 2017.

18. Quoted and translated by Peter Hessler, "The Peace Corps Breaks Ties with China," *The New Yorker*, March 9, 2020.

19. Statistics compiled from UNICEF, the World Bank, and other sources. See "Figure 2.1: GDP Per Capita, 1978–2017," UNICEF, 2018, and "GDP Per Capita (Current $)," World Bank, 2019.

20. See Chen Guidi and Wu Chuntao, *Will the Boat Sink the Water?: The Struggle of Peasants in 21st-Century China* (trans. Zhu Hong), Fourth Estate, New York, 2006, pp. 151–54.

21. In Chinese: 水能载舟,亦能覆舟

22. See "Why Protests Are So Common in China," *The Economist*, October 4, 2018.

23. Sima Qian (trans. Geremie Barmé) in Geremie Barmé, "And Teachers, Then? They Just Do Their Thing!," *China Heritage*, no date.

24. See "Charter 08" (trans. Perry Link), *Reporters sans frontières*, December 2008.

25. See Jeremy Goldkorn, "Behind the Great Firewall," *China Story Yearbook 2012: Red Rising, Red Eclipse*, Australian Centre on China in the World, Australian National University, Canberra, 2012, pp. 172–78.

26. See John Garnaut, *The Rise and Fall of the House of Bo*, Penguin, Melbourne, 2012, p. 54.

27. David Barboza, "Billions in Hidden Riches for Family of Chinese Leader," *The New York Times*, October 25, 2012.

28. See Teddy Ng, "Hu Jintao Warns Graft Threatens Existence of Party and Nation," *South China Morning Post*, November 9, 2012.

29. Josh Freeman, "Illiberal China," *Los Angeles Review of Books China Channel*, September 20, 2019.

## CHAPTER 15: THE NEW ERA OF XI JINPING

1. See Geremie R. Barmé, "Chinese Dreams," *China Story Yearbook 2013: Civilising China*, Australian National University, Canberra, 2013, p. 9.

2. A viral phrase coined by Geremie R. Barmé.

3. Neil Thomas, "Members Only: Recruitment Trends in the Communist Party of China," *Macro Polo*, July 15, 2020.

4. In Chinese: 命运共同体

5. Geremie Barmé, "China's Season of Major Political Anniversaries," Asia Society, New York, November 13, 2019.

6. See Sean Mirski, "The South China Sea Dispute: A Brief History," *Lawfare*, June 8, 2015.

7. In Chinese: 明犯强汉者虽远必诛 (Western Han general); 犯我中华者虽远必诛 (*Wolf Warrior II*).

8. Zi Zhongyun (trans. Geremie Barmé) in "1900 and 2020—An Old Anxiety in a New Era," *China Heritage*, 28 April 2020.

9. See Yun Jiang and Adam Ni, "Dynastic Cycle: Mao and Xi," *China Neican*, July 12, 2020.

10. See Paul Bischoff, "Surveillance Camera Statistics: Which Cities Have the Most CCTV Cameras?," *Comparitech*, August 15, 2019.

11. In Chinese: 天网恢恢, 疏而不漏

12. Josh Rudolph, "Regulations on Party Members' Speech and Actions Outside of Work Hours," *China Digital Times*, June 15, 2020.

13. See Anne-Marie Brady, "Party Faithful: How China Spies—And How to Resist," *Australian Foreign Affairs*, no. 9, July 2020, p. 86.

14. In Chinese: 天下之患, 最不可为者, 名为治平无事, 而其实有不测之忧, 坐观其变而不为之所, 则恐至于不可救

15. Yu Ning, "Cotton Industry Symbolizes Xinjiang's Human Rights," *Global Times*, November 14, 2019.

16. See Etam Smallman, "China's Kaifeng Jews Date Back 1,400 years and Have an Unlikely Ambassador—A Teenager from Hong Kong," *South China Morning Post*, March 8, 2020.

17. See Lu Yi-hsuan and Dennis Xie, "New High of 83.2% See Themselves as Taiwanese: Poll," *Taipei Times*, February 25, 2020.

18. See Jeffrey Wasserstrom, *Vigil*, p. 62.

19. Klaus Schwab, *Global Gender Gap Report 2020*, World Economic Forum, Geneva, 2019.

20. See Esther Sunkyung Klein and Victor Fong, "The Changing 'Dream' in the Classroom: Literary Chinese Textbooks in the PRC," *Dreams: The China Story Yearbook 2019*, pp. 43–46.

21. Gong Jingqi, "Whistleblower," *Renwu Magazine*, March 10, 2020.

22. Lily Kuo, "'He Killed a Party and a Country': A Chinese Insider Hits Out at Xi Jinping," *Guardian*, August 18, 2020. "Mafia boss" 黑帮老大, "political zombie" 政治僵尸.

23. In Chinese: 兼听则明, 偏信则暗

## ACKNOWLEDGMENTS

1. Su Dongpo, "A Shared Perigean Moon" (trans. John Minford), *China Heritage*, April 8, 2020.

# Further Reading

Barmé, Geremie R., *The Forbidden City*, Profile Books, London, 2008.

Barmé, Geremie, and Linda Jaivin, (eds.), *New Ghosts, Old Dreams*, Times Books, New York, 1992.

Brook, Timothy, *Great State: China and the World*, Profile Books, London, 2019.

Cao Xueqin and Gao E., in *The Story of the Stone, Volumes 1–5* (trans. David Hawkes and John Minford), Penguin Books, London, 1973–1980.

Confucius, *The Analects of Confucius* (trans. Simon Leys), W. W. Norton & Company, New York and London, 1997.

Davies, Gloria, *Lu Xun's Revolution: Writing in a Time of Violence*, Harvard University Press, Cambridge, 2013.

Gao Yuan, *Born Red: A Chronicle of the Cultural Revolution*, Stanford University Press, Palo Alto, 1987.

Gernet, Jacques, *A History of Chinese Civilization* (trans. J. R. Foster), Cambridge University Press, New York, 1985.

Ha Jin, *The Banished Immortal: A Life of Li Bai*, Pantheon Books, New York, 2019.

Huang, Ray, *1587: A Year of No Significance*, Yale University Press, New Haven and London, 1981.

Lanling Xiaoxiao Sheng, *Chin P'ing Mei (The Plum in the Golden Vase)* (trans. David Tod Roy), vols. 1–5, Princeton University Press, Princeton, 1997–2015.

Lim, Louisa, *The People's Republic of Amnesia: Tiananmen Revisited*, Oxford University Press, Oxford, 2014.

Lao She, *Rickshaw Boy* (trans. Howard Goldblatt), HarperCollins, New York, 2010.

Lao Tzu, *Tao Te Ching* (trans. with an introduction and commentary by John Minford), Viking, New York, 2018.

Lovell, Julia, *The Opium War: Drugs, Dreams and the Making of China*, Picador, Sydney, 2011.

Lu Xun, *The Real Story of Ah Q and Other Tales of China* (trans. Julia Lovell), Penguin Classics, 2010.

McGregor, Richard, *The Party: The Secret World of China's Communist Rulers*, Penguin Books, London, 2012.

Minford, John, and Joseph S. M. Lau (eds.), *Classical Chinese Literature, Volume 1: From Antiquity to the Tang Dynasty*, Columbia University Press, New York and Chichester, West Sussex, 2002.

Moser, David, *A Billion Voices: China's Search for a Common Language*, Penguin Specials, 2016.

Nien, Cheng, *Life and Death in Shanghai*, Grafton Books, London, 1986.

Ryckmans, Pierre, "The Chinese Attitude Towards the Past," Forty-Seventh George Ernest Morrison Lecture in Ethnology, Australian National University, Canberra, July 16, 1986.

Shi Nai'an and Luo Guanzhong, *Outlaws of the Marsh* (trans. Sidney Shapiro), Unwin Paperbacks, Sydney, 1986.

Smedley, Agnes, *China Correspondent*, Pandora Press, London, 1984.

Spence, Jonathan D., *Emperor of China: Self-Portrait of K'ang-Hsi*, Vintage Books, New York, 1975.

——, *God's Chinese Son: The Taiping Heavenly Kingdom of Hong Xiuquan*, HarperCollins, London, 1996.

——, *Mao Zedong: A Life*, Penguin, New York, 1999.

——, *The Search for Modern China*, Hutchinson, London, 1990.

Sun Tzu [Sunzi], *The Art of War* (trans. Ralph D. Sawyer with Mei-chün Sawyer), Westview Press, Boulder, 1994.

Waley, Arthur, *Three Ways of Thought in Ancient China*, Doubleday Anchor Books, New York, 1939.

Wasserstrom, Jeffrey, and Maura Elizabeth Cunningham, *China in the 21st Century: What Everyone Needs to Know*, third edition, Oxford University Press, New York, 2018.

Yang Jiang, *Baptism: An English Translation of Xizao* (trans. Yaohua Shi and Judith M. Amory), Hong Kong University Press, Hong Kong, 2007.

Yang Jisheng, *Tombstone: The Great Chinese Famine, 1958–1962*, Farrar, Straus and Giroux, New York, 2012.

Unknown, *I Ching (Yijing): The Book of Change* (trans. John Minford), Viking, New York, 2014.

# Image Credits

# Index

*Note: where there is both a traditional and a simplified form, the characters are separated with /.*

## About the Author

Linda Jaivin is an American-born, internationally published Australian essayist, novelist, translator, and specialist writer on China. She has previously lived, studied, and worked in Taiwan, Hong Kong, and Beijing.

**lindajaivin.com.au**

## Also available in the Shortest History series

Trade Paperback Originals • $16.95 US | $21.95 CAN

978-1-61519-569-5

978-1-61519-814-6

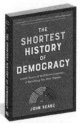

978-1-61519-896-2

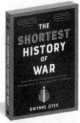

978-1-61519-930-3

978-1-61519-914-3

978-1-61519-948-8

978-1-61519-950-1

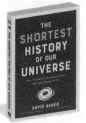

978-1-61519-973-0

978-1-61519-997-6